TRANSFER FROM THE PRIMARY CLASSROOM

Transfer from the Primary Classroom: 20 Years On revisits a number of the schools covered by the ORACLE survey of twenty years ago to look at how changes in education since have affected the process of transition from primary to secondary school. Have the reforms of the last two decades proved an aid to continuity, the result of significant improvements to the curriculum, methods of assessment and monitoring performance, or have they been simply an alternative cause of disruption?

The book covers:

- The last few weeks in primary school and the first visit to the secondary school.
- The attitudes of parents.
- How pupils are inducted into and adapt to a new school environment.
- Differences in teaching the core curriculum subjects – mathematics, English, science.
- The issues surrounding children with behavioural problems and learning difficulties.

Little has been published which supports and examines the transfer from primary to secondary school – a difficult time for pupils. This is a comprehensive and authoritative survey of the subject, based on classroom observation, carried out by a respected and highly experienced team of researchers.

Linda Hargreaves and **Maurice Galton** are based in the Faculty of Education, the University of Cambridge. **Chris Comber** and **Anthony Pell** are at the University of Leicester. **Debbie Wall** is at the Leicester-based Clinical Government Support Unit. They are the authors of *Inside the Primary Classroom: 20 Years On.*

TRANSFER FROM THE PRIMARY CLASSROOM

20 years on

Linda Hargreaves and Maurice Galton

Assisted by Chris Comber, Tony Pell and Debbie Wall

London and New York

First published 2002
by RoutledgeFalmer
11 New Fetter Lane, London EC4P 4EE

Simultaneously published in the USA and Canada
by RoutledgeFalmer
29 West 35th Street, New York, NY 10001

Routledge is an imprint of the Taylor & Francis Group

© 2002 Linda Hargreaves and Maurice Galton

Typeset in Sabon by
M Rules
Printed and bound in Great Britain by
St Edmundsbury Press, Bury St Edmunds, Suffolk

British Library Cataloguing in Publication Data
A catalogue record for this book is available from the British Library

Library of Congress Cataloging in Publication Data
A catalog record has been requested

ISBN 0 415 17021 4 (hbk)
ISBN 0 415 17022 2 (pbk)

We would like to dedicate this book to all the teachers and pupils who took part in the ORACLE and the various follow-up studies, including the unknown child who sent one of us this poem:

The School Move (with the poet's punctuation)

I don't know why,
But I'm getting shy,
And all edgy about the work,
Why can't I stay and lurk,
In corridors and in halls,
In doorways and behind tools,
Nobody will notice I've gone,
Nobody will look for long,
But maybe it will be great,
To walk through that school gate.

CONTENTS

FIGURES

TABLES

CONTRIBUTORS

Chris Comber came late to university education gaining a first-class degree in English and psychology as a mature student. Since then he has developed special interests in the application of ICT in schools and in the underachievement of boys, the subject of his doctoral thesis. He was one of the researchers on the ORACLE replication project and is now a lecturer at Leicester University.

Maurice Galton is a former Dean of Education at Leicester University and now directs several research projects in the Faculty of Education at Cambridge University. He has published widely on various aspects of classroom practice in primary schools including the effects of class size, grouping and group work and the implementation of the National Curriculum in rural primary schools. His last book, *Inside the Primary Classroom: 20 Years On* (Routledge), replicates research carried out two decades ago as part of the ORACLE project and is a companion to this current volume.

Linda Hargreaves gained her doctorate at Leicester University and worked at Leicester and Durham Universities before moving to Homerton College, Cambridge. A former primary teacher, she has collaborated with Maurice Galton on several research studies in addition to directing her own projects. Her latest work is an investigation of interactive teaching in the Literacy Hour.

Tony Pell completed his doctorate at the University of Leicester having previously undertaken a master's course on Research Methods at Lancaster University. A former physics teacher, he now specialises in research methods and statistical analysis. He is currently a member of a project team on transfer and transition co-directed by Maurice Galton for the Department for Education and Skills.

Debbie Wall, a former secondary teacher, was a researcher on the ORACLE replication study. Since then she has worked with various departments at Leicester University helping to review their quality assurance procedures for teaching and learning. A gifted artist, she is responsible for the design of the 'New School Gates' picture that features on the cover of this volume.

PREFACE

This book is the companion volume to *Inside the Primary Classroom: 20 Years On*. That volume covered the changes in primary education since the first ORACLE (Observational Research and Classroom Learning Evaluation) Project was completed in the late 1970s. ORACLE, one of the most cited studies of primary classroom practice, followed children as they moved through the last two years of primary school and into their first year after transfer to secondary school. The findings on transfer were published under the title, *Moving from the Primary Classroom*. Two decades later those of us who retained a link with original study embarked on a replication of that earlier research. Going back to many of the same schools and using the same research techniques, this research has been one of the rare studies to chart the changes in teaching and learning over time by means of carefully structured observations. The main conclusions from the primary study were that the advent of the National Curriculum had created a situation where the teaching at the top end of the primary school had become very like that which was seen in the transfer schools back in the 1970s. There were dramatic increases in class teaching during which teachers talked *at* rather than *with* children. The present volume explores the consequences of this change for pupils when they move to the present-day transfer school.

Twenty years ago the move from primary school resulted in a decline in pupils' attitudes and a hiatus in progress. At the time we attributed these dips to the rather limited challenge provided by the curriculum in the lower secondary years compared to the pupils' experiences in the primary school. Our findings were supported by others with greater experience of the secondary school system, notably by Professor David Hargreaves in his (1982) book, *The Challenge for the Comprehensive School*. Some LEAs, notably Suffolk, have more recently conducted reviews of the transfer process and concluded that these dips were still very much in evidence.

The National Curriculum was supposed to change all of this. Within its framework it was argued that it would be easier for schools to provide continuity and progression as children moved through the different key stages. However, it now appears that dips in progress and attitude are not just a feature of transition to secondary school but occur across the entire educational system when, for example, pupils move to Year 3 in the primary school and when they move to Year 10 at the secondary school.

Transfer from the Primary Classroom: 20 Years On examines three stages of transfer, from first school to the 9–13 or the 10–14 middle school and from the primary to the secondary school at eleven. We are able to show that in some respects there have been considerable changes in the present transfer procedures compared to two decades ago. On the other hand, we can also show that the curriculum and much of the teaching appear to have remained largely unchanged. The consequences for pupils' academic performance and attitude have also been explored.

Although various members of the research team have written individual chapters it is intended that the book should be read as a whole. Chapter 1 reviews the literature on transfer and sets out the main themes of the study. Chapter 2 looks at liaison and induction, particularly during the final summer term before transfer takes place. Chapter 3 looks closely at what happens in the first three days after transfer. We then move away from mainly qualitative accounts and begin to present more systematic evidence concerning the effects of transfer on teaching and learning. Chapter 4 examines the teaching that pupils receive in the transfer schools. Two chapters that attempt to assess the consequences of this teaching then follow. In Chapter 5 the effects on pupils' attitude, self-esteem and attainment are explored, while in Chapter 6 the impact on pupil behaviour is examined. Finally, in Chapter 7, we look to the future and suggest what might be done to improve the present situation. While we accept that many of the changes associated with the government's Key Stage 3 strategy will have an impact on transfer, we also argue that there are systemic problems involving the organisation of the curriculum in the lower secondary school. These need to be dealt with if real progress is to be made.

We owe several debts of gratitude for help with this book. First of all to our fellow researchers, Chris Comber, Debbie Wall and Tony Pell, who have contributed to chapters and also helped with the data collection and the analysis. Second, to Lynn Smolinski and Chris Rouse, who acted in a secretarial capacity to the project when we were based in Leicester at the University School of Education. Since our translation to the Homerton site, Cambridge, these burdens have been taken on by Judy Stevens to whom we offer thanks. We also have to thank the Economic and Social Research Council (ESRC) for a grant. Finally, our thanks and gratitude go to the teachers and the pupils who so willingly gave up their time to help us with the research and allowed us the privilege of entering their classrooms. Without their cooperation there would be no book.

Throughout the writing we have struggled with the terminology with which to describe the schools. At some points we have called them pre- and post-transfer schools while at other times we have referred to the former group as 'feeders'. This terminology is no longer welcomed by some primary headteachers because they feel that it implies that their task is merely to groom pupils for what then takes place when pupils move to 'big' school. We have more usually referred to the transfer from *primary* to *secondary* school although readers need to bear in mind that some of our sample moved to a 9–13 middle school.

In England, the issue of transfer has recently attracted widespread interest. Most LEAs now feature a section on the issue in their Educational Development plans. This is not just the result of the introduction of the Key Stage 3 initiative. All around the world, governments have recognised that tackling the problems connected with transfer and transition is an important constituent in the drive for school improvement. Our results, we feel, can make a contribution to these efforts and we hope, therefore, that they will be useful to teachers and policy-makers alike.

Maurice Galton and Linda Hargreaves

1

TRANSFER AND TRANSITION

Maurice Galton and Linda Hargreaves

Unlike any other educational system, that of England and Wales requires a sizeable number of its schoolchildren to engage in a process which, at its best, research suggests causes slight apprehension, while at its worst provokes deeply felt anxiety. It is a process that takes up a considerable amount of some teachers' time and effort – time which some would argue might be better devoted to classroom teaching – and results in some pupils underachieving in comparison to their performance in the previous years. The process, known as transfer,[1] concerns the movement of a whole year group of pupils from one school to another. Each new school year, apart from pupils aged 6, 15 and 17, large numbers of children will start life in a new school where they will come face to face with new teachers and other pupils whom they do not recognise. This can be a moment of great apprehension. The children may have spent the summer vacation attempting to come to terms with the impending change, perhaps wondering whether the various rumours about 'strict' teachers or what the older pupils do to the 'new kids' are true.

The youngest children to experience transfer are those who move at age 7 from 'Infant' (5–7 years) schools covering Key Stage 1 (KS1) to 'Junior' (7–11 years, KS2) schools. Most of these KS1 'feeder' schools will come within the 546 nursery schools recorded in the DfEE (1999) statistics. However, these figures do not always distinguish clearly between schools which operate according to different age ranges. For example, some all-through primary schools, that is those which cover both KS1 and KS2, contain nurseries and would be included in the quoted figure of 546. There are similar problems with middle schools where a distinction is made between a primary school '*deemed middle*' (8–12 years) and a secondary school '*deemed middle*' which could cover either the 9–13, 10–14 or 11–14 years age ranges. Moreover, some 5–8, 5–9 and 5–10 years '*first*' schools feeding into middle school will also contain nursery units. Children going to school in LEAs with middle school systems will therefore move school at either 8, 9, 10 or 11 years of age and again at either 12, 13 or 14 years respectively. Local Education Authorities also operate different systems at

1

secondary level. Some have 11–16 schools followed by transfer to a sixth form college or college of Further Education, while others favour '*all-through*' (11–18 years) schools. Hence the statement at the beginning of the paragraph that every autumn, with the exception of those aged 6, 15 or 17, some children, somewhere in England and Wales, will be engaged in the process called transfer.

To the outsider the system must seem remarkably complicated and difficult to manage. Most other countries around the world uniformly adopt either two- or three-tier systems. Our more complex arrangements came into being mainly as the result of secondary school reorganisation during the 1970s. Faced with a need to create a comprehensive system without spending vast sums of money, most local authorities reorganised the education system around the existing stock of buildings and then sought, subsequently, to provide an educational justification for the chosen scheme. Thus, as Andy Hargreaves (1980) argues, a notion of a particular phase of development between childhood and adolescence was invented where homogeneity was said to exist in physical, moral, emotional and intellectual growth. This period, known as the *middle years* (Hargreaves 1980: 96) was said to differ markedly from other phases of children's development. However, whether it began when a child reached the age of 8 and ended at 12 or occupied the years between 9 and 13 often appeared to be influenced by the state of existing buildings, the size of catchment areas and projected population growth.[2] Those seeking to justify reorganisation based on transfer at 8 and 12 saw in middle schools the opportunity to extend the best of primary education for a further year (Sharp 1980). Elsewhere in other local authorities, those arguing for a 9 to 13 system provided the alternative justification that able children in the top half of the primary school could gain access to specialist subject teachers who had previous experience in secondary schools (Marsh 1980).

Transfer and curriculum continuity

Whatever system was eventually chosen, however, it was soon established that there were problems in managing transfer so that a satisfactory degree of curriculum continuity was maintained. This was particularly important when three tiers of reorganisation were involved since transfer at 13 (and even more so at 14) left upper secondary schools little time to prepare students for the public examinations at 16. Over time, therefore, the justification for the middle school system changed. Instead of merely offering opportunities for either extending primary practice or introducing secondary specialisms earlier, many schools now claimed to provide a curriculum for the middle years that closely matched this putative 'unique' stage of children's intellectual development. Not surprisingly, tensions between upper and middle schools in matters of curriculum developed. A middle school, for example, might have favoured local history as a source of project work, part of an integrated humanities scheme, to the frustration of the upper school which included social history as one of its main options for what was then the GCE Ordinary Level examination or the alternative CSE (Certificate of Secondary Education). Children from this particular middle school would then be expected to cope with aspects of the industrial revolution with little knowledge of the political context, whereas pupils from another feeder school might not be similarly disadvantaged.[3]

In the 1970s, as the comprehensive system rapidly expanded, schools tended to deal with the issue of transfer in one of two ways. Some believed in a 'continuity' model, believing that pupils would adjust more easily if the ethos in the first post-transfer year remained as similar as possible to that of the primary school. These schools tended to keep their first year pupils away from their older peers by providing a separate play area, holding first year group assemblies and, most importantly by retaining the system where the form teacher took the pupils for most of their lessons. Other schools, however, argued that transfer was a 'rite of passage' marking the emergence of adolescence, and this needed to be symbolised by a distinct shift in the pattern of schooling. These schools introduced specialist subject teaching, often accompanied by setting and banding for key subjects such as English and mathematics from the first day of the autumn term. Identifying the more able children and those with learning difficulties on entry to these schools so that they could be placed in the appropriate sets was problematic, since accurate information about the pupils' previous performance prior to entry was unreliable. With the ending of the eleven plus, few primary schools favoured standardised testing and suitable alternative diagnostic tests were not readily available. Faced with the choice of either a wide-ranging mixed ability group or a set with a small number of 'difficult children', secondary teachers (many with only previous grammar school experience) adopted the strategy of a 'fresh start'. Under either of these arrangements, able children could easily become bored by repeating work they had already mastered, while slow learning children could find the rapid pace of these revision classes too much for them. In both cases, therefore, academic progress might be retarded as a consequence.

The consultative document, *Education in Schools* (DES 1977), acknowledged that there were substantial problems of these kinds at the points of transfer and argued that the whole problem needed the urgent attention of Local Education Authorities. Gorwood (1986) reported that one primary headteacher discovered, while lecturing to a group of secondary principals, that many never looked at the transfer documents which were passed on from primary schools, a situation which, according to some LEA advisers, still persists in many schools. Most of these principals supported their staff in adopting the '*tabula rasa*' policy in respect of new pupils described in the previous paragraph. In support of this approach it was argued that a secondary school's objectives were necessarily more academically specific

3

than those adopted by most primary schools. Consequently, secondary teachers could more efficiently ascertain a child's ability in their specialist subject without reference to primary records, particularly since these were often regarded as vague and sometimes misleading (Orsborn 1977). Another study of transfer procedures in the Isle of Wight (Stillman and Maychell 1982) reported on attempts to develop some general guidelines for producing the transfer record. This aimed to establish uniformity in presentation, comparability of assessments and information which was *needs related*, in that it provided what receiving (*transfer*) schools wanted. At around the same time, across the country, numerous working parties on record-keeping were set up as LEAs attempted to respond to the 1977 DES circular in an effort to improve curriculum continuity. The general conclusion, however, was that these working parties were only partially successful and many enjoyed 'a chequered history' (Gorwood 1986: 142).

Early studies on transfer

Much of the earlier research on transfer, therefore, focused on the issues discussed so far; particularly on establishing greater continuity in the process and reducing anxiety among pupils. Nisbet and Entwistle (1969) carried out one of the earliest and largest studies. This attempted to establish the best age at which to transfer to secondary school in order to minimise such problems. These researchers followed 3,200 9-year-old Scottish children over a 5-year period (what in England is now known as from Year 5 to Year 9). The main focus of the study was the linkage between intelligence and academic progress during transfer and beyond. Verbal reasoning scores were found to be accurate predictors of attainment between the ages of 9 and 11 but the inter-correlations between the two variables fell thereafter. This suggested that there was little to be gained by keeping children in primary education in order to increase the accuracy of the selection process, in schools where pupils were streamed by ability. Nisbet and Entwistle found that other factors such as socio-economic status, parental involvement, pupils' ambition and their social maturity were stronger correlates of success, with ambition and social maturity particularly important for girls. Nisbett and Entwistle concluded that the youngest and least mature pupils were those at greatest risk during the transfer process.

Murdoch (1966) who analysed 550 post-transfer pupil essays adopted another approach. Only 11 per cent of boys and 8 per cent of girls said they found transfer a 'wholly enjoyable' experience. Nearly two-thirds of both boys and girls experienced difficulties of some sort. However, after one term in the new school 80 per cent of pupils said they preferred it to their primary school. Taken together, therefore, these two studies suggest that while the negative social effects of transfer wear off reasonably quickly for the majority of pupils, the impact on academic progress does not.

The organisational features of the transfer process were explored by the then Birmingham Education Department which carried out a large-scale survey of Birmingham schools, most of which transferred pupils from primary to secondary at the age of 11 (BEDC 1975). The Birmingham Department team found little evidence of liaison between the primary and secondary schools, and that which did exist mostly consisted of visits of secondary teachers to the primary school, with little or no movement in the other direction. With regard to the attitudes of the pupils, the survey found that few had any notion or experience of what the prospective transfer school would be like although the vast majority eventually enjoyed their first year, liked the challenge, and the variety of activities. They particularly appreciated being treated as adults by the new teachers. The most popular subject was physical education followed by English which was liked more than geography and history. The sample was equally divided on mathematics but didn't like religious education. Liking a subject seemed to be strongly associated with the liking for an individual teacher. Thus, where there was a hiatus in progress, it seemed to be heavily influenced by the relationship with the new teacher. In this regard it is of interest to note that the survey found that even a year after transfer, 33 per cent of children said that they still missed their primary teacher, compared with 44 per cent who felt this way prior to the move. Nevertheless, in accord with other studies around this time, the Birmingham team seemed to suggest that most pupils settled fairly quickly into the routine of the new school. The main recommendations of the Report focused on such things as the need for better liaison, better communication between the home and the school and a new record system including a transfer card which would inform the new school about a pupil's attendance record, his (her) attainment, background and behaviour.

Another large-scale study was that of Youngman and Lunzer (1977) who followed 1,500 pupils in rural and urban schools through and beyond the transfer period. As elsewhere, the majority of pupils were found to express satisfaction with their new school, but a small proportion, around 10 per cent, continued to find the experience distressing for at least the first two terms after transfer. In addition to attitudes to school and measures of social and personal academic self-concept, scores in IQ, reading and mathematics were collected. Cluster analysis, carried out based on these ratings of social and academic adjustment, yielded six pupil types. Of particular interest was a 'disenchanted' group who had moderate positive, social adjustment ratings, and initially performed well academically, but whose performance subsequently declined gradually over time. The other set of pupils perceived to be seriously at risk was the 'worried' group who had negative social adjustment ratings, low academic ability and whose performance continued to decline over the twelve-month period during which the research was carried out.

5

As we saw earlier, some secondary schools attempted to ease the transfer process for these groups of children at risk. Maintaining a primary ethos in the first year after transfer and gradually introducing changes during the whole year, rather than in the first few weeks in the new school, were said to have a marked effect by Nisbet and Entwistle (1969), but Dutch and McCall (1974) were less convinced of the effectiveness of this strategy. They agreed that compared to a control school, where pupils changed to a secondary-style curriculum immediately after transfer, there were consistent though slight improvements in attainment, attitude and personality measures. However, they argued that these outcome measures were confounded by other variables such as ability. Nash (1973) was also unenthusiastic about such schemes and argued that, in any case, so-called integrated approaches in primary school did not operate at the 'top junior' end of the school and, therefore, there was little point in introducing and maintaining them in the first year after transfer.

In summary, therefore, these groups of studies identify the children most at risk from the transfer process as younger, less mature, less confident pupils; ones of non-academic disposition, often from a poor socio-economic background. These children found difficulty in adjusting to the physical and academic organisation of the new school, and the standards of work as well as experiencing problems with pupil and teacher relationships. The most successful pupils, therefore, were the academically able who were self-confident, more socially mature and tended to receive strong parental support (Spelman 1979).

The ORACLE transfer study

The researchers cited above did not follow the actual events taking place during transfer. Most, like Youngman and Lunzer's (1977) study, measured the attainment and attitudes of pupils while they were still in the feeder schools and then again after a certain time in the new school. The problem with this approach is that while it identifies which pupils are adversely affected by the change, it is unable to put forward detailed explanations of why this might be so (Youngman 1978). While it alerts teachers to a problem, therefore, it can offer only limited advice on how best to deal with it.

The ORACLE transfer study (1975–80) adopted a different approach. Pupils were followed into the new school from their feeder school, after first having been observed for two years previously in the primary school. The work was published in two volumes, *Moving from the Primary Classroom* (Galton and Willcocks 1983) and *Inside the Secondary Classroom* (Delamont and Galton 1986). The main focus of the ORACLE study was on the observation of teachers and pupils, but pupils' academic performance was also tested in the final term before leaving the primary school and again at the end of the first school year after transfer.

6

Attitude inventories as well as a questionnaire measuring anxiety levels were also administered. The latter, known as WIDIS (What I Did In School), was first used by Bennett (1976) in his study of formal and informal practice. WIDIS was administered in the June before transfer, again in November and again in the June after transfer. Thus it was possible to determine whether anxiety levels began to fall within the first few weeks in the new school. In fact, the patterns of anxiety were very similar to those found by both Nesbit and Entwistle (1969) and by Youngman and Lunzer (1977). Anxiety was highest in June just before transfer, had declined in November and had fallen further by the following June. An exception to this trend was found in the two schools that maintained a primary ethos throughout the first year after transfer. In both schools anxiety increased during the first year, reaching the peak just before the children departed from the primary area at the beginning of their second year in the new school. This was attributed to the fact that setting and streaming started in Year 2 and the pupils were clearly conscious of the importance of doing well in the end of the first year examinations. Further, being reorganised into sets and streams could result in being separated from close friends. Some of these friendships may have only begun during the post-transfer year.

The main focus of the ORACLE study was on the curriculum; the way teachers delivered it and the manner in which the pupils responded to this teaching. Eight target pupils (one boy and one girl drawn from the top, middle and bottom achieving quartiles of the class) were observed throughout the school day in every school during the first three days of the new school year when pupils were adjusting to their new circumstances. Thereafter, teachers and target pupils were followed over the course of a single day at regular intervals throughout the transfer year. These observations confirmed previous claims that, in general, there was very little attempt to maintain continuity between the two phases in respect of either the curriculum content or the teaching methods. For the most part, teachers started again from scratch either as a form of revision or because it was assumed that what went on in the primary school was not serious or disciplined work. In one example, an art teacher talked about the children engaging in 'a bit of splash and fun' while at their primary school. He continued by telling them that they were now going to do 'serious art' and 'really think about drawing and the basic elements of design' which were 'line, colour, shape and form' (Galton and Willcocks 1983: 114). In mathematics, many children had to learn new ways of carrying out procedures such as long division and subtraction. They also had to master new terminology and were forbidden to use words such as 'sharing' or 'take-aways', instead having to talk about 'dividing' or doing 'subtraction'.

Subjects encountered for the first time gave rise to particular difficulties. Before transfer most pupils said that one of the things they were most looking forward to was science. When pupils were asked what 'doing science' involved they talked about 'doing experiments' of 'making bangs and smells'. The reality, however, was somewhat different. Typically, a lesson consisted of lighting a Bunsen burner, observing the different colours of the inner and outer flame cones for a few minutes, and then drawing a picture of the apparatus in their books and colouring in the flame. They would then copy notes about the Bunsen burner from the blackboard or fill in a worksheet and stick it into their homework books. In home economics, pupils who had planned and purchased the ingredients for a meal for four, and then cooked and served it while at primary school, now began their secondary course with making a 'hot snack and drink'. This turned out to be a slice of buttered toast and a cup of tea. In the first week pupils copied instructions from the blackboard, then drew and coloured in a teapot and a cup and saucer.

To the researchers, it seemed that the effect of this rather restricted curriculum diet was that some children began to concentrate less on the work. In the primary school of the 1970s, much of the teacher's time was taken up interacting with individual children. The class would have a brief introductory period together before being sent off to their tables where they either worked on their own or in groups, but on individual tasks. The teacher would then either rotate around the tables offering advice and checking progress or call children out to the front of the class in order to mark work at his or her desk. When the teacher was involved with a particular group or an individual pupil, other children, if minded, could relax in the knowledge that 'Sir' or 'Miss' had his or her back to them and couldn't easily see them. In these circumstances, the main way for pupils to slow down their rate of task engagement was to indulge in what the ORACLE researchers called 'intermittent working'. This involved pupils working when the teacher was either nearby or periodically monitoring the class behaviour. However, at other times they engaged in off-task conversations, mainly to do with social matters such as what was on television or what they were going to do over the weekend (Galton et al. 1980).

In secondary school, however, pupils mainly sat in rows facing the front of the class so that they were under surveillance by the teacher for a greater proportion of time. To cope with this pupils developed a new strategy which the researchers termed 'easy riding'. This involved giving the appearance of working while doing so as little as possible. In mathematics, for example, some pupils would spend considerable time ruling margins or underlining answers. In this way they avoided being given another page of sums to do because they had finished early. In English, pupils might be told to write 'at least two sides' in their roughbooks and then to correct it and copy it into their best book for homework. Some children told the observer that they would 'write bigger' in such circumstances so covering the page with fewer words. This had the added advantage that teachers, rather than start a fresh topic, would often let anyone who finished start making their 'fair copy' during the remainder of the lesson so cutting down on the amount of homework.

Thus children who had occasionally indulged in intermittent working while at primary school now more often were observed easy riding. In this way a climate of low expectations was created. Teachers would come to feel that Wayne, Dean or Tracy had done well if they managed to do five sums during the period or if they managed a whole page of writing. One consequence of this lack of effort was that nearly 40 per cent of the pupils scored less on the same tests of basic skills in June following transfer, than they did in the final term in their feeder school. An interesting feature of these downward shifts in attainment was the maintenance of pupil position within the class or set structure. Pupils who were in the top quartile of their class in the feeder school, were still likely to be found in the top quartile of the set in the transfer school even though they were now grouped with other pupils, some from different feeder schools. There were also greater differences between those pupils who made or failed to make progress after transfer in terms of the time they spent on their task. The picture that emerged was of sharper differentiation between pupils who continued to work hard in their new school and those who gradually eased off and settled for doing the minimum.

These differences between primary and secondary schools therefore reflected the different teaching approaches used and the pupils' response to these varied strategies for managing their learning. After transfer, the easy riders could be contrasted with another group of pupils called '*hard grinders*'. These pupils, as their name suggests, worked extremely hard and were difficult to distract, and were similar to a group at primary school called '*undeflected workers*', so named because they refused to be distracted by the other children sitting on their table. Whenever a conversation started on their table these pupils would remain silent and continue with their task. It appeared, therefore, that many pupils established their attitude to learning early in the primary school but modified their behaviour in accordance to a particular teacher's approach. In the primary feeder schools, the pupils adjusted to different teaching styles, while in the transfer schools they learned to cope with the different subject specialisms. In the transfer schools teachers often sought to slow down the quicker pupils and speed up the slower ones up in order to manage the class or set and avoid the need to provide *enrichment* tasks for the more able. One means of doing this, as we have seen earlier in the case of English, would be to start an activity in class and leave the slower pupils to finish it off for homework. We shall consider some of these findings in more detail when we deal with them again in specific chapters later in the book.

Later studies of transfer[4]

Another research study, adopting a very different approach from ORACLE, was undertaken by Measor and Woods (1984). These researchers used participant observation to study only one secondary school and one of its feeder schools and focused specifically on pupils. In addition to observation, unstructured interviews were carried out with pupils who were moving from an 8–12 middle school to a 12–18 comprehensive school. Much of their work confirms the earlier finding that the last term in the feeder school was characterised by high anxiety, tinged with excitement and 'optimistic expectation'. Children used words like 'being frightened', 'worried', 'nervous' and 'scared' to describe their feelings prior to transfer. These utterances were particularly related to concerns about work, bullying by older children, their new status and their separation from friends as a result of setting, banding or streaming. Measor and Woods argued that what was at stake over transfer were basic questions about the pupils' identity, as they shift from the known homely, cosy world of the primary school, to what they perceive to be the largely hostile, unknown and bureaucratic world of the larger comprehensive. In making these adjustments, the children evaluate themselves against others, particularly those within their newly developing friendship networks. Making new friends during the first few weeks in the new school is, therefore, very important.

Pupils in the Measor and Woods study found the induction day process and the parents' evenings helpful in dispelling some of the more obvious rumours and myths about transfer, but the anxieties on this score tended to return during the school holidays. However, the first few days of the new school were generally rated as being routine and very boring. The eager anticipation of going into a laboratory to do science or using the gymnasium for PE was rapidly diluted when these lessons turned out to be very similar to others with note taking, copying and great emphasis on routines. Again, Measor and Woods found that the children's reaction to the different subjects taught depended very strongly on the relationship with the teacher, although they also reported gender differences in both subject preference and attitude to learning. Boys tended to react strongly against domestic science and the girls to physical sciences. For example, while girls were more likely to show their opposition to the new school by using avoidance strategies, boys tended to engage in more direct resistance. Measor and Woods concluded that the 're-incorporation' into schooling is not as quick as many of the studies, including the ORACLE transfer study, would suggest.

This concern with pupils' identities and the impact of the 'labelling' systems in schools on the pupils' self-image is a recurring theme of more recent research on transfer (Murdoch 1982). Beynon (1985) also looked closely on the development of teacher and pupil relationships. Like Measor and Woods (1984), Beynon found that judgements about one's teachers, based on initial classroom encounters, had more to do with personality than the quality of the teaching. Teachers who treated you 'like a proper person' were well regarded, for example. More extensive evidence on pupils' reactions to secondary school comes from a study by Rudduck et al. (1996). Pupils from three comprehensive schools were followed from Year 8 up to Year 11. As part of a series of interviews, pupils were asked to recall retrospectively their feeling on transferring to the 'big school'. In this part of the study Rudduck found that, on looking back at the experience, pupils did not regard the move to be as dramatic as that characterised by Delamont and Galton (1986) ten years earlier. Part of the change could be attributed to the increased effort made by secondary schools to help pupils 'feel at home'. Induction days were more frequent and schools produced 'user friendly' booklets to help new pupils 'find their way around' (Rudduck *et al.* 1996: 25). More important, in Rudduck's view, were the discontinuities in learning experienced by pupils. Only in Year 10, when the importance of getting some qualifications in order to secure employment was more fully appreciated, did pupils come to see the value in building up good study habits in such matters as homework and attendance from the beginning. By then the realisation that what was taught in the first years of secondary school could have a bearing on later performance came too late for some pupils to catch up and make good the gaps in their knowledge. Rudduck *et al.* (1997) argue that Year 8, in particular, is a key year, since it often lacks a clear identity, coming as it does before the serious business of preparing for the National Curriculum Tests in Year 9 which is then followed by two years of intensive preparation for the 16+ examination. Lacking the novelty of the transfer year, Year 8 is regarded by many pupils as a 'fallow year' in which the 'dynamics of friendship groups become all-consuming'. Thus the transfer process is but part of a larger issue, that of transition, in which the year-by-year move to new teachers and fresh topics brings with it the danger that some pupils become increasingly unable to manage the learning and fall further and further behind.

Gorwood (1986) takes a different approach. Concentrating on the issue of curriculum continuity in his survey of typical practice in several LEAs, Gorwood claimed his findings strengthened the case of the middle school as a vehicle for ensuring smooth transition between a typical primary and typical secondary curriculum. Although his evidence was based largely on what LEAs *claimed* to do, rather than the kind of detailed observation of lessons undertaken in the earlier ORACLE study, the survey, carried out in 1984, appeared to demonstrate that transfer and transition were of increasing concern. Nearly 85 per cent of the Local Education Authorities had organised conferences on the theme of continuity, for example, while 42 per cent had produced documents listing various strategies for successful transfer. However, less than a quarter had advisers with specific responsibility for liaison, despite the fact that nearly three-quarters of LEAs responding said that they were experiencing some or major difficulties with curriculum continuity. These difficulties were generally ascribed to the limited time available for managing transition, to teacher attitudes, and to the large number of feeder schools, including the scattered nature of some in rural areas. In some cases there were also general communication problems between schools and the

LEA. One Chief Education Officer reported that 'there is too much for inspectors to do and they need to make considerable effort to overcome the natural inertia of schools' (Gorwood 1986: 160).

Continuity was thought to be most successful in mathematics and least successful in the humanities. Gorwood's recommendations were eminently reasonable. They included such things as the introduction of posts of responsibility for transfer (what is usually now called the 'first year coordinator' role), greater liaison between primary and secondary headteachers, attempts to devise common syllabuses and the passing on of pupils' work. The use of active tutorial worksheets during personal and social education was also recommended, as in the suggestion from Gorwood (1986: 176) that before transfer pupils should write down short biographies of themselves and of their class mates and raise questions about what it will be like in their new school, such as 'How many pupils will there be in my new class? How will the make-up of each class be decided? Where shall I go if it is raining at breaktime or dinnertime?' and 'What happens if I do not like school dinners?'

Subsequent reports would indicate that some of the above suggested innovations were in fact already well established by the time Gorwood published his review of LEA procedures. However, there has been considerable disagreement about their beneficial effect. Brown and Armstrong (1986), for example, studied the essays of 220 junior school pupils about to move to five secondary schools, concerning their feelings about transfer. The exercise was repeated with just over a third of the sample once they were judged to have settled into their new schools. Brown and Armstrong found that before transfer, the array of negative concerns was much longer than the list of positive aspects, but that this trend was reversed once pupils had adjusted to life in their new school. Commenting on such findings, Rudduck *et al.* (1996), as we have seen, argue that although on the surface children nowadays appear to settle more readily, as measured by anxiety inventories or by essays of the kind reported by Brown and Armstrong (1986), a much longer process is also involved during which pupils come to terms with their identity and status as secondary pupils, echoing the point made by Measor and Woods. Hence Rudduck *et al.* (1997) contend that there is the need to see transfer not just as a shift from institution to institution or key stage to key stage, but as a particular case of *year-by-year transition*, a viewpoint which has received relatively little attention thus far.

The impact of transfer on pupil progress[5]

In the review of the 1975–80 ORACLE transfer study it was pointed out that some pupils had failed to make progress on standardised tests of English, mathematics and reading comprehension at the end of their first year in the transfer school when compared to their performance in the final term in the feeder schools (Croll 1983). In mathematics 45 per cent of boys and 35 per cent of girls failed to make progress. The corresponding figures for English language skills were 56 per cent and 44 per cent respectively, while for reading 57.5 per cent of boys and 27 per cent of girls failed to make further progress. The measure used was the *raw score gain*, that is the difference in absolute terms between the scores achieved by pupils on each test on two occasions. Each test contained 30 multiple choice items taken from the *Richmond Tests of Basic Skills* (France and Fraser 1975). When the scores on all three tests were combined, then the average gain during the transfer year was 3.4 marks compared to a gain of 7.5 marks during each transition year in the primary feeder schools. Analysis showed that the smaller gains after transfer were not merely due to 'ceiling effects' of the test (i.e. where pupils' scores at the end of primary school were so high that there was little room for further improvement). Nor did lack of progress appear to be a function of age of transfer, nor the approach adopted by a particular school. For example, schools which attempted to preserve a primary ethos during the first year after transfer did no better and no worse, overall, than schools which adopted a secondary style by introducing streaming and specialist subject teaching from day one.

On the other hand, irrespective of individual pupil gains or losses, there was a remarkable degree of continuity in terms of a pupil's ability relative to the rest of the class. Pupils in the primary school were classified as high, medium or low ability according to their quartile scores within the class. After transfer, pupils in a particular quartile would then be placed in classes with either a mixture of pupils from other schools, or, in some cases they would be placed in sets or bands. Yet when the pupils in these new classes were ranked according to their combined score on the three tests, between 77 per cent and 86 per cent of pupils in the 'top quartile' in the feeder school remained in the same quartile after transfer. The same was true of around two-thirds of pupils in the bottom quartile.

However, the numbers of pupils in the ORACLE sample for whom scores for two years in the feeder school and one year after transfer were available were relatively small (less than a hundred). The question of whether these results were generalisable to other transfer schools was therefore at issue. Unfortunately, few, subsequent studies of transfer have included measures of pupil performance. A notable exception has been Suffolk LEA which has monitored pupil progress in the age range 6+ to 12+ over a number of years, establishing consistent dips in progress as pupils move from school to school (Suffolk LEA 1997). For the rest, evidence that dips in progress do occur during transfer has to be inferred from other sources. OFSTED inspectors, for example, are required to estimate the degree of progress they expect pupils will make by the end of the year on the assumption that the lessons continue to be of a standard observed during their brief visit to a school. These ratings are then aggregated over all inspections and summarised in the

Annual Report of the Chief Inspector of Schools. There are indications of a small dip in Year 3 of primary school where only 35 per cent of lessons were thought to result in pupils making 'good' or 'very good' progress compared to 38 per cent and 37 per cent in Years 2 and 4 respectively (OFSTED 1999). Further evidence comes from the analysis of the Qualifications and Curriculum Authority's (QCA) Key Stage 1 optional tests (Minnis *et al.* 1998). In reading, only 52 per cent of Year 3 pupils made one or more level of progress compared to 71 per cent in Year 2. For writing, the corresponding figures were 44 per cent and 66 per cent, while for mathematics they were 52 per cent and 66 per cent respectively.

At secondary level, however, it was Years 8 and 9 rather than Year 7 that were singled out for attention by OFSTED, although the inspectors also reported on a steep rise in the number of unsatisfactory lessons observed in Year 7 compared to Year 6. At the beginning of secondary school, pupil attainment was judged to be 'unsatisfactory' in 50 per cent of the inspections (OFSTED 1998). Given that the pupils take the 'high status' National Curriculum Tests at the end of Year 6 it is perhaps not surprising that performance was judged to fall off in the following year. The different perspectives of primary and secondary OFSTED inspectors who may not be using similar criteria in reaching a judgement may exacerbate this view. Nevertheless, whichever way these effects are evaluated, it is clear that they are not of a large order of magnitude, confirming the pattern established in the ORACLE study by Croll (1983), where the *raw score* losses were generally within one standard deviation for the test. For this reason it is important to talk about a *hiatus* rather than a decline in pupils' progress whenever they transfer to a new school.

The effect of the National Curriculum

The election of a Conservative government in 1979 saw the beginning of increasing state intervention in the field of education which was to take place throughout the next decade, despite the rhetoric of the 'market forces' philosophy. This included breaking the power of the teacher trade unions over pay and conditions of service and taking control of the curriculum (Tomlinson 1992: 47). LEAs were also marginalised by channelling innovations, including the Technical and Vocational Educational Initiative (TVEI), through other departments such as the Department of Employment rather than the Department of Education. At the same time conditions were put in place for a new education reform bill. Its aim was to make an irreversible change in the public education system such as that already achieved in other aspects of social and economic policy such as trade union legislation, council house sales and the privatisation of nationalised industries (ibid.: 48). Central to this education bill was the setting up of a National Curriculum, having as one of its main objectives the establishment of curriculum continuity, thereby avoiding the unnecessary 'duplication which many children suffer when moving from one school to another' (Baker 1993: 192).

From the start, as recounted by Galton (1995), the National Curriculum debate was dominated by secondary concerns with only the token primary teacher being placed on various subject committees. Being in a minority, these representatives of primary education were hard placed to stand up to the secondary subject experts' views. Indeed, given the attitudes of secondary principals reported by Orsborn (1977) and Gorwood (1986), it was always likely that the main concern of those involved in the discussions concerning continuity would be to establish a syllabus for each subject in which content, previously first introduced at secondary school, was now 'pushed down' to Key Stage 2. Whereas, as we have previously mentioned, secondary teachers had bemoaned the fact that art in the primary school was 'all splash and fun', they could now ensure the KS2 pupils were taught about 'colour', 'shape' and 'form'. In mathematics, meanwhile, older primary children could earlier be introduced to the 'proper' words such as subtraction instead of using 'slapdash' terms like take-away. This emphasis on subject knowledge and correct terminology was reinforced by the replacement of the first chief executive of the National Curriculum Council (NCC), Duncan Graham, by Chris Woodhead, an ex-English teacher, and later Her Majesty's Chief Inspector who, judging by the frequent use of a quotation from Matthew Arnold's *Culture and Anarchy*,[6] regarded the text as his 'educational bible'.

The consequences for primary teachers of the introduction of the new curriculum have been well documented. Writers such as Campbell and Neill (1994) have clearly established that it resulted in substantially increased workloads, mainly due to the need to cope with increased subject matter and attendant increases in administration and bureaucracy. The substantial overloading of subject content led to a review by Dearing (1993). This resulted in the allocation of 20 per cent of curriculum time for *discretionary* activities, together with a commitment not to introduce further reform during the next five years. Subsequent research has shown that this discretionary time was mostly taken up with additional mathematics and English lessons as schools attempted to improve their National Curriculum Test scores in response to the government's decision to publish these as 'league tables' in the local and national press (Galton and Fogelman 1998), thus continuing a process set in train by the previous, Conservative government, as part of its project to create an 'education marketplace'. The PACE (Primary Assessment Curriculum and Experience) Project which followed pupils over a five-year period during the early 1990s (Pollard *et al.* 1994; Croll 1996a) came to similar conclusions. More recently, Woods *et al.* (1997) in their study of primary teachers argue that what used to be a fulfilling job distinguished by professional dilemmas, has increasingly become merely a technical activity. Because a decision to teach *this* rather than *that* is a statutory requirement, it is no longer mainly determined by the pupils' needs. As a result, the majority of teachers in Woods *et al.*'s (1997) study were compliant and did not relish changes in role but sought to 'accommodate, concur and allow changes to impinge upon them' (ibid.: 60).

The impact of such factors on transfer is not likely to be positive. Indeed, the survey by Suffolk LEA inspectors of what happened when pupils moved schools at the age of 9, 11 and 13 years concluded that, despite the introduction of the National Curriculum, there were serious discrepancies between the work pupils were given before and after transfer. In mathematics, for example, pupils who had achieved level 4 on the Key Stage 2 tests were engaged in tasks of level 2 standard after moving to the new school (Suffolk LEA 1997). Reports by the Schools Curriculum and Assessment Authority (SCAA 1996) point to similar problems. All in all, therefore, the problem of curriculum continuity at transfer appears to be a somewhat intractable one.

Gorwood (1991), in bringing his earlier work up to date following the introduction of the National Curriculum, has also argued that one of the main objectives of those designing the primary phase statutory programmes of study was to increase children's initial progress at secondary school by introducing greater specialisation at Key Stage 2, thereby improving continuity and coherence. He pointed out, however, that many secondary schools still appeared to start pupils on the same level, regardless of individual achievement in the primary school, and argued that the National Curriculum does little to solve this problem. Although schools he surveyed now focused to a greater extent on transfer procedures with the appointment of special coordinators to manage the transition, Gorwood recommended that discussions needed to extend beyond the teachers charged with managing liaison and those in Year 6 in the feeder schools. He recognised, however, that this approach involved issues relating to whole school policy in both sectors since 'by their very training, teachers in our schools have been encouraged to maintain fundamentally different philosophies of primary and secondary school' (ibid.). Other critics such as Marshall and Brindley (1998) have pointed to the problems of comparability between levels of attainment at Key Stage 2 and Key Stage 3 as a major source of difficulty. In English, differences in perspective between primary and secondary teachers have sometimes meant that the latter did not recognise information passed on by Year 6 colleagues because it 'was not relevant to their [i.e. *secondary teachers*] understanding of English and the kinds of tasks they were asking pupils to do' (ibid.: 125). Similar conclusions are drawn by Stables (1995). Stables, in her study of teaching in Year 6 and Year 7 technology and design lessons, found strong discontinuities in the approach used in the different sectors, such that the ratio of pupil–teacher or pupil–pupil *discussion* to pupil *listening* to teacher was almost the exact reverse in Year 6 to that in Year 7 classes. Like Marshall and Brindley (1998: 133), Stables doubts whether more efficient ways of passing on information about pupil performance on Key Stage 2 Tests, as suggested by SCAA (1996), constitute an effective answer to these problems.

Other factors affecting transfer

There are other concerns with the process of transfer from one school to another besides that of curriculum continuity. The desirability of curriculum continuity arises, in part, because of an assumption that it eases problems for pupils as well as for teachers. Because the work will be familiar, pupils will feel less stress and anxiety about whether they will cope in their new school. However, moving from one school to another involves more than simply coping with work demands. There is also the problem of getting used to the new surroundings for the transfer school is likely to be much larger than the feeder school. Finding one's way round the corridors to the various class-rooms, knowing where to store one's P.E. kit, or how to order and pay for one's dinner are all matters which loom large in the new pupil's thoughts. Transfer schools also include pupils from other feeder schools, some of whom might have been in not-so-friendly rivalry with each other. Thus, while the transition provides opportunities for making new friends, it also offers the possibility of making fresh enemies. Moreover, whereas in their final year in the feeder schools these children were the oldest, they are now, after transfer, the most junior and have to find ways of coping with fears about what the much bigger, older pupils might do to them. In many countries the same myths abound concerning the initiation practices on entry to secondary school. New pupils will be chased by older children and rolled down grassy banks, or will have to suffer the horrors of the 'royal flush'[7] and so on. While most of these tales do indeed turn out to be allegorical, the anxieties of the newly arrived pupils are real enough

For most pupils, however, getting used to new teachers and their particular ways is more important. In the ORACLE study of transfer, for example, an English teacher, Mr Steele,[8] told pupils on their first day in the new school that 'each teacher you come across will have their own way of setting out work, and this is my way' (Galton and Willcocks 1983: 128). What is true for English will be true for every other area of the curriculum. Each teacher may have their own idiosyncratic ways of doing things. This contrasts sharply with the situation in the final year of the feeder school, where most lessons are delivered by the same teacher or by someone who has been the class teacher in a previous year

All these factors – new surroundings, new pupils and new teachers – are likely to have adverse effects, no matter how successful is the attempt to provide continuity during the immediate period preceding and following transfer. As Measor and Woods (1984) have pointed out, transfer to secondary school can be seen as a 'status passage' (Glaser and Strauss 1971) during which the pupil begins a journey through adolescence. Associated with this passage are rituals and procedures. In this view, if these practices do not change in the move from primary to secondary school, because continuity is all embracing, then pupils will not know that they have completed the process of transfer successfully. Thus school coordinators, charged with managing the transfer process, have to strike a reasonable balance, creating conditions whereby the effects of the move are minimised for most pupils while still maintaining a certain amount of disjunction (Measor and Woods 1984: 171).

In selecting which aspects of transfer they should seek to improve and which they can afford to ignore, school principals and their staff may reasonably look to researchers to help identify the consequences of opting for different solutions to the transfer problem. As the previous paragraphs have demonstrated, the transfer process has, indeed, been the subject of some research, although it would appear that certain crucial questions remain unanswered, particularly those concerning the extent of the hiatus in pupil progress and the best means to reduce or eliminate it.

The ORACLE replication study

The fact that, since the introduction of the National Curriculum, no systematic research of substance had been carried out which examined the impact of transfer on pupils' progress suggested that it might be useful to repeat the original ORACLE study. This would not only investigate whether the efforts of those charged with reform of the curriculum had succeeded in improving progression and continuity, but also whether any such changes had affected pupil performance since the issue was first examined two decades earlier. Further, conducting fieldwork in the primary feeder schools would make it possible to look at changes in teaching methods which had been the source of considerable controversy during the early 1990s (Alexander 1997). A bid was therefore made to the Economic and Social Research Council (ESRC) for funds to carry out the research and agreement was reached for a three-year study to begin in the 1995–96 academic year. However, whereas the funding for the original ORACLE programme allowed for three full-time research assistants and several part-time observers, the replication study employed only one research assistant. It was therefore necessary to reduce the scale of the study by, for example, observing for only one year in the feeder schools instead of two or three. Furthermore, only feeder schools which sent the majority of pupils to the selected transfer schools were included and as will be explained later, one of the original pair of transfer schools in an LEA some 75 miles distant from Leicester University was replaced by others that were only 15 miles away. In addition, other changes were made to the research design in the light of the experience gained during the original ORACLE study.

The original ORACLE transfer study broke new ground in that it combined both systematic and participant methods of observation when following pupils in the transfer schools (Galton and Delamont 1985). In contrast, the main research technique employed in the feeder schools was that of systematic observation or interaction analysis (Croll 1986). Over two or three years, depending on the age of transfer, eight pupils from some sixty classrooms together with their teachers were observed on three days each term. Their behaviour was coded every 25 seconds under a number of pre-specified categories using two instruments, the Pupil Record and the Teacher Record (Boydell 1974; 1975). These schedules were described in detail in Galton *et al.* (1980) and are reproduced in Galton *et al.* (1999b) in Appendix A of that book.

One of the problems with the first ORACLE study was that the transfer schools had to be selected at the beginning of the project in order to identify the feeder schools in which the eight target pupils would be selected for observation. Thus there was a delay of two years before the fieldwork in the transfer schools actually began. Inevitably, this resulted in a certain degree of attrition in the sample. When selecting a number of target pupils from a particular class in the primary school there was no guarantee that these pupils would end up in the same forms, groups or sets after transfer two years later. Accordingly, after transfer, it became more difficult to select classes containing a reasonable number of target pupils who had been observed over two years in their feeder schools. This was particularly true of mathematics where children were mostly placed in sets from day one after transfer. In the more extreme cases it was not possible to find a set with more than six original target pupils. Partly for this reason, systematic observation was used only in limited amounts for English and mathematics and data in the other curriculum areas were collected across a wider sample using the alternative technique known as participant observation. Unlike a systematic observer who adopts the role of a 'fly on the wall', the participant observer takes as active a part as possible in the classroom in order to understand what it is like to be part of this process. Each observer writes detailed case notes of all that is seen and heard and these can then be supplemented by interviews with both teacher and pupils in order to compare and contrast different points of view.

It was particularly important, therefore, to carry out participant observation during the pupils' first three days in their new school. Thereafter, on subsequent visits, systematic observation was carried out during English and mathematics periods in two sets containing the highest numbers of pupils from the top and bottom quartiles respectively. During the remainder of their time in each transfer school each researcher continued to use a participant approach when other lessons were being observed.

Mindful of the problems and limitations resulting in the decision to use only eight target pupils in the original ORACLE project, it was decided to adopt a different sampling technique for this replication study. On each visit six children in the primary school class were selected randomly. No attempt was made to stratify the selected sample of pupils by ability, although it was possible, retrospectively, to determine whether they were in the top, middle or bottom quartiles, as in the original ORACLE study. Teachers were asked to name pupils who, by reason of special learning or behavioural difficulties, were unrepresentative of the normal range of pupils in the school and these few cases were excluded from the observations. In the course of a year most pupils in the primary classes were observed on at least two visits. Consequently, when selecting at random a sample of pupils for observation in any two classes or sets in the transfer schools, it was highly probable that these pupils had also been observed in the feeder school. This provided a larger sample for comparative analysis even though the amount of data available for each pupil was less than in the original 1975–80 study. After the first three days further visits were then made to the transfer schools during each term of the 1997–98 school year in the manner similar to ORACLE.

On each visit two observers were present to provide what Cohen and Manion (1980) termed *investigator triangulation*. In the original ORACLE research at least three observers visited each transfer school during the course of the year. In the present study schools were assigned pairs of observers. In ORACLE all fieldnotes were passed to the most experienced fieldworker with a background in Anthropology. She then collated and indexed these notes in order to locate several examples of significant events. The subsequent analysis in which themes were identified was then discussed with the other observers before being written up as part of the report.

In the replication study a different approach was adopted. Pairs of observers took responsibility for a particular theme based on a general discussion following the school visits. Thus, for example, induction day visits and the first three days of the school year were selected for particular attention. In the present case all observers had the advantage of having the themes developed in both Galton and Willcocks (1983) and Delamont and Galton (1986) as a framework for these discussions. Differences and similarities between what was reported in the 1970s and what was observed in the present research were noted. Pairs of observers then went away and wrote a draft on a particular theme using illustrative examples taken from their fieldnotes. These drafts were circulated and the other pair of observers then examined their fieldnotes for examples that either supported or questioned the various propositions put forward in the draft. Further revisions would then be made.

In addition to the collecting of observation data, pupils were also tested at the end of the primary phase and at the end of the first year in the transfer school using the same tests as in the original ORACLE study. These were modified slightly to allow for changes in interpretation over the two decades and details of these modifications are presented in the companion volume dealing with the primary year of the present study (Galton *et al.* 1999b).

Table 1.1 Timetable for observation and testing in the 1996–97 transfer study

Summer term 1996	Autumn term 1996	Spring term 1997	Summer term 1997
Test pupil in basic skills (Richmond)			Test pupils in basic skills (Richmond)
Administer attitude, motivation and self-esteem measures	Administer attitude, motivation and self-esteem measures		Administer attitude, motivation and self-esteem measures
Systematic observation (2 days)	Systematic observation (First 3 days) Eng, Maths and Sc only + participant observation of other subjects. One further visit after half-term	Systematic observation (2 days) Eng, Maths and Sc only + participant observation of other subjects	Systematic observation (2 days) Eng, Maths and Sc only + participant observation of other subjects
Attend parents evening and assess their concerns on transfer			
Attend pupil induction day and administer projective measures 'going to new school'	Administer projective measures on different subject settings		
Question class teachers about pupils at risk			Question form tutors about pupils at risk

Unlike the original ORACLE study, however, much more information was collected about children's attitudes and feelings towards transfer. A series of instruments were developed, measuring not only liking for school and opinions about the transfer process, but also the children's confidence and self-concepts. These instruments will be discussed in greater detail in the relevant chapters. Finally, use was also made of semi-projective techniques in the form of a cartoon representation of children entering the new school which, again, will be described in greater detail in the appropriate chapter. Table 1.1 presents a brief description of the various measures used, together with the timetable giving the administration details. It will be seen that unlike the Richmond Tests which were administered on two occasions in June 1996 and June 1997, pupils completed the attitude questionnaire and other measures on a third occasion during the first term after transfer. This was in recognition of the findings from previous research to the effect that for a majority of pupils the uncertainties of transfer had been satisfactorily coped with during the early weeks of the first term in the new school.

During the final term in the feeder schools teachers were interviewed and asked to identify pupils whom they felt might be *at risk* in the period after transfer. Subsequently, the form tutors in the classes selected for observation in the transfer schools and the first year coordinator responsible for liaison were interviewed and asked to identify pupils who had failed to settle down in the new school. Pupils were not interviewed formally but when the occasion presented itself either individuals or groups of children were engaged in extended conversations during, for example, lunch or in the playground. Parents were also asked to say how well they thought their children had settled in at the new school. In these ways, therefore an element of *between method triangulation* was also introduced to support the observations. In general, the research team feel that the various changes made to the design of the study, to the measures used and to the form of analysis undertaken did not depart radically from the original approach developed for ORACLE. If anything, within the limitations of funding, they offered a more efficient and robust framework in which to address the various issues concerning the transfer process.

The transfer schools

In the original ORACLE study, three different transfer situations were examined in three different local authorities situated within some seventy miles of Leicester. These were designated as *Local Authority A*,[9] where transfer was to 9–13 middle schools, *Local Authority B*, where transfer was to 11–14 high schools, and *Local Authority C*, where transfer was to 12–18 secondary schools. In the present study, both Local Authority A and B were retained but Local Authority C was excluded on grounds of costs and manageability, it being the farthest away from the university base. A further reason for this decision was that in the intervening period between the two studies, the age of pupils entering the two high schools in Local Authority B had changed from 11 to 10. As a result pupils would be taking the Key Stage 2 National Curriculum tests at the end of their first year in these transfer schools. Given the 'high stakes' nature of this examination, following on from the decision to publish results in the form of league tables, it was possible that classroom practice might be unduly influenced by the need to maximise pupils' scores on the tests. It was therefore obviously important, in this context, to have another pair of schools where transfer took place at 11 years after the Key Stage 2 examinations had already been held in the primary feeder schools. Accordingly, a pair of 11–14 transfer schools on the edge of Local Authority B was chosen as replacements for those in Local Authority C.

In selecting the six transfer schools for the original ORACLE study two main criteria were used. First, the two transfer schools from the same local authority tended to share a catchment area or, at least, had adjacent catchment areas so that as far as possible the social mix of the pupils was very similar. Second, a distinction was made between schools who attempted to maintain the primary ethos into the first year after transfer and those who adopted a more typical secondary pattern. In *Moving from the Primary Classroom* (Galton and Willcocks 1983) these schools were labelled by letter such that *AST* denoted the secondary style transfer school in Local Authority A, while *APT* denoted the primary style transfer school in the same local authority. Schools in the two remaining LEAs were similarly labelled *BST*, *BPT*, *CST* and *CPT* respectively.

However, in subsequent publications, particularly those based largely on the participant observation such as Delamont and Galton (1986), each school was given a pseudonym. Schools with a secondary style ethos were named after Walter Scott novels, while those with a primary ethos were named after Thomas Love Peacock. Thus AST became *Guy Mannering* and APT became *Gryll Grange*. Table 1.2 shows the main characteristics of the six schools used in the present study. For the pairs of schools in Local Authority A and B, the characteristics used in the original ORACLE study to define their ethos are placed in brackets.

Table 1.2 Main characteristics of the six transfer schools

Local Authority	A		B		C (new authority)	
1977 identity type	AST	APT	BST	BPT	n/a	n/a
Name	Guy Mannering	Gryll Grange	Kenilworth	Maid Marion	Channings	Danesbury
Age range	9–13	9–13	10–14	10–14	11–14	11–14
First year base	yes (no)	yes (yes)	no (no)	yes (yes)	no	no
First year play area	no (no)	no (yes)	no (no)	yes (yes)	no	no
First year assembly	yes (no)	no (yes)	no (no)	no (yes)	no	no
Mainly one teacher	yes (no)	no (yes)	no (no)	no (yes)	no	no
School uniform	yes (yes)	yes (no)	yes (yes)	yes (yes)	yes	yes
Sets in maths/Eng	no (yes)	yes (no)	yes (yes)	yes (no)	yes	yes
Setting elsewhere	no (yes)	no (no)	yes (yes)	no (no)	no	no
Stars/credits given	yes (yes)	yes (no)	yes (no)	no (no)	yes	yes

It is generally obvious that in the intervening two decades the distinctive characteristics which identified a secondary or primary ethos have generally become blurred so that schools are no longer distinguishable in these terms.

For example, in Local Authority B neither Maid Marion (BPT) nor Kenilworth (BST) now holds regular first year assemblies. There is also less emphasis on having one particular teacher responsible for most lessons, the result, in part, of increased specialisation at the top end of the Key Stage 2 National Curriculum. Decisions about banding and setting are less clear-cut. For the two replacement 11–14 high schools the respective profiles are entirely similar. To distinguish them from the original ORACLE transfer schools their names have been taken from the works of Mrs Henry Wood and they are named Channings and Danesbury respectively. However, it is interesting to note that if Channings had been chosen as a transfer school in the earlier study it would then have been defined as having a distinctive primary ethos.[10]

The recurring themes of transfer

In this chapter we have discussed some of the major issues concerning the transfer of primary pupils to secondary school. Much of the research on the topic is dated and, in particular, that dealing with the impact of transfer on pupil progress is over two decades old. Although from time to time most local authorities have been sufficiently concerned about the transfer problem to encourage schools to attempt various initiatives, with the notable exception of one or two LEAs, scant evidence has been collected about the success or otherwise of these attempts to ease the move from primary to secondary school. There is some research to suggest that pupils are now less concerned than previously about the move to the bigger school, but almost no evidence to indicate that, as hoped by the then Secretary of State, Kenneth Baker, the introduction of the National Curriculum has solved the problem of curriculum continuity. Information about the effect of transfer on pupil progress remains fragmentary and is mainly based on professional judgement rather than on empirical evidence.

However, since the introduction of the 1988 Education Reform Act (ERA), the circumstances concerning the governance of the schools involved in the original ORACLE study have changed enormously. Two of the schools in the sample from that first transfer study have since opted for Grant Maintained status and are now independent of the local authority. Perhaps more importantly, in the context of transfer, has been the shift in thinking brought about by ERA and all that followed. The push for a 'market forces' approach to education has meant that the local authority is no longer able to protect individual schools from the winds of competition. Schools now have to compete for pupils both within and outside their traditional catchment areas. Hence, as will be shown in the subsequent chapters, the increased emphasis on liaison with the feeder primary schools is not just due to concerns about the social adjustment of future pupils. Providing prospective parents with a positive image of a school is now regarded as essential if they are to exercise their parental choice in its favour at transfer. One consequence of this increased need to 'market' the school has been the shift in the date on which the transfer procedures begin. Twenty years ago, it was generally the case that the first and only meeting with prospective parents would take place in the second half of the summer term preceding transfer. Today, parents are invited into the transfer schools in September at the beginning of their child's last year in the primary school. This will be the first of several meetings, including in some cases individual appointments where the concerns of a prospective pupil will be explored in some detail.

Another important factor has been the increase in public accountability through the imposition of the statutory testing programme. The National Curriculum Assessment Tests, in theory at least, now provide a baseline whereby pupils moving from the primary school can be allocated to appropriate sets according to their level of performance at Key Stage 2. Yet the results from a survey carried out by Worcester LEA (1997) show that few headteachers in the transfer schools regard this information as valid. Whereas 80 per cent of respondents said that they made use of the pastoral information supplied by the feeder schools, less than half said they paid attention to the statutory assessment results or other test data. Fewer than 20 per cent made use of portfolios of pupils' work or records of achievement.

Perhaps, even more important, has been the change in culture within the feeder primary schools as a result of political and media pressure. As discussed in *Inside the Primary Classroom: 20 Years On* (Galton *et al.* 1999b), this unprecedented campaign, described by one commentator as 'a Reign of Terror' (Brighouse 1997) has led to a shift in the balance of classroom organisation towards the greater use of whole class teaching. However, this shift has not generally been accompanied by a change in the use of different teaching tactics, that is the moment-by-moment exchanges between teachers and their pupils. For the most part, teachers still talk *at* rather than talk *with* their pupils so that the ratio of statements made to questions asked by a teacher has stayed remarkably stable over the two decades. This despite the calls for greater use of 'whole class interactive teaching' (Reynolds 1998).

The impact of these changes has been most noticeable in a subject like science. One might expect in an empirically based, experimental discipline, that children would be engaged in cooperative activity on the grounds that 'a problem shared is a problem solved'. Instead, Y6 primary pupils are now taught as a class for nearly 50 per cent of the lesson during which time the emphasis is on transmitting information rather than on problem solving or hypothesis generation. This didactic approach has resulted in a tendency for pupils to engage in what twenty years ago was largely a practice observed in the secondary schools; namely that of easy riding, described earlier in the chapter. Science offers many opportunities to indulge in this form of behaviour, as there are plenty of legitimate reasons for pupils to leave their places, as when, for example, they are required to collect or return pieces of equipment such as a stopwatch or a metre rule. In a crowded classroom it is not too difficult for a student to take a circuitous route to the storage area and once there to engage in extended unnecessary housekeeping activities such as repackaging the stopwatches in their box (Galton *et al*. 1999b).

In Galton and Willcocks (1983) it was argued that these practices were developed by pupils as a response to the rather routine and somewhat monotonous curriculum offered in the first months at secondary school. Similar conclusions were reached by David H. Hargreaves (1982: 3) who likened such lessons during a typical school day to 'seven very dull television programmes, which could not be switched off'. Now it would appear that these avoidance strategies have been adopted by some primary school pupils in response to the teachers' attempts to cope with the huge increase in subject matter in the National Curriculum by increased use of didactic whole class teaching. It is pertinent to ask what these same children will now do when faced with a secondary curriculum which in many respects may be very similar to that offered in the final year of Key Stage 2.

These, then, are the major themes of our research. In the next chapter we begin by looking at the changes which have taken place in the liaison strategies adopted by schools and we make an attempt to gauge their effects. As we have argued, twenty years ago, liaison consisted for the most part of an evening event for single parents during the summer term prior to transfer. Pupils also visited their new school for a brief conducted tour and occasionally secondary teachers would visit the feeder primary school to answer questions. One of the main purposes of the parents' evening would be to advise on the purchase of school uniform and to offer guidance on how it should be labelled and so on. How far this situation has changed, and the extent, to which any such changes have brought about more effective liaison, will be considered in the next chapter.

Notes

1 Some authors use the words transfer and transition interchangeably. Here we use the term *transfer* to denote the move to a new school and *transition* to indicate the move from one year group to the next within the same school.

2 Thus several Local Authority Education Officers in their submissions to the Council would use the identical sentence beginning 'There is a time in the development of a pupil somewhere between the end of early childhood and the onset of adolescence. This period is generally taken to occur between the ages of . . .'. Then would be inserted 8 to 12 or 9 to 13 years as appropriate.

3 Even greater difficulties could be encountered in modern languages and science. Some middle schools offered both French and German and this tended to guarantee a place in the double language option for GCE. These pupils were able to drop another subject and so would be timetabled together for the compulsory core options. Similar problems occurred in allowing choices of additional

mathematics or extra science. In effect, fast-track streams were established at the outset which then had a knock-on effect across the remaining broad ability bands. Thus one of the key arguments in establishing comprehensive education, putting an end to the rigid streaming of the grammar schools was subverted by lack of cooperation between the middle and upper sectors.

4 I am indebted to my Homerton colleagues, John Gray and Jean Rudduck who contributed material to this section in a review on transfer and transition which we jointly undertook for the DfEE (Galton *et al.* 1999a).

5 Again, my colleague, John Gray, collated the material for this section of our DfEE review on which the section of the chapter is based.

6 See Chapter 1 in Galton *et al*'s (1999b) *Inside the Primary Classroom: 20 Years On* for a detailed evaluation of Mr Woodhead's contribution to the education debate. The oft quoted section from *Culture and Anarchy* refers to culture as the study of 'all matters which most concern us, the best which has been thought and said in the world' and reflects the then Chief Inspector's view that education is essentially concerned with the transmission of subject knowledge (see Woodhead 1995 for an example of the argument).

7 This term is used in Australia to describe the practice of having one's head pushed down the lavatory bowl while someone pulls the chain. In all our research into transfer during 1975–80 and more recently during 1995–97 we never had a case of this kind reported to us by pupils we interviewed.

8 Not his real name.

9 In Delamont and Galton (1986) local authority A became Ashburton, B became Bridgehampton and C became Coalthorpe.

10 This conclusion is based on conversations with several retired lecturers from the local University School of Education who placed PGCE students in the school and a headteacher of another high school in the same Local Education Authority who began his career at Channings in the late 1970s.

2

'GETTING USED TO
EACH OTHER'

Cross-phase liaison and induction

Linda Hargreaves and Debbie Wall

> This is your chance to make a really good start. I know you are
> a really well-behaved class because our class has won the award
> in assembly. I know you're really quiet. So enjoy your day.

With these words of encouragement from their teacher, 30 10-year-olds set
off along the road to spend a whole day in the local neighbouring school
where they were destined to go after the summer holiday. A few minutes earlier the same teacher had been re-compiling the children's records in response
to a last minute request from a secondary colleague in the transfer school.
This last minute request was neither expected nor welcome, since she and the
other teachers in her school had devoted considerable time to the preparation
of assessment information and records which they had already passed on.
The probable futility of the exercise had not escaped her.

> They phoned this morning. They want the children's records for the
> whole of KS2, not just the current year, . . . and they've [the records]
> got all out of alphabetical order . . . probably won't be looked at
> anyway, not all those years back.

The children, meanwhile, were leaving behind their bright, airy, and carpeted
classroom with its tables put together in twos and threes, and its colourful and
informative displays such as a paper 'homophone tree', and panel of huge
paper blooms entitled 'Flower power'. The room contained two computers, a
class library, and equipment for mathematics and science. As the human crocodile moved along the pavement on its way to the new school, hopping over
cracks and dark patches some children emitted nervous comments, such as:

> I'm scared
> I'm real nervous

I can't feel my legs
I don't want to go.

Similar journeys were taking place all over the region as the oldest children in each local primary school began their 'Transfer' or 'Induction' days. These have now become a standard feature of cross-phase transfer procedures, although twenty years earlier, when primary to secondary transfer was studied during the ORACLE project, only one secondary school, Maid Marion, had instituted such a day. By the time that this ORACLE replication study took place, however, all five cross-phase liaison options identified two decades earlier were features of transfer liaison schemes. Delamont and Galton (1986: 26) identified the following practices:

Option 1: Teacher visits to the feeder schools
Option 2: Pupil tours of the destination school
Option 3: Parents evenings in the destination school
Option 4: Pupils spent a whole working day at the destination school
Option 5: Teachers from destination school teach at feeder schools.

Delamont and Galton had been denied permission to observe Option 4, the full transfer day, but they noted subsequently, the 'relative ineffectiveness of four of the five options at reducing anxiety', in comparison to the full working day which 'reduced anxiety to a significant extent' (ibid.: 27). A few years later, in the early 1980s, however, Measor and Woods (1984) were able to describe induction schemes which included a full day's visit to the transfer school, followed by a further half-day visit, as well as an open evening for parents. In their observation of such a scheme, Measor and Woods identified 'Socialisation, reassurance, demystification [as] the order of the day' and noted the teachers' dilemma between maintaining the children's excitement, and demonstrating that the school was a caring but also disciplined place. They concluded that 'if the aim was to make the pupils feel at home, it was accomplished in other ways as well.' (Measor and Woods 1984: 33).

While the teachers' dilemma was still evident to the observers carrying out the present study, the embryonic pre-transfer programmes described by Delamont and Galton had expanded considerably to become pre-planned, structured programmes which extended almost throughout the school year before transfer. These transfer programmes can be divided into two parts. The first of these parts we call 'induction' and this covered all events which involved children. The second part we term 'liaison'. This included a new layer of administrative and professional contacts between teachers. Such 'cross-phase liaison programmes' were an attempt to increase curriculum continuity and ensure pupil progression. They had emerged from local meetings set up for the moderation of teacher assessment proposed originally by the Task Group on Assessment and Testing or TGAT (1988). These meetings between schools within and across key stages began in the early 1990s. Their limited success will be evident below.

Table 2.1 Primary and transfer schools' liaison and induction activities

Liaison and induction activities	GM	GG	K	MM	D	C
Cross-phase liaison activities involving staff						
Regular meetings involving head-teachers	♦	♦	♦	♦	♦	♦
All Transfer senior staff involved in curriculum liaison			♦			
Transfer liaison co-ordinator visits primary teachers	♦	♦	♦	♦	♦	
Teachers meet to discuss new intake			♦	♦	♦	♦
Teachers meet to discuss curriculum	♦		♦	♦		
Secondary teachers visit primary to observe/assess children			♦	(♦)		
Primary teachers visit secondary school						
Staff share professional development days		(♦)			♦	♦
Induction activities involving staff						
Transfer Head or deputy meets children in primary schools		♦	♦		♦	
Transfer Head or deputy takes assembly in primary schools			♦		♦	♦
Secondary teacher teaches in primary schools					♦	
Induction activities involving children						
Autumn term Open evening to look round with parents	♦	♦	♦			♦
Induction day – full day in transfer school	♦	♦	♦	♦	♦	♦
Liaison co-ordinator visits primary to see children	♦	♦	♦	♦	♦	
Opportunities to use transfer school facilities for, e.g. gym, library, music, school grounds			♦		♦	♦
Secondary pupils visit/contact primary children				(♦)	♦	
Primary and secondary schools fund SEN transfer scheme			♦	♦		
Head of Intake year visits all children with SEN	♦	♦				
SENCO visits children in primary schools						
Full day at Transfer school prior to main induction day						♦
Letters from secondary to primary SEN children				♦		
Induction activities involving parents						
Open evening in autumn term		♦	♦	♦		♦
Parents' evening	♦	♦	♦	♦	♦	♦
Secondary representatives attend primary parents' evening			♦			
After transfer, transfer school contacts new intake parents					♦	

Notes: ♦ Event was established, (♦) Event had taken place once or was planned.

The range of activities encompassed by the induction and liaison schemes is listed in Table 2.1 where the transfer schools are identified by their initials (e.g.

MM = Maid Marion). Some activities, such as the full transfer day, were common to all the transfer schools; others were unique to individual schools. Induction events began as early as October in the final primary year, and served as much to sell the schools to prospective children and their parents, as to inform them about secondary school life. This advertising function was a consequence of schools' competition for pupils following the introduction of local management of schools in the 1988 Education Reform Act. Thus, by the time of transfer in the autumn, most children in the present study would have:

- attended an open evening with their parents;
- met the transfer head teacher or deputy head teacher in a primary assembly;
- met the primary liaison teacher during the year;
- spent a full working day at the transfer school;
- been discussed by their primary school and transfer school teachers;
- had records of their achievements, attendance, behaviour and health compiled and transferred.

Table 2.1 also shows that schools such as Kenilworth and Danesbury placed particular importance on the liaison and transfer processes. Primary schools close to Danesbury were encouraged to make use of the library, ICT and sports facilities. In addition, some of the Danesbury Year 8 students, along with their design and technology teacher had been working in the primary schools. Another joint activity involved children from primary schools close to Kenilworth. Those who could play a musical instrument were invited to take part in after-school music sessions in this transfer school's keyboard suite culminating in a concert for parents.

The proliferation of paperwork and record keeping in primary schools necessitated by the National Curriculum and its assessment arrangements (Campbell and Neill 1994) contributed to an expectation that similarly detailed records would be transferred from primary to transfer school. Several of the schools were in the process of trying to streamline this process, and to agree locally standardised formats, as we shall see later in the chapter. The primary teachers who had to compile the documents were understandably sceptical about the value of this time-consuming work, for while the transfer schools asked for these records, they were not necessarily passed on to the form or subject tutors unless problems arose about a child. Typically the records remained with the teachers responsible for transfer liaison who would inform the form tutors of any critical concerns as or when necessary. Only one school's liaison coordinator held regular meetings with the new entrants' teachers after transfer to review how well children were adjusting and to discuss any potential difficulties.

One important development since the 1970s, however, concerned children with special educational needs (SEN). This was particularly significant where children transferred from Year 5 into Year 6 at the end of Key Stage 2 and

31

so would take the statutory assessment tests within a year of entering the transfer school. One family of schools, including Maid Marion and Kenilworth, the local upper (14–18) school and eight primary schools had set up a scheme to focus on SEN in which the schools' SENCOs met regularly and the schools jointly funded a part-time teacher to work with children across transfer. While these schools pooled funds to pay for these liaison activities, the lack of targeted financial support to help SEN pupils cope with the move was a limitation in some of the other transfer schools. In one of the other transfer schools, for example, the SENCO was part-time and worked only three days a week. She therefore had no time to visit the primary schools in the pyramid and meet the children. In another school, the SENCO had just been given full-time responsibility for a tutor group and was extremely concerned about coping with the incoming statemented children. In all cases it was clear that form tutors and class teachers were relied upon to play a major supporting role. As one SENCO put it, when eighteen children were to share thirty hours of ancillary support and fifteen of these hours were designated for one child, a 'creative use of timetabling' was essential.

However, before looking more closely at what actually happened during the liaison and induction events, we shall report on the hopes and fears which children still had about transfer after the transfer days.

Hopes and fears at the new school gates

The 'New School Gates' task presented children with the ink drawing[1] shown in Figure 2.1, which depicts two girls and two boys in a group approaching the gateway of their new school. We asked the primary children to imagine what two of the children in the picture might be saying to each other and to write this down in the spaces provided. Since the task was being done after the transfer day visit, the children's projections were based on some knowledge of what lay ahead and this was evident from some of the responses. This activity made it possible to use the same stimulus to collect open-ended responses concerning various issues associated with transfer from 600 children who completed the task. After an initial survey of the data, responses were classified in terms of their content (e.g. social relationships, buildings and facilities, work and the curriculum, and routines, etc.) in addition to the expressions of feelings and attitudes. Whether or not the comments of speaker 1 and speaker 2 in the picture were in agreement, disagreement, or unrelated and whether they referred to a boy or girl pupil in the picture was also recorded. The incidence of the major content categories is shown in Table 2.2 but first we shall consider the expressions of emotion.

Delamont and Galton (1986) pointed out that the children often had a mixture of feelings about moving school, a phenomenon which Measor and Woods (1984) interpreted as an aspect of identity formation. The school gates activity allowed children to make two responses about transfer, so that

Figure 2.1 The 'New School Gates' activity.

they could express mixed emotions without implying personal inconsistency. Typical of the things that children wrote (children's words, punctuation and spelling retained) were the following:

BOY 1: 'Yikes! Well, here we are. I really nervous – and take note I put the emphasis on really!

BOY 2: 'you can't be more nervous than me. And anyway we'll adapt to it.

GIRL: I'm realy scared and nervous.

BOY: I'm not scared one bit. I'm going to enjoy it.

BOY: "I'm pretty ushure about this place". "I'm realy nervous". "I hope I don't have to sit next to someone I don't know". "It's weard first you're the oldest and then you're the youngest".

GIRL: "Yes, it is weard, but at the moment I've got mixed feelings im excited and scared". "Well here it goes".

GIRL: I didn't want to come here today.

BOY: Neither did I but my mum says I need my education.

As well as allowing for mixed responses, this method also showed when responses reinforced each other. A significant number of girl pupils (18 per cent of those completing the activity) invented a supportive comment for speaker 2 compared to boys (11.6 percent). For example:

GIRL: O my God I m realy exsighted but what if someone bothers me what shoud I do.
BOY: Well I will come and help just call my name and I will come and help you (*Y5 girl pupil's response*).

A very high proportion of the children attributed negative feelings to the children in the picture, such as being worried or nervous about the situation but girls (88 per cent) were more likely to do so than boys (71 per cent). Girls (74 per cent), however, were also more likely than boys (66 per cent) to ascribe positive feelings to the pupils in the picture such as:

GIRL 1: It's big. there is lots of big kids. I'm worried
GIRL 2: Me too, but I bet we'll get used to it. Oh look, theirs our friend we met on induction day. (*Y5 girl pupil's response*)

It is immediately noticeable from Table 2.2 that social and practical concerns were mentioned more often than the curriculum or schoolwork. It could be, of course that the induction days increased these practical concerns, such as worries about getting lost, while reassuring children about the curriculum. The categories parallel those identified in the 1970s by Delamont and Galton but the frequencies might appear small. We might expect a majority of the children

Table 2.2 Major categories of children's comments about going to a new school, based on 'New School Gates' activity (as percentage frequency of occurrence)

Content of children's comments	Boys $N = 294 \times 2^2$	Girls $N = 298 \times 2$	All $N = 601 \times 2$
Social relationships			
with other children	11.3	19.8	15.3
with teachers	10.4	9.7	10.3
The school itself			
'new school'	12.4	12.8	12.6
size of school	8.2	11.6	9.7
finding way around/			
moving between classes	7.1	7.2	7.0
Curriculum and work	6.2	5.6	5.4
School routines (e.g. dinner times)	4.5	3.7	4.4

to have had some views on gaining and losing friends, getting lost, or learning French. The relatively low frequencies are probably a by-product of the decision to ask for limited open-ended responses rather than asking children to complete to a typical inventory, which would have forced children to respond to all issues raised. Such a method would result in inevitably higher frequencies since all children would be asked to respond to questions about 'stricter teachers', doing science, or being bullied. The present methods enabled us to identify the children's uppermost, spontaneous concerns, following their induction visits. The main categories of response are validated by children's responses to another task, reported in Chapter 5, in which they were asked to list three things they were most and least looking forward to at the new school.

Boys' and girls' responses were surprisingly similar in most categories, but girls were more likely than boys to write about social relationships, and to mention the size of the school. Comments expressing social concerns, about other children, teachers and about getting lost or the size of the school constituted nearly 30 per cent of all the children's comments. Typical comments, using the children's spellings, included:

GIRL: I think our new school is going to be great
BOY: Are you kidding – look at the size of the school we re bound to get lost
   (*boy's response, aged 11*)

On the induction days, several children commented on the size of the buildings, how far it was to walk from class to class, and how tiring it was to go up and down stairs. The strong impression of the size of the transfer schools, compared to the primary schools, was evident in many of the responses:

GIRL: That school is massive comparied to our other school isent it?
BOY: yea it is like a grasshopper on an ant. (*Y5 boy's response*)

The most common comments made by both boys and girls were about social relationships, and confirm Demetriou *et al.*'s (2000) findings, based on interviews, about the importance of friendships. Table 2.3 provides more detail about these social comments. While 22 per cent of responses, made by boys and girls, referred to making new friends, girls were more likely to comment on losing friends. Boys were much more concerned about the new headteacher and 'stricter teachers'. On the Induction Days, the observers' notes showed that boys were more likely to be mixing with boys from other primary schools (and older boys already in the school), in communal games of football (where this was allowed). Girls tended to stay in primary school-defined groups rather than mix with other children. It appeared that relatively few children were anxious about bullying, since this appeared in less than 3 per cent of the total comments, although more girls (3.5 per cent) than boys (2.0 per cent) referred to it.

Table 2.3 Comments on social matters from the 'New School Gates' task (percentage frequency of occurrence)

Comment	Boys $n = 294 \times 2$ % social responses (% total responses)	Girls $n = 298 \times 2$ % social responses (% total responses)	All $n = 601 \times 2$ % social responses (% total responses)
Peer relationships			
New or more friends	22.3 (4.8)	21.3 (6.2)	21.4 (5.4)
Lack of friends	2.3 (0.5)	8.5 (1.7)	4.8 (1.2)
Opposite sex	4.7 (1.0)	2.4 (0.7)	3.2 (0.8)
Older/bigger children	6.5 (1.4)	7.6 (2.2)	6.8 (1.7)
Siblings/relatives	1.0 (0.2)	2.0 (0.6)	1.6 (0.4)
Other social	5.6 (1.2)	12.8 (3.7)	1.0 (2.5)
Being bullied	9.3 (2.0)	12.1 (3.5)	11.1 (2.7)
Fighting	0.0 (0.0)	0.1 (0.2)	0.4 (0.1)
Teachers			
Teachers/headteacher	32.6 (7.7)	26.2 (7.6)	30.6 (7.7)
Stricter teachers	12.6 (2.7)	7.9 (2.3)	9.9 (2.5)
Being shouted at	0.0 (0.0)	1.0 (0.3)	0.8 (0.2)

Typical of the children's comments about friends were:

GIRL: Oh no we don't know anybody and worse yet they could be horrible.
BOY: They will probably be nice and comforting, welcoming and might want to be friend's I wonder if I'm right?

BOY: I'm pretty scared but we'll probably make lots of friends.
GIRL: I bet you'll make lots of friends because you know what every boy likes in the world, FOOTBALL!

As can be seen in Table 2.2, references to school work or school routines constituted a very small proportion of the comments. Only 2 per cent mentioned work being harder or easier, tests or exams, or making mistakes, while direct references to curriculum areas were made in only 3.5 per cent of the children's comments. Finally school routines such as dinner times and home time featured in about 3 per cent of responses, with boys mentioning dinner times more than twice as often as the girls (2.4 per cent boys; 1 per cent girls).

In their attitudes to the new school, girls were significantly more likely to use negative words like 'nervous' and 'scared' than boys (12.7 per cent and 9.4 per cent respectively) and significantly more girls (6.2 per cent) than boys (3.1 per cent) used the word 'worried'. At the same time, more girls than boys made positive comments (74 per cent: 66 per cent respectively) though this difference was not significant. Figures such as these suggest that more girls than boys expressed their feelings, thus tending to confirm feminine and masculine stereotypes.

The 'New School Gates' task was completed very soon after the induction days, but surprisingly perhaps, only 13 per cent of the children referred to induction day events. Of these, science and English were mentioned significantly more often than mathematics. Overall, it can be concluded that this task revealed that the children's concerns a few weeks before leaving primary school were mainly social, were focused on gaining or losing friends, and to a lesser extent, about meeting their new teachers and headteachers. In the following pages, therefore, some of these induction events will be described, but before doing this, we shall concentrate on the liaison programmes which preceded them.

Liaison programmes

'Liaison programmes' refer here to the communication and transfer of documents between schools and teachers about the curriculum and the new intake of children. All six transfer schools had some kind of liaison programme, as shown in Table 2.1, but these differed in emphasis, extent and formality. One might expect the age and educational stage of the children to underlie such differences but this did not appear to be the case. At Gryll Grange and Guy Mannering, where transfer occurred at 9+, liaison and induction procedures consisted mainly of visits by the liaison coordinators. Regular headteachers' pyramid meetings existed as a matter of course, possibly precluding the need for more detailed liaison arrangements. National Curriculum programmes of work had been designed to maximise curriculum continuity. The transferring of documents was under review as the schools were trying to develop a town-wide system. Table 2.4 lists the documents, and their transfer dates, which were being considered for the new scheme, and which the Year 4 teachers would be asked to compile. The exchange of these detailed records was apparently the extent of preparation for transfer for the youngest children in our sample.

In contrast, the arrangements in Kenilworth and Maid Marion where transfer occurred two terms before the Key Stage 2 (KS2) National Curriculum Tests, and where competition for pupils was an issue, were more formal, particularly at Kenilworth, as we shall see in detail below. The two remaining schools, Channings and Danesbury, were taking in children after the end of KS2 and with some three years to the next national assessment point. These schools belonged to a well-established town cluster. Here, the academic achievement levels for the new children had implications for the schools' results in the league tables, which at that time did not include in-take characteristics as part of the 'value added' measures. Nevertheless in spite of these similar conditions, there were differences between the schools in their approaches to liaison. We shall report below on the most structured of these, at Kenilworth, which won praise from OFSTED in an inspection shortly after the end of the project.

Table 2.4 Proposed transfer documents for each pupil in one pyramid

Document and delivery date	Contents	
Basic personal details	Name	Date of birth
On disk or printout	Gender	Ethnic origin
	Address	Contact number
Friday after summer half term	Medical info.	Guardians
	Doctor	Religion
Summative transfer document	*Curriculum information*	
1st Friday after summer half-term	English, Maths, Science SATs	
	Reading age (test specified)	
	Noteworthy strengths	
Y4/Y5 face-to face meetings	*Work habits*	
About Summative Transfer	Motivation	
Documents	Ability	
By penultimate Friday of summer	Attendance	
term	Behaviour	
	Friendships (working/unproductive)	
	Special educational needs	
	Stage on SEN register	
	School arrangements	
	Special arrangements	
	Medical	
	Dietary needs	
	Involvement of other agencies	
Yellow folders	Indicative samples of Y4 core subjects	
	Current reading record	
Penultimate Friday of summer term	Reports to parents (R – Y4)	
	NC summative sheets – all subjects	
	Relevant correspondence	
	A4 sheet showing:	
	Detailed medical information	
	Extra curricular activities	
	Noteworthy aptitudes	
	Specific social information	
	Child's educational history	
Special needs folders	Current SEN stage	
By penultimate Friday of summer	Target sheets Y4 onwards	
term	All official letters/documents	
	N –Y4	
	Evidence from targets	
Face to face discussions with	Test results	
Coordinator or SENCO in June	Statements	
	Behavioural difficulties	
	Parent support	
Curriculum maps	Y3/4 curriculum to be passed on to Y5	
	(one in each yellow folder)	

The liaison activities listed in Table 2.1 vividly reveal the advances on the five options shown by Delamont and Galton in the 1970s. Three of the six transfer schools had what one coordinator described as 'a structured annually repeated transfer programme' although another coordinator described his school's programme beyond the parents open evening, induction day and the intake parents' evening, as 'haphazard'.

A crucial element in the establishment of inter-school communication and hence the possibility of effective liaison, however, is the degree of trust between the participating institutions. During the 1980s, schools had begun to form cooperative clusters or pyramids, and at least one of the participating LEAs had set up cross-phase Development Groups, partly as a way to manage the hand-over of INSET funds to the schools themselves. Local Management of Schools, introduced in the early 1990s, unfortunately had had the effect of turning partners into rivals as geographically close schools competed for pupils (see Husband and Bridges 1996) except where inter-school trust was already well established. The Channings–Danesbury group of schools was such a cluster and, officially at least, they posed no threats to each other. The fortnightly meetings of the cluster headteachers enabled them to discuss new initiatives, hold shared INSET sessions and track changes in the schools' intake patterns. However, although the headteachers, knew each other well, there was less direct contact between the teachers, and Channings and Danesbury differed considerably in their liaison and induction programmes.

We observed the April meeting of the Channings Y7 tutors with the primary Y6 tutors which was the first of its kind, whereas Danesbury had held joint meetings with its partner primary schools in previous years. The Channings meeting began with tea and cakes, followed by a short welcoming speech from the headteacher. The meeting aimed to give the staff the opportunity to get to know each other, to set dates for the Head of Year 7 to visit the primary schools, and to provide feedback on the previous year's intake. The aims were achieved to some extent: dates were made, concerns about SEN children expressed and the teachers looked at the photographs of the previous years' children in their new classes, and talked about their progress. Comments such as 'Very bright. Best at my subject', 'Hangs on. Nice kid, yes!', and 'He's tried it on once or twice but I sorted him out,' were made by the secondary teachers.

However, although the maths and English tutors conversed with primary teachers, other Channings tutors spent much of the evening talking to each other. Despite a gradual mixing of the groups, there was still an assumed superiority in the language of the secondary teachers, who talked of 'coming down to the primary school', and, 'course structures filtering down'. The observer concluded, however, that the evening, 'appeared useful', and while there was no formal discussion of curriculum continuity, it did enable teachers to make contact with each other.

Since this meeting at Channings was the first of its kind, it was not surprising that it took a little while for the teachers to begin to interact. Kenilworth and its main partner primaries, on the other hand, had a well-established curriculum liaison programme. Observers attended two of the 'Curriculum Continuity' meetings which will be described below, as well as two parents evenings, and the Autumn Open Evening.

Curriculum continuity meetings

Kenilworth's programme of liaison meetings included one round in October, which was covered by the schools' in-service training budgets, and a further round of meetings in teachers' own time in April. The observers' independent reports of the mathematics and science coordinators' meetings tended to suggest that despite the familiarity of the set-up, a clash of values and cultures was evident at both meetings.

The schools had agreed to compare assessments of process skills, or 'Ma1' and 'Sc1', or Attainment Target One in Mathematics and Science respectively, by discussing some marked and annotated examples of children's reports of investigations in mathematics or science respectively. The meetings were mainly about the assessment of children's investigative skills in science and mathematics. The staff also discussed, however, the secondary headteacher's proposal that they should spend half a day visiting each other's schools to observe the children work. This would have meant that the primary teachers would no longer need to prepare thumbnail sketches about each child as they did under the present regime. Visit dates were set up but not before the secondary heads of department had protested:

If it's out of my INSET budget, the answer's 'No'.

How much can realistically be gained? It's nice to meet the teachers and children but how useful is it compared with a record sheet?

The next issue discussed was testing. The groups had been trying to select standardised tests which the children could take prior to transfer. In this case the Y6 National Curriculum Tests, designed to serve such a purpose, were of no use because transfer took place a year before the children took the examination. The mathematics team had agreed on a published test but the science group was still trying to decide which test to use. The eventual decision was that the Year 5 pupils would take the Year 6 QCA examination paper. The primary teachers would mark the paper and pass the results back to the transfer school. 'In the interim,' said the head of science, 'I shall continue to test on entry.' In saying this he clearly indicated, if unwittingly, to his primary colleagues that he did not place great value on their present extensive efforts.

The final agenda item was the discussion of the marking and grading of children's investigative skills according to the National Curriculum level descriptors. It was soon evident that the two phases had very different interpretations of these levels. The main issue for the transfer staff was whether the children had recorded their decision-making processes and justified their conclusions. The head of mathematics pronounced the mathematics examples, 'unmarkable':

> This is not an investigation. No child has said what they are trying to do, what they found out . . . I couldn't give any Ma1[3] here. It's below the level I normally work. I don't know Level 1 . . . Have you done any work with them?

The primary teachers then apologised:

> We were clutching at straws . . . We criticise ourselves, not the children. It's our fault . . . but in maths, at primary level you can spend all day writing down saying what they are doing, and in science, we have to teach children to write factually, to get the main points . . . to structure it.

However, it was clear that although the focus was the assessment of investigative skills, the children had undertaken very different challenges. The Transfer school children had had to find which of two pieces of wire, of different thickness, would make the best spring, following a demonstration of what to do, and given a limited choice of apparatus. The pupils had recorded their investigation on a standard report sheet, having decided whether to use a bar chart which would achieve Level 4, or a line graph, to achieve Level 5. Thus the assessment largely depended on the outcome (the written report) rather than the process of investigation which could have involved the children using some or all of such skills as raising questions, planning and measuring.

The primary teachers' focus was just the opposite, as one of them explained:

> What we tend to say is what it's focusing on, for example, . . . on measuring, *or* on prediction, or on setting out the work. Then we have one activity, which covers all, rather than a very constrained context for a fair test. For example, if they were finding the strongest of 4 magnets . . . We'd let them find a way to do it, and if they can't do it, it doesn't matter. It gives children the opportunity to show what they think.

A further example was the work of two Year 5 boys whose task was to find the most waterproof of a set of fabrics. The teacher explained:

> I didn't give them a chart, but they decided to tabulate [the results]. There was no measuring. The children decided to give the fabrics a star rating [for waterproofness].

The boys had constructed a table with three columns headed *Fabric/estimate/ answer* and had inserted their 'star' ratings, which represented an attempt to quantify 'waterproofness'. In other words, in Year 5 the assessed learning process had been the boys' understanding that they needed to quantify the dependent variable and their attempt to do so. The secondary teacher's response to this was to reiterate the criteria on the Transfer school's 'indicator grid', namely that non-numerical observations could not achieve Level 4, that to progress beyond Level 3 needed the use of standard measures, and that to progress beyond Level 5 required repeated measures.

Other similar mismatches in grading were discussed, each one illustrative of this difference in emphasis on process or product. The value of these meetings, however, despite the lack of agreement, was that the teachers themselves became aware of the culture gap between them. As the primary teachers put it:

> All three of us have failed . . . it's interesting that there's a big divide.

> It's a breakdown in communication – us knowing what you want and you knowing what we've done.

This meeting took place in the context of an established family of schools, and highlights the considerable time and effort which teachers need to devote in any attempt to bridge the primary–secondary gap. Clearly, different aspects of learning are valued at each stage. What is needed is a transitional stage to help the children adapt to working in a more prescribed way with a reduced problem-solving element as they move from one assessment regime to the other.

These different cultures illustrate vividly two phases of Jerome Bruner's (1966) spiral curriculum which mapped a progressive path from one conception of education to the other. As Bruner put it:

> In teaching a subject you begin with an 'intuitive' account that is well within reach of the student, and then circle back later to a more formal or highly structured account, until, with however many more recyclings are necessary, the learner has mastered the topic or subject in its full generative power.
>
> (ibid.: 119)

However, in this case, the process of school transfer and the imposition of statutory assessment within months of the transfer, meant that the children had to cross a chasm, rather than work up a gently ascending spiral. Where the children's primary science records were closer to what Bruner (1996)

42

called a narrative account, secondary science report forms usually offer a more structured, formal account. What is lacking is an intervening stage to help the children make the necessary stylistic leap. As we shall see in Chapter 5, where pupils' performance before and after transfer will be addressed, not all children managed this successfully. Perhaps what is illustrated most vividly here is the considerable distance still to go before constructive cross-phase communication is established.

If the Liaison meetings highlighted a cultural divide between the primary and secondary teachers, the next section, which will focus on the Induction Days, reveals the cultural divide which the children had to cross.

Induction days

It's a day for you getting used to us and us getting used to you.

Thus spoke a transfer school headteacher in his welcome to the new entrants. In addition to 'you getting used to us' and 'us getting used to you', however, a third process, that of 'you getting used to each other', had to take place too, as children from several different primary schools were meeting for the first time. Earlier in the chapter, we saw that worries about friendships were salient amongst the children's hopes and fears about transfer. For children from small primary schools, this was likely to be even more of an issue. Danesbury was aware of this and held a 'pre-induction day' especially for them and also included children with special educational needs. This event took place a week before the official induction day.

The balance achieved between 'you getting used to us' and 'us getting used to you' during the induction days varied considerably. To the observers it begged the question of whether the induction programmes were set up to reassure the children and demystify secondary school life for them, or to induce apprehension at what was to come. Where the latter appeared to be the case, the purpose of the day was to initiate pupils into a society bound by strict rules and routines to which they would be expected to conform unquestioningly.

Twenty years ago, Maid Marion was the only school which had had a full day's programme for the new intake children, and was the most successful in reducing the children's anxieties about transfer. In the present study Maid Marion stands out again for an induction day which concentrated on social activities designed to encompass the three processes of getting used to each other, to the exclusion of curricular activities. Table 2.5 shows how the six induction days were divided up:

- initial meeting with headteacher;
- curricular activities, e.g. science, maths, music, etc.;
- social activities, e.g. ice-breakers, name-learning names, 'getting to know you';

Table 2.5 Summary of induction day programmes

Transfer school (intake year)	Danesbury (Year 7)	Channings (Year 7)	Kenilworth (Year 6)	Maid Marion (Year 6)	Gryll Grange (Year 5)	Guy Mannering (Year 5)
Welcome from headteacher	Hi! Wonderful programme. Ask questions	Rate us Ask questions Enjoy the day	Always do your best Class lists read out	Make friends Ask questions	School is for work not play Class lists read out	Nice to see you Parents present
Curriculum	Languages, Design and Performing Arts Science, PE, Humanities	PE, Humanities, Science	Music, Science, Maths with IT	No curriculum activities	Maths, English	Maths, English
Social cohesion activities	Inter-form sports: 'It's a knock-out' with Year group Disco with other year groups	Ice-breakers in class; PE relays with another class Village Fete with older year groups	Individual writing about 'Ourselves' in class	3 'getting to know you' activities; Welcome booklet adjectives task and listing friends	Activity sheets: 'Me', school crest, neighbours in class, design a pencil case, map of school	Icebreaker name game; Activity sheet and 'who goes where' class
Rules and routines	3 main rules: Treat everybody as you want to be treated' No sweets or chewing gum No smoking	No mention of rules	Strong emphasis on rules for moving about, behaviour in class, break and lunch procedures Fashion show of School Uniform	No explicit emphasis 'Code of Conduct' in Welcome booklet	Rules about cloakrooms, changing shoes, out of bounds areas, working in silence is implicit	Rules about traffic flow, lining up, opening doors, classroom behaviour, setting pages out (Reasons were given)
Lunch time routines for new intake	12.10–1.35 Cafeteria system Last to be served	12.30–1.35 Cafeteria system First to be served	12.00–1.30 Cafeteria system First to be served	11.30–1.10 Meal selected in advance from menu First to be served	12.40–1.50 Opt for meat or vegetarian meal Last to be served	11.30–12.55 Cafeteria system Served in first half of lunch hour
Classroom administration	Timetable, lockers, folders for holiday tasks	Class time spent on social activities	Timetables, dinner money, worksheets	Welcome booklet –	Welcome sheet	Name cards Fire drill
School tour?	No tour (Tour on parents' visit)	No tour (Tour on parents' visit)	Tour with form tutor	Tour with different teacher	Tour with deputy head	No tour (Tour on parents' evening)
Total time with form tutor	1 hour	< 30 mins	1 hr 25 mins	1 hr 45 mins	> 4 hrs	> 3 hrs

- routines and procedures, e.g. break and lunchtimes, tours of the school;
- classroom administration, e.g. timetables, dinner money, time, with form tutor.

Several features stand out in Table 2.5, such as the different timings and duration of the lunch breaks, different proportions of time devoted to social versus curricular activities, and the amount of time spent with the form tutor. This last information, along with the curricular activities differentiates the induction days by age of transfer. The schools which took in the children at Year 5 spent most of the day with their future form tutor – or at least with the same tutor, whereas in the schools whose intake was at Year 7 children spent an hour or less with the same tutor. If we look at Tables 2.1 and 2.5 in conjunction, it is interesting to note that the schools which emphasised academic rather than social activities, had also set up the most structured liaison programmes. While Table 2.5 allows a quick comparison of the contents of the induction days, Table 2.6 is a highly condensed account of the qualitative information contained in the observers' detailed field-notes. These revealed variations in the school ethos conveyed in the nature of interactions between teachers and children, the ways in which the activities and curriculum areas were presented, and the attempts made to welcome the children into a new community. For example, although Table 2.5 shows similarities in emphasis on the curricular activities at Kenilworth and Channings, Table 2.6 indicates that the way in which these lessons were conducted differed considerably. We suggest that the children's experiences of induction could be characterised as either a possibly upsetting initiation into a new culture, or the beginning of a safe passage from one culture to another.

Table 2.6 summarises the 'styles' which were implicit throughout the induction days in each transfer school. Although there were differences in the ways in which the teachers worked with the children between schools, there was greater evidence of consistency in approach within schools. Comparative examples of the beginnings and endings of the day, taster 'lessons', and social activities, taken from a wide range of equally telling accounts, will be used below to illustrate this.

Beginnings and endings of transfer day

The headteachers' introductions at each of the schools had taken place by 9.30 and lasted between 2 to 15 minutes. They all included a welcome greeting, acknowledgement of probable anxieties and invitation to ask questions during the day. In their different ways the headteachers offered reassurance. Subsequent reflection on our observations showed that they also epitomised the tone for the day. At Kenilworth the theme was rules, while the 'reassurance' was that everything would be fine as long as they always did their best:

There are lots of rules to learn, but I'm going to tell you just one. The first rule of the school is, 'You do your best.' I'll forgive lots of things but I won't forgive you if you don't try your hardest and do your best.

Table 2.6 Summary of characteristics of two types of induction day

Induction day feature	*Induction as initiation*	*Induction as safe passage*
Head's address	You are here to work Always do your best Follow the rules to avoid punishment	Enjoy the day Make friends Tell us how we can improve this day
Allocation to tutor groups	Children's names read out in hall on induction day	Class lists given out at Parents' Evening prior to induction day
Classroom environment	Formal layout Desks in rows Minimal display	Mixed or informal/flexible layout Tables rather than desks
Rules, routines and procedures	Statements of rules without explanation Strict enforcement of rules Minimal disruption of school routine	Inductive approach, working out the rules where necessary Reasons given for rules Extra time allowed for some routines initially
Teacher/pupil relationships	Authoritarian 'Yes Mr X' Children speak when asked to do so Teachers seem powerful and infallible	Authoritative Questions and suggestions invited Teachers fallible Show sense of humour
Lessons and activities	Demonstrations; work sheets; individual tasks	Participation; hands-on activities; co-operative tasks
Pupil–pupil interaction	Discouraged Children work in silence	Encouraged Activities encourage interaction between boys and girls, and groups from different primary schools
Process of change	Conforming to new culture Use of new terminology Devaluation of primary culture 'Get used to it.'	Assimilating new culture, over time and with support 'It will seem strange but we will help you.'

Rules began to proliferate as soon as the children left the hall, by their designated doors, and encountered monitors standing in line down the centre of the corridor, enforcing the 'Walk on the left' rule. Within the next 30 minutes children had been introduced to the following:

No talking when I'm talking.
No calling out.
Use ink pen – not biro or pencil.
You are not allowed inside between 11.00 and 11.15.
No sweets.
No eating in the classroom at all.
Stand in this area when eating snacks.

At Gryll Grange, the head's welcome address to the assembled 9-year-olds left them in no doubt as to what lay ahead:

I'm looking forward to you starting in September . . . As far as I'm concerned, you come to school to learn. It's not a fun factory. It's not a holiday camp. If you come to school thinking that, then you and I are going to fall out very quickly.

Later in the day these Year 4 children spent 1 hour 40 minutes writing while sitting in tightly packed rows of pairs of desks all facing one way. After an hour, the observer's notes read:

12.00 Some children are getting restless, twisting and turning. . . . Daniel very occasionally lets out involuntary noises. Richard – doing very little. . . . Quite a bit of yawning now. No doubt the children are genuinely tired.

At the end of the day this observer noted the rule-bound nature of the regime:

The induction day finishes and what a long long day it was. I didn't think the morning would ever end . . . The 'Intake day' seemed to be about showing children what the school's expectations were . . . you knuckle down to the task; you work in silence; you stay rooted to your seat and put your hand up if you want anything . . . children were quiet and subdued. The 'characters', suppressed.

At these two schools, then, induction meant being personally responsible for adapting to the new school and avoiding a confrontation with the head. In complete contrast, at Maid Marion, the only school which provided chairs for the children to sit on rather than floorboards, the head's theme, and the day which followed, focused on social matters:

> There are 17 schools represented here, a wide variety. Some of you will be saying, 'I don't know anyone', but, hopefully, by the end of the day you can go home and say, 'I know someone'.

The day consisted of activities designed to get children to learn about each other. Each teacher had been given a sheet of 'Ideas for induction day' which listed several 'ice-breaker' games. In one class, when the boys and girls were reluctant to shake hands and introduce themselves, the teacher, who joined in the game, intervened so that not only boys and girls but also children from different schools interacted with each other. These icebreaker activities were interspersed with reading sections of the 'Welcome to Maid Marion' booklet, such as the lunch menu, details of the play areas, and the Maid Marion 'Code of Conduct'. This included, 'Always try to be honest, take responsibility for your actions, . . . to show consideration for others', etc. and was expressed in positive terms throughout. One page, headed 'Induction day', which listed adjectives such as worried, sad, relieved, small, excited, asked the children to circle four words which best described their feelings at the time. While this induction day certainly addressed the children's main concerns about school dinners, making new friends, etc., it provided little idea of the curriculum that lay ahead.

A third approach was evident at Channings. The children were asked to rate the day and report back to the headteacher at the end:

> Come back here at the end of the day and tell me about your day. Give marks out of ten. If you give it four, five or six out of ten, I will want to know. If you give it nine or ten, I shall be pleased. I need to know so that we can do it better.

The Channings day struck a balance between introducing the secondary curriculum and involving the children in the school's social activities. The main feature of this was an annual 'village fete' organised by the Year 8 students to raise money for charity. The stalls included cake stalls, a bran tub, and 'beat the goalie' and '. . . a kind of stocks at which you throw wet sponges with the deputy head as one of the stooges'. 'An early opportunity for the children to see the staff as human', as one observer put it. This event gave the new children a chance to chat, meet other pupils, including older ones from their own primary school and to have some fun. A few were apparently disconcerted and bewildered, however, and one of the observers speculated that they might have welcomed slightly more structure or even some rules. This was a particular problem for children who were coming from outside the normal catchment area and had no peers from their own school to link up with. They tended to stand on the edge of these social events and watch rather than participate.

The endings of the days were characteristic too. The Kenilworth children were told:

> So, please go home and tell your parents the truth – that you have enjoyed your day and you're looking forward to coming back in August.

At Gryll Grange, the headteacher seemed determined that Induction Day would not disrupt the school routine in any way. For example, the new intake children took lunch last, at 1.15, over an hour after their normal lunchtime. This was so that the newcomers would not delay other classes' lunches and prevent the afternoon lessons from starting on time. There was no 'Cook's tour' for pupils as this would disturb classes. At the end of the day, there was no farewell, or mention of looking forward to the new term. It was left to a child to do this, as the observer's notes record,

> The afternoon has just drifted apart rather than [the teacher] being able to summarise or speak to the whole class about what they've done. . . . One child said, 'See you in September Mr J . . . '

At Channings, the headteacher listened to the children's accounts and evaluations of the day, thanked them for coming and said that she looked forward to seeing them in the new term.

These beginnings and endings to the day typify the events that they enclosed. To complete this part of the chapter we shall look next at the curricular experiences provided for the children during the Induction Day.

The curriculum

Table 2.5 shows that the schools which took the older children included a wider sample of the curriculum in their programmes, that is with the exception of Maid Marion, which did not include any curricular activities and will be described later. Guy Mannering and Gryll Grange, which took children in at age 9-plus, focused on mathematics and English. Kenilworth and Channings offered three curriculum areas, and Danesbury included four. The lessons on offer introduced the children to different types of school and classroom organisation. At Guy Mannering and Gryll Grange the children stayed in their class bases and with their class teachers for these curricular experiences but different styles were evident. At Guy Mannering the children were presented with a fairly familiar classroom setting with tables for four to six children. Parents accompanied them to their new classrooms, but soon left when it was clear that they were not needed. The children were not only allowed to talk to each other, but were encouraged to do so for collaborative activities. The day's programme was broken into shorter segments by a fire drill, early lunch and an afternoon break. For the children attending Gryll Grange, the day was probably a shock. The classrooms were set out formally with pairs of desks, tightly packed in rows facing the blackboard. Silence was expected and maintained, although the teacher moved around the class, talking to individuals and exhorting others to concentrate. This was necessary during the 1h 40 minute period before lunch. Continuity across the summer break was reinforced, however, as the induction day work was completed and then displayed in the classrooms in the first few days of the new school year.

Kenilworth, Channings and Danesbury offered a greater variety of curriculum areas, as well as different classroom arrangements and conventions. The children therefore experienced working in several new settings, such as art rooms, laboratories and music rooms. At Danesbury the children tried valiantly to write down the day's timetable from the teacher's dictation. It was the standard Y7 timetable. By 9.10 a.m., within 40 minutes of entering the school, they were in effect the new Year 7. Each of these three schools included a science session which will now be described.

Three science taster sessions

Kenilworth's session was the most spectacular of all. The children were seated in two rows at one side of the laboratory. At various points in the performance a few of them were invited to assist in the demonstrations. The Van der Graaf generator charged up two pupils so that their hair stood on end. Two more had their noses unexpectedly sucked into rubber tubing, when they volunteered an explanation for one of the effects which was being demonstrated. The *pièce de resistance* was the discovery that science teachers could breathe fire. In the absence of any further explanation or discussion, the children might have concluded quite justifiably that, 'Science teachers are indeed dragons', as one observer surmised.

In complete contrast, the science lessons at Channings and Danesbury involved pupil participation and interaction. At Channings, the children worked in groups, to answer questions about what they would be learning in science. Despite a high noise level, the children had answers ready when asked to share their thoughts. The teacher went on to demonstrate various safety points, and asked children to bring her pieces of apparatus. She invited and answered questions, while demonstrating the use of the Bunsen burner to heat water in a beaker on a tripod and gauze. The children asked, 'Does the beaker crack? Where does the air come from in the bubbles?' and were congratulated on their knowledge of scientific vocabulary.

This science session, while including a demonstration, was interactive, and offered a fairly realistic preview of what the children would be doing in two months time. It gave the children a chance to show their knowledge, participate in the lesson and at the same time to learn some key points about working in a laboratory.

The science lesson at Danesbury was of yet another variety. It was a hands-on practical session in which the children worked in groups. At the beginning, a volunteer read out the instructions from a worksheet and the teacher, in this case the headteacher, showed the children what to do *without* actually demonstrating it. The children then mixed pairs of solutions together in boiling tubes, heated them up over Bunsen flames, and described the effects. The children set to work with alacrity, donning goggles, mixing chemicals, and recording their observations. The groups of girls but not the boys managed to write down some hypotheses when asked 'to have a guess why' the chemicals reacted with one another. This lesson, which included a brief but vivid run-down of important safety aspects, gave the children hands-on experience of the kind of secondary science that many were anticipating. They were confronted with a new kind of science, with some decisions to make about which chemicals to mix, but all in the context of a structured task. This session appeared to sustain these pupils' excitement about science, and was a genuine preview of one of the science modules that they would cover in their first year.

These science lessons demonstrated three different approaches to induction. At Kenilworth, induction meant spectate, and this was reinforced at the subsequent 'fashion show', staged to teach the children about the school uniform. At Channings, the children were participants in the science session. At Danesbury, they were scientists. What is notable is that the approaches illustrated here, were broadly typical of other sessions in the same schools. The music sessions at Kenilworth and Channings exemplify this point further.

Two Music taster sessions

At Kenilworth, music took place in the school's highly impressive networked keyboard suite, equipped with enough keyboards for each child to have one to themselves and this clearly provided a very exciting prospect. The lesson began thus: . . .

MISS MARTINDALE: This is the quietest room in the school, Who knows why?

CHILD: We have headphones.

MISS MARTINDALE: You can all hear me through the headphones – yes? (*The children all nod.*)
Now play some notes. Can you hear the notes through the headphones? (*The children shake their heads.*)

MISS MARTINDALE: No ! You shouldn't because I have turned your keyboards off.

A little later Miss Martindale, like her science colleagues, revealed her 'magical powers' by informing them that she not only 'had the power' to tell immediately if someone had pressed a 'demo' button, but that she could check without them knowing whether they were doing the work. 'You'd be surprised at the conversations I hear.'

The 'magical' powers of the music teacher to read (and anticipate) the children's thoughts were further demonstrated throughout the lesson. It subsequently transpired, however, that the first music lesson of the new term took place in an ordinary classroom and the children used rulers rather than keyboards as sound sources.

The music session at Channings, one the other hand, bore greater similarity to music at primary school. The children sat in a circle, listened to an extract of a piece of music, described the mood it evoked, its instrumentation, and said whether they liked it. Next they learned 'The bug song', and the teacher exhorted them to sing:

> Sing out loud. You'll feel silly at first, but you've come into the land of silly here!

Pupils completed a questionnaire about their own musical skills with a promise from the teacher that he would not 'tell of them' to other staff.

These two music lessons epitomise the different approaches to induction adopted by the schools. At Kenilworth, the message conveyed was one of control, of the need to conform, with just a glimpse of curricular wonders included. At Channings, the taster sessions encouraged interaction, participation, and a realistic vision of lessons to come.

Given the considerable changes that the children faced at some of the schools, a major omission from these induction days was any discussion of the new ways of learning, new forms of organisation and new styles of teaching that the children would need to get used to. Although at Danesbury the modern languages and humanities sessions introduced the children to new curriculum content, they did not discuss the learning and teaching processes involved. Induction at Guy Mannering and Channings seemed to offer the prospect of continuity or supported transition. At Gryll Grange and Kenilworth, however, it plunged the children into unfamiliar contexts and learning cultures with minimal warning or guidance.

Conclusion

In summary, this chapter has considered the children's hopes and fears about transfer as they reached the end of their primary careers. The 'New School Gates' task revealed that the children's main concerns were social: the girls worried about whether they would lose or gain friends, the boys, about having harder work or stricter teachers. The schools' liaison programmes ranged from being highly structured to almost haphazard, but several revealed the continuing gap between primary and secondary cultures of learning and assessment. The need for teachers to observe each other teaching in both phases and to discuss their observations was very clear. To engineer a gradual transition from the more open-ended, interactive and process-oriented emphases of primary school to the convergent, individualistic outcome orientation of some of the transfer schools takes time even in well-established clusters. This conclusion was borne out more strongly when we considered the transfer or induction days themselves. While some could be characterised as a genuine attempt to provide a 'safe passage' from primary to secondary school, others appeared more concerned to impose their ways of working *on* the children regardless of the children's previous histories, their excitement or their anxieties. Greater emphasis upon the transition to a new set of learning styles and to a new school regime would clearly benefit the children involved. This, of course, assumes that these taster sessions during induction are representative of the children's experiences in the first few days of the following autumn term in the new schools. The next chapter which will describe the children's initial experiences immediately after transfer will explore, among other things, whether Maid Marion maintained its social focus, Channings its realism or Gryll Grange its austerity.

Notes

1 Artist: Debbie Wall.
2 The 'New School Gates' activity allowed for two responses per respondent.
3 Mathematics Attainment Target 1.

3

MOVING UP TO BIG SCHOOL
The first few days

Chris Comber and Maurice Galton

It is 8.30 on a bright, early autumn morning.[1] Along the roads and streets of a city suburb walk small groups of smartly dressed children, heading for their new school. As they near the entrance, twos and threes become sixes and sevens, until eventually there is a small army of new recruits, marching through the gates and into a new and as yet largely unknown world. The children look around for familiar faces, and huddle together in friendship groups for reassurance, but here and there are a few who seem lost in the crowd, standing on their own, bewildered and anxious.

The children are mostly gathered around the main building – only a few have dared to venture out onto the playing fields – and there is an excited buzz of conversation, as they catch up with one another's lives, and exchange fears and hopes about what they are about to encounter. At this point, they might momentarily reflect on the last time that they visited the school, as primary pupils who had come to look around, and to find out about their prospective school. Then, a variety of style and colour identified them as members of different communities, the school holidays were to come, and the end of August seemed a long way off. Now, the holidays are over, and they are dressed all alike, the pristine new uniforms signifiers of a new and larger community. Only their bags and rucksacks, many newly bought, single them out as individuals.

A teacher emerges from a side door, a whistle blows, and there is a sudden hush. The teacher's voice echoes across the playground, telling the children to go into the school. As they move off, the conversation begins again almost as quickly as it had stopped, but as they file into the school hall the children fall silent. Uncertain now – the old rules no longer apply – they wait to see what will happen next. The silence is broken by the Head of Year who is standing on the stage. 'Well, Year 7, don't you all look smart . . .'.

Life as secondary pupils has begun.

First encounters in the transfer school

The first day at secondary school is a unique moment in a child's educational life. Children move from what is generally a secure and known world, and from a position of being the oldest and most experienced pupils, to become naïve initiates in a new and often bewildering environment, where all the certainties of their primary school years are behind them. Writing twenty years ago on the transfer schools in the 1975–80 ORACLE study, Delamont and Galton (1986) likened arrival at the new school to passing, in grim silence, through 'Disasters Gate'.[2] Although few researchers since then have painted quite such a portentous picture, most agree that in the first few days or weeks this is still a time of considerable apprehension for many children (Measor and Woods 1984; Gorwood 1986). The degree to which their anxieties are balanced by excitement and enthusiasm has been a matter of some debate, however. Pupils in Brown and Armstrong's (1986) study had many more positive feelings about their new school than negative ones. More recently Rudduck *et al.* (1996) have also argued that the portrayal of pre-transfer children as distressed is now outmoded. The process of transfer, she suggests, has become a much less daunting prospect than before, something of a reversal of what Measor and Woods (1984) describe as 'anxiety tinged with optimism', partly as a result of the increase in liaison procedures described in the previous chapter. Rudduck's pupils, it should be remembered were not being asked about their experience of transfer as it was taking place. She interviewed pupils in the following year when perhaps some unpleasant memories had dimmed or had been overtaken by more pressing concerns. This may account, in part, for differences in the findings.

As we saw in the opening chapter (p. 10), however, writers such as Murdoch (1982) and Rudduck *et al.* (1996) while claiming that any initial anxiety occasioned by 'fear of the unknown' is short-lived, nevertheless argue that there are longer-term effects which have more to do with the form and structure of secondary schooling. The effects of streaming and setting on the pupils' self-image and for Rudduck, in particular, the impact of friendships, gained and lost, are part of a continuing process during the early years of secondary school. These anxieties which arise from the pupils' search for identity and status as junior members of the school are far more important than uncertainties about paying for school dinners, finding one's way from the form room to the laboratory or working out a means of remembering what PE kit to bring. This view is supported, in part, by the findings of the present replication study, as we will see when we come to examine the attitude data in Chapter 5. This will show that in this sample of schools at least, children enter their new school with much less apprehension than they did at the time of the original ORACLE studies of twenty years ago. This much then, has changed, but to what extent have these increased efforts towards inter-school liaison, and other externally imposed changes – notably the introduction of a National Curriculum[3] – affected other features of children's first encounters with their new world?

From induction day to first day at the new school

As we saw in the last chapter, in the past two decades the induction or 'transfer' day has gradually replaced a variety of much less comprehensive and unsatisfactory arrangements. Typical of these earlier schemes was the 'whistle-stop tour' of the destination school, which achieved little by way of lessening children's anxieties, and may even have been counter-productive (Delamont and Galton 1986: 29–32). Nowadays children arrive on the first day with much more realistic expectations of what they are likely to encounter. In many cases, collaboration between secondary schools and their primary feeders enables access to sporting and other facilities well before the children transfer, so that at least some aspects of the 'big school' will already be familiar to them.

During the induction day the children will have spent time in their future 'base' room – that is their form-room or classroom and will have met their prospective classmates as well as their class teacher or form tutor. In moving from teacher to teacher for 'taster' lessons (and in participating in the still obligatory 'school tour'), they will have experienced, albeit briefly, something of the specialist nature of the secondary curriculum and will have gained some sense of the size and geography of the buildings. Finally, and critically for most children it would seem, they will have tried out the school dinners, explored the play areas and located the toilets.

In a sense these and other familiarisation procedures now fulfil some of the functions which traditionally belonged to the first day at school. But beyond reassurance, how successful were induction days in preparing the children for transfer, and how representative were they of the secondary school life to come? For some schools, simply putting children at their ease appeared to the observers to be the primary objective of the induction process, so that if children left at the end of the day with little to worry about over the school holidays, it had served its purpose. In other schools, however, there was a different, or additional agenda, which was to signal clearly to the children that secondary school was different, or more specifically, that it was not like primary school. This, as we shall see, often involved the invocation of at least as many stereotypes about primary school culture as there are myths in feeder schools about life at secondary school. What Measor and Woods (1984) refer to as the 'status passage' was thus set in train on induction day itself so that for these schools, success was measured by children ending the day already beginning to think of themselves as secondary pupils. Indeed, some teachers made great play of telling their prospective classes or forms that they were already 5LC, 6CK and so on and would use this form of address throughout the day.

> In five minutes time 5BS, I want you to line up and walk quietly down to the hall.

Right 6CK. Grab those chairs and place them in a half circle around the piano.

The extent to which these different approaches were precursors of life in the secondary school was already becoming clear from the earliest stages of the autumn term. By the end of the first day, for example, despite a high degree of similarity in terms of the structure and content of introductory activities, which we examine shortly, the philosophy of the school which was presented to pupils on induction day proved to be a reasonably accurate reflection of what they were about to receive. There were, as might be expected, some specific deviations from this general pattern; for example, the presentation of science as a kind of magic show in one school bore little resemblance to the actual science curriculum that the children would be required to follow. Nevertheless, in terms of the overall impression gained of what their prospective school was 'about', what the pupils saw was more or less what they got. Thus, for example, where there was a strong emphasis, on induction day, on rules, appearance, behaviour and the virtues of independence and hard work, these were the qualities which were central to the school's philosophy and were reinforced in every classroom encounter in every assembly and even during breaks from the beginning of the first minute of the first day. In one instance, for example, the edited version of the field-notes recorded the following incident:[4]

We are directed to the hall by Head of First Year, Mr Baines. I sit behind three girls sitting silently together. Suddenly, a class of older pupils comes around the corner on the way to the gym (or perhaps the science block) and pass by the big side windows. Suddenly the girls begin to wave. I lean forward and ask one of them,

'Were you waving at someone you recognised from your old school?'

'No,' she replies, 'It's her boyfriend.' (pointing to her companion)

In the hall there is a hum of conversation although quite a few children don't join in. Form tutors stand around the edge talking to each other. Suddenly, the head, Mr Sheffer, appears on stage (he has slipped in through a side door). Some children haven't seen him and continue talking.

'Right Year 6 settle down.' (Still conversations continue)

You boy!' (shouting) 'You in the middle row (pointing) 'Yes! I mean *you*. Stand up.' (continues to shout) 'When I talk *you* don't! (he emphasises the *you*) Do you understand? Now stay standing.'

He continues in a normal voice to address the whole assembly, 'After that little distraction, welcome to Maid Marion.'

(Maid Marion (BPT) 10–14 school)

On induction day, although as we saw in the previous chapter the day mainly focused on social rather than academic concerns, at Maid Marion part of the morning was spent writing out the school and class rules. If one took the first letter in each rule it formed the name of the school.

Similarly, in those schools which presented a different face, where offering reassurances and encouraging pupils to ask questions were the order of the day, for example, the approach to induction day turned out to be fairly representative of the way in which these schools operated. At Channings, for example, no rules had been explicitly stated on induction day. Instead, during the course of the day pupils had been set various problems to solve including, 'What you could do if,

> You have a PE lesson and ten minutes before it starts you look in your bag and find you've left your shorts at home?
> You want to phone home?
> You want to come to school on a bicycle?
> You feel ill at school?'

Children at Channings were sent to the hall as they arrived in school and they continued to talk when the head of first year, Mrs Diepers, attempted to give them information about going to various classrooms. Like the head-teacher at Maid Marion she has to shout to be heard, although her approach to the problem is somewhat different from Mr. Sheffer.

> 'I have a little problem. I find it difficult to talk when there's lots of noise going on. This is a big hall and it's difficult to hear. If I shout even my dog can't hear.' (noise level drops and she continues in a quieter tone)
> 'I know it's exciting but there's a time to talk and a time to be quiet. When you come in here you sit quietly.'
>
> (Channings 11–14 school)

The first morning at the new school[5]

Whichever strategy was used on induction day, whatever underlying philosophy informed its deployment, and however successful it was in preparing the children for the beginning of their life in secondary school, it rapidly became clear that the routine business of 'settling them in' still occupies most of the first morning, just as it has always done. A great deal of what occurred during this first period in present study has strong echoes of the first-day events described by Delamont and Galton (1986: 43–63). Moreover, just as was found then, the organisation and content of such events showed remarkable similarity across the different schools, although, as we shall see, the manner in which this was delivered varied considerably from school to school.

Delamont and Galton (1986: 48) provide an account of the first half-day at Waverley School in Local Authority C (this was one of the schools replaced by Channings and Danesbury in the present study). The day at Waverley began with an assembly for the new intake. This opening event, described as 'clearly control oriented', immediately makes explicit the power structure which operates within the school. Following a perfunctory 'Welcome', the head of year sets out a series of rules governing conversation, appearance, movement and time. Further contributions from two senior teachers reiterate the message, adding new warnings about behaviour and hard work. All three make it clear that swift and firm sanctions will follow any contravention of the rules. The assembly ends with the reading out of class lists, and the children leaving in turn with their respective teachers.

Although we are unable to make a direct comparison, events at Waverley were said to be 'essentially similar' to those in the other schools in the 1977 study. In 1997 Channings was alone, however, in choosing to start the day off with an assembly, albeit a very brief 'welcoming' affair for the new intake, the major purpose of which was to greet the children formally as a year group (accompanied by comments on their smart appearance and one or two basic rules or procedures) and to briefly outline the shape of the rest of the day. Kenilworth adopted a similar, if slightly longer-winded strategy a little later in the morning.[6]

At first glance, then, it would seem that schools have largely dispensed with the kind of 'opening event' described as typical of schools in the original ORACLE study, perhaps as a result of the modern induction day during which, as we saw in the previous chapter, schools took the opportunity to address the children collectively, and to assign them to their different tutor groups or classes. However, four of the six schools, Guy Mannering, Gryll Grange, Maid Marion and Kenilworth, held a full assembly at some time during the first day. For the new intake at these schools therefore, one of their earliest experiences was to sit in the hall as novices in front of a large crowd of their older 'school-wise' peers. Comparing the accounts of these gatherings with those recorded twenty years earlier at Waverley reveals both remarkable similarities and marked differences and we shall come back to examine some of this issue in greater detail later in the chapter. In the meantime, let us return to the newly arrived pupils who have by now gone off to find their base rooms to be registered, and to begin their first period as secondary pupils.

This first session at least was generally 'off schedule', a period of settling in with their teacher or tutor before the first encounter with the timetable proper, which in most cases followed the morning break, although in two of the schools this experience was held over until the afternoon. Delamont and Galton (1986: 47) note that although there had to be some content or task during this first period, its prime purpose was to 'establish the teacher's regime', an objective which, despite induction days and other pre-transfer visits, still remains central to much of what goes on during this time. But it is also represents a period of enforced acclimatisation, mainly achieved by keeping the children occupied (or more accurately pre-occupied) with the mundane; like the buttering of a kitten's paws when introduced to a new home, the children are provided with tedious and relatively undemanding activities designed to so totally engage them that adjusting to the new environment becomes an almost unconscious process. At Guy Mannering (9–13), for example, it's 9.04 a.m. on the first morning and the form teacher, Mrs Staunton, is giving out places while taking the register

> Alex Patrelli hasn't got a place, Clare isn't here and Seymour has to be told twice to answer 'present'. Most children answer 'yes'. Some say 'yes Mrs Staunton'. Mrs Staunton makes no comment but says, 'Two people who can find their way to reception?' Hands go up. Mrs S picks Clare and Jenny. Someone calls out.
> 'Yes! I know. There are two Clares. That one' (points). She gives the register to Clare to take to reception with Jenny and continues,
> 'Next time at registration I want all of you to say "Yes Mrs Staunton"'
> 'I'm pleased to see you've got your coats off. That's sensible. Those who haven't, do so and put them over the back of your chair. In a moment we will go downstairs to find our classroom pegs, then we will come back here and do the timetable.'

In 1977, pupils at Waverley school also began their secondary lives by copying out the timetable from the board. According to the observer's notes,

> Twenty minutes pass. Several need new pieces of paper and have to start again because they have 'made a horrible mess of them'. Question from boy. 'Sir, do we do any lessons today? (Teacher)' 'Yes, this afternoon.'

As is clear from Table 3.1, timetable-reproduction remains a key feature of the first day, occupying, in one case, over an hour of the first morning as children were required to write it out first in rough and then in 'best'. Delamont and Galton contend (1986: 49) that in addition to absorbing pupils, presenting them with undemanding tasks such as this allows the teacher to assess writing and reading skills and the ability to follow basic instructions. Like many aspects of this initiation period, however, the extent to which such an objective was part of the process in the present study was not easy to determine. Certainly some teachers made claims for this strategy, but how such an informal assessment was to be used, or by whom, was rarely explained with any clarity. Given that detailed information regarding the literacy levels and general aptitude of each pupil was provided by the primary

Table 3.1 Main activities in one class in each school[7] from the opening session up to the first subject lesson

Year 5		Year 6		Year 7	
A	B	C	D	E	F
Go to base	Go to base	Go to base	Welcome	Go to base	Welcome
Registration	Registration	Registration	Assembly	Registration	Assembly
Routine info Rules/ procedures	Routine info rules/ procedures	Routine info rules/ procedures	Go to base Registration	Copy timetable	Go to base Registration
Distribution of h/w diaries	Tour cloakroom	Copy timetable	Copy timetable	Routine info rules/ procedures	Icebreaker/ name games
Copy timetable	Copy timetable	Whole school Assembly	Routine info rules/ procedures	Tour of lockers/toilets	Copy timetable
Discuss timetable	Distribution of exercise books	Copy timetable (contd.)	Copy timetable (contd.)	Q & A	Routine info
Copy timetable (contd.)	Write names on books	Write in H/W diaries	Distribution of H/W diaries		Mini-tour of school
Routine info	Whole school assembly	Make and decorate 'name cards'	Make and decorate 'name cards'		
Make and decorate 'name card'					
Whole school Assembly					

Note: Breaks and dinner times have been omitted.

schools, this strategy also seems difficult to justify in educational terms. An assessment of literacy skills based on the completion of a timetable, during what was a confusing and tense period for most children, would appear to be a poor substitute for the primary teacher's evaluation. An uncharitable conclusion would perhaps be, therefore, that such activities were as undemanding for the teachers as they were for the pupils, and represented just as much of a 'gentle easing in' to the term.[8]

Two decades ago, back at Waverley, and the session continued in much the same vein. The teacher gave out letters to parents, and provided a great deal of information; mostly in the form of what they, the pupils, couldn't do (eat in certain places, wear certain jewellery) must do (line up for dinner – an activity which they then 'practised'), and various bits of information concerning routine procedures. At the end of this first hour or so, the teacher briefly reminded the pupils that they are 'bound to lose their way' during the first few weeks and that they must always ask for directions. As far as can be ascertained from Delamont and Galton's account, no attempt other than this was made to reassure the children, nor were they invited to ask questions, but were instead required to sit passively listening to or watching the teacher, or copying from the board. These activities took the class (and teacher) up to the first bell, and thus first break.

Events at Guy Mannering, twenty years later were remarkably similar to those in the above paragraph. While waiting for Mr Hudd (PE and in charge of cloakrooms) to send for them, so they can be allocated a peg with their name attached to it, Mrs Staunton asks the class:

> 'What's it not a good idea to leave down there?' A boy (I think it's Carl) answers,
> 'Money.' Mrs Staunton continues,
> 'Yes. It's a big temptation.
> 'Pencil cases should stay in the classroom, Jumpers? Possibly in case they fall off.
> And another thing, lunch boxes since some children love to pilfer other people's food.'
> On the way back to their base, after visiting the cloakroom Mrs Staunton instructs the class on how to walk down corridors. They are to walk in pairs and the front pair has to hold the fire doors open for the rest of the class. When everybody has passed through the pair then join the back of the column. There are three such doors en route to the classroom so this procedure is rehearsed several times. Back in their base, Mrs Staunton announces,
> 'Next it's the timetable which comes down to what you need to bring. I'd like you to write in pencil. Then you can write in again in ink when you are certain it's correct. I'll bring mine written up on Monday so I'll know where I'll be.'

Given the much greater emphasis on continuity, and the importance attached to the liaison and induction process since the account of the first day at Waverley was recorded, it might have been predicted that schools would have introduced different, and more interesting ways of inducting the new pupils into the life of the new school. Some schools did provide 'transfer booklets' for pupils to complete during the school holidays, potentially providing a 'bridge' between the old and the new, and the possibility of introductory activities on the first day. We saw little evidence, however, that these books were used in any systematic way during the first few days. Indeed, in some cases they were not referred to nor were the answers checked for accuracy, strengthening our general conclusion that induction day was an almost entirely separate event from the process of initiating pupils once they 'officially' joined the school, and that it served mainly (and admittedly successfully) to lessen anxieties. Table 3.1 – which lists the major events of the first day for one target class/group in each school – shows quite clearly that instead the first morning was taken up with a series of activities of a very similar nature to those which were observed two decades previously, and which were, moreover, remarkably alike across the six schools.[9] These included copying the timetable from the board, the distribution of, and the writing of names on exercise books, 'rough' books and homework diaries (often accompanied by detailed explanations of how and where to write names and dates, procedures for underlining and so forth) and the making out and decorating of name cards for desks and drawers.

A second notable feature of the first morning (and, indeed as we shall see, almost every first encounter of any kind) was the bombarding of pupils and the observers with more information than they could possibly assimilate; about uniform, sports kit, jewellery, breaktimes, homework, dinner money, where, when and what they could eat, the selection of monitors, and so on, and so forth. That much of this repeated what pupils were told on induction day did not, in the opinion of the observers present, make it any the less overwhelming. Even though the children were still coming to terms with the novelty of their new world, the teachers' enthusiasm for acquainting the new intake with every school rule or class procedure appeared undiminished. At Guy Mannering, for example, Mr Hudd, while allocating coat pegs went through a similar routine as Mrs Staunton regarding not leaving money, sweaters, lunchboxes and so forth in the cloakroom but taking them to their classroom. He ended by asking the pupils,

'Why do we have rules?' (and without waiting for a response continued)
'Because it's not all messy. So we know where we are' (and then he sends them away with) 'Right 5BS. Have a nice day!'

As at Waverley, and we presume most if not all of the ORACLE 1977–78 transfer schools, these routine activities were generally completed by the children individually, with little in the way of pupil–pupil interaction. For the most part, the teacher remained at the front of the class and the children were expected to listen rather than ask questions or discuss. Questions which did arise tended to seek clarification of rules or procedures or explanations of particular terms such as 'PSE' or 'humanities', and were generally dealt with briefly. Genuine effort on the part of teachers or form tutors to find out much more about the children than was gleaned on the induction day was rare, and because inter-pupil interaction was largely discouraged, children got to know one another in the playground and at the lunch table rather than during this 'familiarisation' session.

In many ways, then, these first activities served to confirm for the children that their understanding of the 'secondary way' which had in most schools already been signalled to them on induction day was substantially correct. There was rarely anything beyond a few introductory remarks which addressed or acknowledged the children's anxieties before teachers set the pupils the task of listening to or copying out rules and procedures. Here as a further, more detailed example of the start to a first day is an account of one class at Gryll Grange taken from the observer's field notes. Explanatory additions are in brackets:

> 8.52 (The children have filed into the classroom)
> Mrs Silver (Form tutor): 'Try and find a seat where *you were* sitting on Transfer Day . . . Coats on back of chairs and bags under the table . . . (Registration) 'Could you try and answer your name. Say Yes Mrs Silver if you're here.' All do so . . . Mrs Silver asks if anyone knows where Barry is.
> 8.54 Mrs S: 'Could you just sit quietly for a moment. I'll be back in a second' (leaves the room).
> 8.55 (Mrs Green from another class looks in) 'Are you all looking forward to your first day here?'
> 8.57 (Mrs S comes back) 'Right, I'd like to welcome you all. Some of you are probably excited; some probably very nervous. You don't need to go home and worry about things – this being your first week. This morning is off timetable. We will start by filling in your homework diary . . . in it are basically the rules of the school, the things that you need to do (for) homework. Parents need to sign the diary at the end of the week – when you take it home. In it are sections for parents to write something in.'
> 9.00 Boys and girls are asked to give the diaries out.

The observer comments at this point that 'Not a word had been uttered' by the children during these first 10 minutes of their first day, and save for the briefest interaction between pupils when they are shown their pegs in the cloakroom, this atmosphere continues for most of the next 40 minutes of the lesson as children fill out their timetables. After 50 minutes, the observer made the following entry:

> 9.42 Mrs S (to class): 'Are there any questions you'd like to ask?'

Seemingly presaging a change in the routine but this proves to be a false assumption as the observer further notes:

> 3 (children) put their hands up and then put them down again as she adds 'about your timetable'.

The remainder of the period until break (some two and a half hours) continues in much the same vein and consists of writing names in diaries, reminders about uniform regulations, a daily 'check list' of things to remember, the ongoing filling in of the timetable (first in pencil and then in 'best'), and so on.

In the same way at Channings in Miss Fielder's class, she takes the register while they wait to go to the first assembly. Her first words to the children, however, are not of welcome:

> 'Can you take your coats off? We're going to do some writing. If we start off with how I want it you will get the hang of it.'
>
> 'So when we take the register it's "Yes Miss Fielder" or "Yes Miss" and "not Yeah".
>
> And when we write we do so in silence.
>
> Everyone must have a pencil and eraser. If you haven't brought them today don't worry but I don't want to talk to your teachers and be told my class is always having to borrow pencils and pens.'

Only after these initial rules have been established and the register taken does Miss Fielder soften her tone and continue,

> 'Can I welcome you. Nice to see your faces. Is anyone nervous? Put up your hands.' (a few go up then gradually more as Mrs F puts her own up) 'I'm new here too. Anyone go somewhere brilliant in the holiday?'

What we have so far described was pretty much what all children experienced during this first session and we could provide similar accounts from almost all of the classrooms we observed, even in the most 'welcoming' of schools. What this confirms, therefore, is that despite the development of inter-school liaison procedures, induction days, parents' evenings and the like, once the children actually get into school, it is business as usual and the opening session in today's secondary classroom is almost identical to that of twenty years ago. There was, however, one notable exception to the rule which is worth detailing since it serves to throw into relief the general lack in other cases of any attempt to provide children with opportunities to ask questions and clarify information, or to acknowledge their anxieties beyond the somewhat bland reassurances of the kind noted above.

In this class, the first hour was occupied by exercises designed to reassure the new pupils, to give them the opportunity to ask about aspects of school life which went beyond rules and procedures, and in particular give the children a chance to get to know one another. The teacher began by welcoming the children and inviting them to ask questions 'no matter how trivial' adding that she wanted them to go home after their first day 'having learned something and knowing what to do'. The morning began with a story supposedly written by a previous student entitled 'My first day at school' which, in raising issues about anxieties and worries – about being the smallest and youngest, being bullied, learning new subjects, doing homework and so on – provided the opportunity for the pupils to express their own apprehensions and concerns. This was followed by a 'getting to know you' exercise whereby each pupil had to talk to and collect the 'autograph' of everyone else in the group (including the teacher, who wrote her full name, rather than Mrs Lake) which immediately generated a buzz of conversation and laughter as the children went about the task. Although these activities lasted no more than an hour, by the time the children moved on to the more mundane tasks of filling out timetables and so on, the atmosphere was relaxed and good humoured, and, at least it appeared to the observer, that compared to other classes visited, a clear sense of group identity was already emerging.

The first assembly

In the earlier account from Waverley school, we saw that the first assembly presented an immediate opportunity to signal the difference between primary and secondary cultures, and to get across what was expected of pupils during their time at the new school. In the previous chapter, however, we noted that the modern form of induction day now enables some of this to be accomplished before the children arrive. Nevertheless, in all schools a full school assembly was held sometime during the first couple of days. Such gatherings were a far cry from what the new intake had been used to in primary school, and served (or so it seemed to the two observers) to reinforce the pupils' novice status. In place of an event where the emphasis was often on participation (for example, where different classes give a performance or presentation based on a religious, moral or curricular theme), the assemblies in the transfer schools were almost exclusively adult-led affair in which pupils were a passive audience.

Where the findings of the present study depart from those of ORACLE is in the typicality of these events. Delamont and Galton report the Waverley assembly as being typical of the other transfer schools. There were, it is true, a number of common elements to the assemblies we observed. The whole school gathered in one place to formally usher in the new academic year. The address from the headteacher set the tone, delivering the message of 'what this school is about'. There were common themes too; of the role of education; of the importance of community, of rights and of the structures that were in place to ensure that the school operated efficiently. But it is the differences in the way that these themes were addressed which revealed quite different educational philosophies, reinforcing and confirming the 'message of induction day'. If the new children still had any doubts on day one about the culture of the community they were now members of, then this first assembly where its ethos was most clearly demonstrated should have clarified matters.

We present three accounts of an opening assembly which emphasise the difference in school cultures. The first, at Kenilworth, bears a marked likeness to that experienced by the Waverley pupils (and, we must assume those in the other 1977–78 ORACLE schools). The assembly lasted for 55 minutes.[10]

The children move off to the hall, and are directed to their places by the various form tutors. The new pupils are required to sit at the front and face the stage, and there is a strong emphasis on silence as the others arrive. A boy is picked out for talking. The Headteacher, Mr Rudd stands on the stage and speaks through a microphone.

Mr Rudd begins by reflecting on the past year's sporting and academic successes, and looks forward to a new year of further successes and hard work, but laments the fact that over the Summer holidays 'some people seem to have the tendency to forget the rules', although he does not expand on this comment. He then turns to the purpose of education, which is encapsulated in the statement 'You come to school for one reason – to work hard.' He then talks of the importance of adopting a responsible and thoughtful manner towards one another. The maxim 'Each one of us is equally important' is underpinned by three main rules. It is pointed out that the first two, which prohibit of any form of physical violence or 'name calling' together constitute bullying, and the notion of rights, that is the right not to be bullied, is invoked, with the forceful addition that 'violation will not be tolerated and you all know that'. The third basic rule is also founded on the notion of rights. 'You are sent here to get a good education' and any wilful disruption constitutes a denial of another's 'right to hear what's going on'. Again, the gravity of this rule is made clear with the comment that the older year groups 'know exactly what will happen' if it is broken, adding that the new intake 'will be told soon'. The importance of correct uniform is then stressed, with the comment that the children all look very smart, although disapproval is shown of the 'one or two who think it's a fashion show'. The Head's address ends with remarks about homework, that is that there will be more ('the bad news'), but shorter ('the good news') assignments will be set this year, that parents must sign homework diaries, and that it will not be acceptable to write 'none sent' in them.

The Mr Rudd then cedes the microphone to one of the Deputy Heads, Mr Jarman, who begins by outlining changes to what is in or out of bounds. He then proceeds to list three things which are forbidden in the school, of which the first is going to the toilet in lessons, since 'you are all getting older and should be able to control when you need to go'. The second prohibited behaviour is the wearing of jewellery for which there will be 'no amnesty' reinforced by a supposedly real-life example of a student facing the choice between death or losing a leg as a result of a jewellery-induced infection. Finally, the bringing in of peanuts into the school is absolutely forbidden since 'there is a boy (here) for whom it is very serious if he just comes near a peanut', presumably a reference to a serious allergic condition, although the connection between the possession of peanuts and the nature of 'very serious' consequences for the boy in question is not explained further. The whole of Mr Jarman's message, which takes around 5 minutes, is delivered in a tone described by one of the two observers present as in the manner of a sergeant major, suggesting serious consequences if any of these rules are broken. The microphone is then returned to the Headteacher, who gives out general announcements and details of the remainder of the day. He ends with the hope that the children 'have a good and successful year'. With this the pupils are dismissed, and they leave, as they arrived, in complete silence.

The second example is taken from one of the 9–13 Middle Schools, Guy Mannering, and takes 20 minutes. It follows the mid-morning break, but pupils first go to their classes and then move off to the hall in line as previously demonstrated when they visited the cloakroom earlier.

Before they leave the classroom Mrs Staunton tells the class they must walk in silence and stay silent once in the hall. This doesn't apply to teachers, however, since as they pass by the cloakroom area, Mr Hudd, joins us and walks beside Mrs Staunton talking loudly. Once in the hall, the various class teachers direct the children to their places. There is a great deal of emphasis on sitting in straight lines and facing the front. Although music is playing as they enter, absolute silence is required of the children as the others arrive. This is reinforced when two boys who were talking are told to stand up with their arms by their side in front of whole school.

The Headteacher, Mrs Parish, starts the proceedings with 'Good morning ladies and gentlemen' and begins her address by extending a 'very warm welcome' from herself and all the staff to the returning pupils and 'a special welcome to our new Year 5. It's a new year with new challenges.' She then turns to her main theme, which is about standards. She begins by acclaiming the high reputation of the school, which is 'known throughout Ashburton,[11] for its high academic standards, its strict uniform code and the good behaviour of its students, and which has led to an increase in requests for places from parents. Children in the school are respectful, have excellent test results, and look tidy and smart. The buildings are tidy, and there is no litter or graffiti. These standards are to be kept up not just within school, but also walking to and from it. 'We are judged every day by what we do, what we say and how we behave.'

Mrs Parish then lists 8 rules which represent the school's philosophy: neatness and respect for the uniform, respect for others, appropriate behaviour, being prepared for lessons, working to high standards, punctuality, completion of homework, care of the school and regular attendance. She reinforces her message by reminding the children that all the teachers expect high standards from them, that they should always be neat and respectful. 'I believe in good manners. I dislike and will not tolerate bad behaviour. You are responsible for your own actions, and I will not tolerate disruption of the life of the school. All the staff here will give you the best education in Ashburton, but you all have to cooperate to ensure that this continues.'

Mrs Parish then suddenly 'changes tack' and introduces a new theme. 'Let us think of those who are in the world who have not these opportunities. I hope there is space in our hopes for them. I shall now say a short Christian prayer.' She proceeds to call down a blessing on their efforts during the year which is then enlarged to include all children and their teachers throughout the world. Most of the staff sit with heads bowed during this brief episode.

The Headteacher ends by saying that she hopes they will all enjoy a happy year in which they can all share. 'Let's hope there are no upsets. Be on your very best behaviour and work hard. I look forward to many successes.'

The Deputy Head, Mrs Lawrence, then takes over, noting 'A good start to year, but two year 7's (the two boys made to stand) let us down. Otherwise a good start and well done. You all look very smart. Very good Year 5. You came in very well.' The assembly ends with general announcements and a reminder to the older children to help settle in the new pupils. 'Remember, you were new not so many years ago.'

The final account comes from Channings, one of the 11–14 schools and like Guy Mannering it occupies about 20 minutes.

The children move off to the hall, and are directed to their places by the various form tutors. An excited hubbub ensues, and continues as pupils and teachers from the older year groups arrive. The Headteacher, Mrs Morris, stands at the front and claps her hands. Within about 20 seconds, the hubbub falls to a hum. The Head claps her hands again and there is silence.

Mrs Morris then begins to talk about her 'thoughts on what schools are for'. She considers, and rejects, some dictionary definitions of what schools are (e.g. 'a collection of buildings') as inadequate, preferring to focus on the Latin derivation of the term (*schola*) meaning 'leisure spent in the pursuit of knowledge'. She recollects some of her own early experiences at school – about a boy called Kevin Berk who was 'always in trouble' with his teacher and was made to stand in a basket when he was naughty. The boy's name, and the story, raises a laugh among the pupils. But now Kevin Berk owns a chain of shops even though he 'didn't always get 10 out of 10'. She then turns to her own relationship with teachers who awakened her interest for learning, a history teacher who 'used to tell us stories', a 'soft, but very gentle' geography teacher who 'encouraged us to do things for ourselves' who arranged trips and excursions, and finally, after she left school and didn't know what to do, a former teacher who encouraged and supported her in her decision to become a teacher herself. Her point was that it is these kinds of relationships which 'change a school from a collection of buildings into a community of mutual support'. She concludes by encouraging the children to have the confidence to ask questions – including being able to ask a teacher why they've been given a piece of work and its purpose – and to be able to ask for help 'and in knowing that you'll get it from staff and from friends', and by citing the school's aims statement: 'self-discipline, independence and cooperation leads to knowledge and successful progression through life'. She finishes by expressing the hope that the children will find 'at least some of these things in coming here' and thanks them for listening.

This is followed by the usual general announcements by other members of staff, which ends with a plea by the Deputy Head to the older year groups to 'use common sense' and recognise that there will be some delays during the first 3 or 4 days until the new children are settled in. As the children are dismissed, the buzz of conversation restarts, and continues as they go off to their first lessons.

These three synopses tell us quite a lot about the culture of these transfer schools. On the face of it, all three Heads are appealing to a notion of community, but the concept is defined in very different ways. In a sense, they all present their version of 'what schools are for'. For Mr Rudd, the question is relatively unproblematic. Schools exist to provide a 'good education', a concept which is assumed to be readily understood, and in need of no further explanation or exploration. The route to this goal, working hard, is presented as equally straightforward. The context in which this is achieved is one in which all are 'equally important' and where pupils have individual rights – the right to be free of fear or intimidation, the right to learn without being distracted by others. Mrs Parish also employs similar arguments, except that the components of a 'good education', and more importantly, a good school, are clearly and repeatedly spelt out. While at Kenilworth the achievement of academic excellence is directly related to the pupils' commitment to work hard, at Guy Mannering it is presented as the natural order, so that pupils have a duty to uphold the standards and reputation of the school. The messages spelt out by both headteachers, however, were clearly 'control oriented', just as at Waverley and the other ORACLE transfer schools two decades previously. References to rules and sanctions predominated, clearly signalling to pupils that the way to get on at their new school was to conform to the pre-existing order.

For Mrs Morris, on the other hand, the question of 'what schools were for' was presented philosophically, and she provided various insights in her attempts to answer it. In doing so, she introduced a note of humour, disclosed information about her own school experiences and clearly implied that academic achievement is not the only criterion of success, and that the development of other qualities is an equally important role of education. At no time during the assembly was a rule or a sanction mentioned. While the message at the other schools was mainly about what was expected of the pupils, then, here at Channings it was as much about what they were entitled to expect.

The remainder of Mr Rudd's comments concerned practical matters such as uniform and homework, although he expresses the wish, at the end of the assembly, that all have a 'good and successful year'. As is clear from the earlier use of this word, success is defined largely in terms of academic achievement rather than personal or social fulfilment. The importance of good inter-pupil relationships is also strongly related to notions of being allowed to succeed unhindered and unafraid. Mrs Parish also uses the word success in a similar context, immediately following the wish that pupils have a 'happy year'. By contrast, Mrs Morris stresses the importance of supportive and enthusiastic teachers, and of the right of children to be able to ask questions and to receive guidance. The key message is summed up in her observation that it is the nature of inter-personal relationships, both between pupils and between teacher and pupil, which makes the difference between a school being an institution and a community.

First lessons

We have seen that the first morning was largely about familiarisation, a series of routine and relatively unchallenging activities which were designed to ease the children into their new environment. For the remainder of the day, and over the next few days, these first lessons (regardless of different classroom arrangements, or indeed subject) were largely characterised by the kind of routine activities that we have already described; listening to or copying out rules, instructions and information about the curriculum, going through safety or other basic procedures or familiarising pupils with the new environment. In the original transfer study, the intention behind many of these activities was made very clear by teachers such as Mr Steele at Merlin Court whose first words to the new pupils were, 'There's a song called my way. . . . This is my way.' He then proceeds to tell them how to set out work (Galton and Willcocks 1983: 126–128).[12]

Regardless of curriculum area, numerous first (and sometimes second and third) lessons involved some form of 'designing' activity – a title page, a folder or exercise book cover which established rules of presentation. As was the case twenty years ago, first lessons in several subjects often involved the copying out of sets of classroom rules or 'exemplars' (how and where to set out margins and underline). Each teacher would have slight variations about underlining titles, using pencil, ballpoint or pen, etc., as if to stamp their own personality upon the class. In Guy Mannering, for example, the children had a PE lesson and a games lesson, the latter involving seven members of staff. These initial encounters were almost exclusively taken up with listing rules, explanations of what activities were to come, the assignment of pupils to different groups, rules about safety, correct kit, behaviour and so on. Despite being required to change into full kit, the children were kept seated on the floor for most of the sessions, getting just 8 minutes physical activity out of a total of two hours.

At Kenilworth, Miss Martindale, the music teacher, gives the new pupils an introductory half lesson (30 minutes):

> The lesson begins with the teacher explaining her procedure for coming in to the classroom, which involves lining up until she arrives, and then filing in according to her seating plan order. She begins to organise the seating and tells pupils that it is the 'first thing to remember'. The second thing, which follows immediately, is that there is to be no talking 'which I'm sure you remember from your primary school' about which they are reminded several times. Most of the rest of the session is taken up with the handing out of exercise books, upon which the pupils are required to write name, form and subject; and completing a worksheet entitled 'How to make a folder' which the teacher talks through, although there is no actual practical activity. The teacher then briefly outlines some of what they will be doing in music, making great play about the fact that they will be using keyboards which 'have lots of voices' (no explanation) and are 'lots of fun'. The fun element of the curriculum is referred to again when the teacher uses as an analogy, shopping at a supermarket or going abroad to compare a willingness or reluctance to experience

new musical forms, that they (currently Year 6) will be doing 'popular music' in Year 9. The pupils have listened throughout. There has been no activity save writing on exercise books. Conversation between pupils, even during this routine task, was strongly discouraged more than once on the grounds that it 'wastes time'. Books and worksheets are collected up again and the lesson ends.

Such a lesson appeared to the observer to contain little to stimulate the pupils' interest in the subject. Nor was there much evidence of fun as the pupils worked in silence. At Maid Marion, the last lesson of the first day is English with the form teacher, Mrs Whistler:

The lesson begins with the teacher announcing that 'We are going to do English' but it soon becomes evident that what they were mainly going to do was what they had already been doing for most of the day. Three exercise books are handed out, and the children write on each one the subject, classroom number, their names and so on. Some children, confused by the fact that the spelling and vocabulary book is actually an A4 book cut in half, write their names on the back instead of the front, and are told to tipex it out later and to write their names in the correct place. Following this, there is a brief discussion of what books they have read over the Summer, before the teacher offers the class advice on homework, at which they are required to get out their homework diaries to write in their task for English – covering books. The teacher continues to explain about filling in the diary, being honest in completing it, getting it signed by parents and so on. All of this has taken around 35 minutes. With around 15 minutes of the day left to go, the observer notes that the children are beginning to wilt (some yawn or let their heads drop on their arms as they write) since everyone has been here since 8.00 a.m. The teacher begins a discussion about the use of English and its importance, and communication in general, before concluding the lesson, and the day with a quick word game. Of the 50 minutes of the lesson, no more than 15 was actually devoted to the curriculum.

In the third example at Danesbury the last lesson of the first day is an introduction to PE and music:

The whole year group gathers in the hall, and the children are told that they will be hearing about music before seeing a video about PE. Speaking 'very rapidly' the music teacher goes through some of the things that they will be doing in music, and outlines some of the extra curricular music activities and groups that are available in the school, adding basic information about charges, letters to parents and so on. This takes around 15 minutes. The head of PE now takes over, and introduces the video. The children's enthusiasm quickly evaporates as it turns out to be training material for teachers, using terminology such as *peripheral circulation* and *synovial fluid*. Despite this, the children, many of whom are by now yawning, are told to 'watch the screen and listen' and to 'try and take some of it in' even though the teacher acknowledges that 'it's been a long day' and that they look 'zonked'. After the video has finished – it lasts around 10 minutes or so, the PE teacher goes over the same kind of ground as the music teacher; outlining future activities, after-school clubs and so on.

There were exceptions to this trend, and some teachers made genuine attempts to involve the children in curriculum-focused work from the beginning. This was particularly true in the two 11–14 schools for modern foreign languages. Teachers in every class that we observed began immediately with oral work or, in one case, a class discussion about European culture.

As Table 3.2 – which provides a school-by-school breakdown of the main activities of the first day – shows, in the vast majority of cases very little teaching took place during the first session in any subject. This was mostly reserved until the second, and in some cases third lesson. In cases where the teachers attempted to provide children with authentic learning experiences so that the pupils were given a taste of a specific subject, this appeared to be the personal preference on the part of the teacher in question, rather than a response to any kind of central school policy. The above descriptions are very similar to those by Delamont and Galton (1986) as part of the ORACLE transfer study and concern issues of movement, use of space and time. For example, Miss Martindale's first utterance is to tell pupils where to stand outside the music room and then how to enter and take their seats. In the same way, in Galton and Willcocks (1983: 126) Mr Evans at Guy Mannering, told pupils:

> 'All you've to do is come in quietly. It's not a club where you come in and talk . . . I've never liked noise or fuss and I never will.' He then sets out rules for when pupils arrive outside the class. 'First wait outside the left hand side of the door side by side; second, don't go to the other side of the door. Miss A lives there and you mustn't steal her space.'

As we begin to explore the pupils' experiences, therefore, we shall be talking more about the effects of teachers on their pupils, and less about the effect of schools since the common elements of the system such as timetables, the rules of moving around the building, etc., are quickly put in place during the

Table 3.2 Main activities in each school for the whole of the first day

	Gryll Grange	Guy Mannering	Maid Marion	Kenilworth	Danesbury	Channings
8.30	Arrive/line up	Arrive	**BASE** Class teacher	Arrive/line up	Arrive	Arrive
8.45	**BASE** Class teacher	**BASE** Class teacher	Registration	WELCOME ASSEMBLY	**BASE** Form tutor	WELCOME ASSEMBLY (Y7 only)
9.00	Registration	Registration Routine info	Copy timetable	(Y6 only)	Registration Copy timetable	**BASE** Form tutor
9.15	Routine info giving	Tour cloakroom	WHOLE SCH ASSEMBLY	**BASE** Form tutor	Routine info	Registration '1st day at school' exercises
9.30	Distribution of h/w diaries	Copy timetable	**BASE** Class teacher	Registration	Tour of lockers/ toilets etc	
9.45		Distribution of exercise books	Copy timetable (contd)	Copy timetable Routine info[13]		Icebreaker/name games
10.0	Copy timetable from board					
10.15	Discuss timetable	Write names on books	Write in H/W			Copy timetable
10.30		— BREAK—	Make and decorate	— BREAK— (early 1st day)		Mini-tour of school
10.45	— BREAK—	WHOLE SCHL ASSEMBLY	'name cards' — BREAK—	**BASE** Form tutor Copy timetable (contd)	Q & A	— BREAK—
11.00	**BASE** Class teacher Copy timetable		**BASE** Class teacher		— BREAK—	— BREAK—
11.15	(contd) + school		MATHS	Distribution of diaries	**SCI RM?** Science tchr Currie work	**FRENCH ROOM** French tchr
11.30	information	**BASE** Class teacher ENGLISH				Currie work
11.45	Make and decorate 'name cards'	Currie work		Make and decorate 'name cards'		
12.00		— LUNCH —	— LUNCH —	— LUNCH —		
12.15	WHOLE SCHL ASSEMBLY **BASE**				— LUNCH —	**MUSIC ROOM** Music tchr Currie work
12.30	Routine info giving					
12.45	— LUNCH —					
1.00						
1.15		**BASE** Class teacher	**BASE** Class teacher			— LUNCH —
1.30	**BASE** Class teacher	Registration	Registration	ASSEMBLY (whole school)	**HALL** Art tchrs	
1.45	Registration MATHS	**MUSIC ROOM** music tchr	ENGLISH	FRENCH	PE tchrs Routine	
2.00	(test)	Currie work	Currie work	**ROOM** Currie work	Arts info Video on PE	**BASE**
2.15						Form tutor Registration
2.30		— BREAK—	HEALTH EDUCN	GYM PE tchrs	**ART ROOM** Art tchr	Routine info
2.45	HISTORY Currie work	**BASE** Class teacher	Currie work	Routine information	Currie work	**HISTORY RM** History tchr
3.00				giving		Currie work
3.15		ENGLISH Currie work	ENGLISH Tchr reads story	END of DAY		Copy H/W task
3.30		Routine info/ letters home etc	END of DAY		END of DAY	END of DAY
	Clearing up/ putting away END of DAY	Clearing up/ putting away END of DAY				

75

first few days. Thereafter children have to learn to cope with the demands of subjects. Although we shall argue that in each subject many of these curriculum experiences were similar across all the transfer schools, this was the privileged view of observers who were all able to spend time in at least three institutions. Pupils, for the most part, had to cope with one teacher of English, one of mathematics, one of French all of whom had their own way of 'going about things'. Observers also saw increased use of formal testing during this initial settling period in the core subjects of English, maths and science, in order to 'set' children, that is to place them in ability groupings. Pupils also began to establish reputations for better or worse. During the first day of the start of the autumn term, for example, Seymour had to come next to Mrs Staunton whenever the class left their places to sit on the floor around the teacher's desk. This was, Mrs Staunton informed Seymour, 'so I can keep my eye on you'. In other schools children stayed in their places during class sessions and pupils like Seymour would be told to sit by themselves in a corner of the room. Part of learning to be a secondary pupil, therefore, involved adjusting to unfamiliar environments. In the following section, we examine these and other themes; the establishment of rules, procedures and authority structures and the ways children responded to them.

The learning environment

We have already said that one of the key benefits of the modern induction day is the opportunity for children to spend time in what will become their form- or classroom while they are still at primary school. In the two middle schools, Guy Mannering and Gryll Grange (9–13) and at Maid Marion (10–14), most of the children's encounters with the new curriculum took place in their base room and, in the case of Guy Mannering, mainly with their own class teacher.[14] The base room came to represent perhaps the nearest equivalent to the primary classroom that they were likely to experience in their new school. Although laid out much more formally, it represented a geographical location which was 'theirs' for at least part of the day, a place where rapport between tutor and pupil developed over a period of a time, and in which non-academic issues could be addressed.

For pupils at the remaining 10–14 school (Kenilworth) and the two 11–14 ones (Channings and Danesbury), however, the introduction of the timetable proper signalled the beginning of the typical secondary pattern whereby pupils went from one curriculum room and specialist teacher to another. For these pupils secondary school life appeared to be mainly about being on the move, much as it was twenty years ago. Because of this, symbols such as the tutor group and the recently acquired bag in which to carry personal possessions for example – become the new signifiers of identity and stability. Just as the primary classroom of today is little changed from twenty years ago (Galton *et al.* 1999b), the typical secondary classroom remains as different from that familiar environment as it ever did. In place of the grouped-together desks or tables of the primary classroom there are parallel rows of desks facing the front. There is no 'library corner' and no carpeted area where children gather around the teacher for stories or registration. Materials and equipment placed in cupboards, stacked on tables or shelves along the side of the room, or displays on the wall no longer reflect a multiplicity of subjects, but relate to a single curriculum area.

While these three schools could be described, in the terms of the original ORACLE studies as of a 'secondary-type', for pupils at Guy Mannering, Gryll Grange and Maid Marion, the change was less dramatic. As we saw in Chapter 1 these three transfer schools retained some of the characteristics which defined them as primary-type schools. Although some of the criteria listed then no longer differentiate between schools – almost all middle and secondary schools nowadays have some form of official uniform, for instance, and most have some system of ability grouping in one or more of the core subjects – others continue to do so. Maid Marion retained its first year base and recreation area, while the layout of the classroom there and at Guy Mannering should have been reassuringly familiar to the children, retaining many of the features of the primary environment. In both these schools this was also where pupils spent the much of their time for lessons, particularly for English, maths and the humanities, and in the case of children at Guy Mannering, being taught mainly by the same teacher. This was very different from twenty years ago when the school offered a secondary-style curriculum. Interestingly this primary-type aspect of school life, remaining in the same class with the same teacher for much of the time, was now only partly a characteristic of Gryll Grange representing a shift, to some degree, away from the ORACLE 1976 study when the school was defined as a primary type.

Whichever arrangement pertained, however, there were common elements to all of the schools which marked them as different from the primary experience. All schools used a fixed timetable system, for example, so that subjects periods began and ended at specific times. Common to all schools too were the 'specialist rooms', spaces specifically designed for particular curriculum activities – the science lab, the computer suite, the artroom, the design and technology workshops, and so on. In other subjects, mathematics, English, the humanities, and so on, all children encountered, to a greater or lesser degree, and in various circumstances, individual subject specialists. In the three schools most closely identified with the 'secondary type' (Kenilworth, Channings and Danesbury) for example pupils went to different teachers, usually in different rooms for all subjects, while at Maid Marion the specialist teachers came to the pupils' 'base', rather than the other way around, although not for science, art, PE and music. At Guy Mannering, the most 'primary' of the six schools, and to a lesser extent at Gryll Grange, there was a mixture of the two approaches. For English, mathematics and humanities, some teachers came to the pupils for certain subjects, while their form teacher took them for others. At Guy Mannering, for example, Mrs Jolly, the mathematics coordinator, took Mrs Staunton's class for one period a week when they did 'investigations'. For the remainder of the maths periods the form teacher took over.

Observers also saw the frequent use of tests for the core subjects of English, maths and science, in order to 'set' children, that is to place them in ability groupings. In Channings and Danesbury children were tested during the first term despite the availability of the Year 6 National Curriculum Test Scores. At Guy Mannering, for example, Mrs Staunton and Mrs Jolly both gave mental arithmetic tests at the beginning of each period from the second day of term. These were recorded for 'sorting out the sets'. In English, the observer recorded the following activity:

> After lunch it's English. Mrs Staunton announces we are going to have a test. The rules are simple. She will read a sentence and then pick out a word which the pupils have to spell. The words get more difficult as the test proceeds. They are to continue until they can do no more. They will get 10 seconds to write down each word. She will time them with a stopwatch. There is to be no conferring and no copying. They are not to worry if they come to a point where they can't go on. She begins,
>   'I am waiting for my friend. The word is friend.'
> and this continues until we reach sentence number 52:
>   'This was the principal reason why I did not go. The word is principal'.
> This last word defeats everybody. Jane and Philippa are the only ones left. The whole exercise took some twenty minutes with a break to console Sammy who had begun to cry because he couldn't keep up. I wonder whether you would score a point if you wrote *principle*. Afterwards, Mrs Staunton tells me that she had come across an old copy of a published test, she thought it was an NFER one. The first year teachers had got together and made up their own version along the same lines. It had worked well last year. They had organised the English sets based upon the scores and 'hadn't found it necessary to move anyone in or out of their group for the rest of the year'.

There were notable developments at a pupil level too, over these first few days, for example, the emergence of new identities, both at an individual and group level; the impact of 'being identified' by teachers, other adults and peers, either formally (e.g. as 'SEN') or informally (e.g. as a 'problem'). In the following section, we examine these and other themes such as the establishment of rules, procedures and authority structures and the ways in which children responded to them.

Through the eyes of the pupils[15]

As the first few days evolved, the patterns of working in each classroom began to stabilise and become routine. Rules were reinforced, sometimes accompanied by shouting if a pupil's behaviour was judged to be too provocative. When such incidents occurred these judgements were then shared with other staff, either informally in the staff room or at year group meetings. One observer recorded the following:

> The first year teachers are holding a meeting but didn't tell me about it so I stayed in the playground with the pupils. As I go past the door I heard one of them say, 'I shouldn't say it but she's the kind of Miss know it all . . .'
>
> The speaker saw (or heard) me and lowered her voice so I couldn't hear the rest of what she said.

In this way reputations are quickly gained. Failing to put a hand up before answering, getting up without permission, forgetting books, pens and PE or games equipment are all taken as indicators of potential problems. At Guy Mannering, for example, day two begins with some changes. Children have been moved to different tables. Seymour is no longer next to Carl, Sammy has moved next to Mario and Jane and Clare J have been separated. There is a large poster on the end wall. It reads:

REMEMBER Use a sharp pencil
          Rule off each piece of work
          Margin on the left
          Underline headings
          Always do your best
          Neat work only
          Swimming kit on Thursday

Seymour, it may be remembered, identified himself on day one by having to sit next to Mrs Staunton whenever the class left their places to sit on the floor around her desk. At the time he grinned, sheepishly, as if he had been expecting this result. Perhaps his primary teacher had been in the habit of using the same strategy when the class were sitting on the carpet for such activities as story time. Over the first three days, Seymour, by his behaviour, suggests clearly why Mrs Staunton and perhaps his primary teacher took this course of action. He is reprimanded for calling out, swinging on his chair, shaking a plastic bag containing sweets, sticking his tongue out at another pupil and whistling out loud. In PE he continues to run around after the instruction to 'stop' and 'stand still' and is asked by the teacher to identify himself by name.

In contrast, Carl and Sammy are singled out for positive reinforcement. Sammy has just moved to the area from another part of the country so that he has no friends from his previous school. He hangs around the entrance door to the playground during break times, cries in front of the class during the mental arithmetic and English tests, and doesn't volunteer an unsolicited utterance until the third day when lets out the information that he has a pet rabbit. Carl appears to be the more outward-going, attempting an unsolicited joke (for which he is not reprimanded) and joining in ballgames during break time with enthusiasm, although he appears to have poor coordination skills. However, he, too, can be easily upset as the following incident illustrates:

> Carl has ink on his fingers. Mrs Staunton tells him to use pencil or a ballpoint. I (*the observer*) offer to take him to the cloakroom. He is near to tears. As I dry his hands and offer sympathy, saying 'it used to happen to me at school' he tells me that 'I don't write well with pencil either'. At break I tell Mrs Staunton the story. She makes a point of going over and telling Carl that he will get extra help to improve. Carl replies that he has to practise at home. Later when they come back from PE Carl has got the wrong button of his shirt in the wrong hole so that the shirt tail hangs out at the back over his trousers. Sammy can't even get that far. His shirt is open at the front except at the top where his tie holds it together and at the bottom where he has tucked it into his trousers.

At Maid Marion Mrs Whistler also rearranges the seating. Initially the desks were set out in rows but on day two they have been pushed together to allow pupils to sit in groups as at primary school. On day three, however, they are put back in rows facing the teacher's desk and the blackboard like any conventional secondary classroom. During English on day two there are continuing problems with noise and distractions. From the start, Wayne causes several problems. He is late, hasn't got a pen, is told off for not using a ruler to draw a line across the timetable, and is rarely on task for any extended period. In English he starts a conversation about girls with another boy at his table:

> WAYNE: Have you got a girlfriend?
> LAWRENCE: I don't like girls. I'm interested in schoolwork.
> The girls at his table jeer. Mrs Whistler looks up and says in a sharp tone of voice. 'Wayne. Stop that noise.'

Wayne is also in trouble with one of the PE teachers, Mr Pike. The boys go into the sports hall and the girls to the netball area. Mr Pike gives them a long list of rules.

Don't make a noise when I am speaking. It will get me annoyed.
Don't come on the carpet with dirty shoes.
For football put your boots on outside, not in the changing room.
If you don't take a shower you will be in trouble – serious trouble.

Wayne is shouted at for drumming his feet on the floor and asked his name when he starts to shuffle out of line. Next day he is sent to the head of year, Mr Baines, for fighting.

Most of these observed incidents involve boys. Girls tended to talk while continuing to work (or giving the appearance of doing so) at their writing or at mathematical calculations. Exchanges might involve passing notes which the recipient would find amusing or refusing to allow a neighbour to borrow a coloured pencil or an eraser and then laughing. Generally, teachers ignored or failed to see such exchanges but in some cases took subsequent action, as when, for example, Mrs Staunton separated Jane and Clare.

At Channings, however, the approach appeared to be more relaxed. Perhaps more significantly, it was noticeable that rather than merely stating rules and leaving it at that, rules were usually accompanied by an explanation of why they were required. Again, this was often done by asking pupils to work out the reason for themselves as in this episode where (as in all the other schools) pupils were engaged in covering books and writing their names on the covers. The teacher, Mrs Redmond, begins by explaining the setting procedure,

> 'You will be in this group for three weeks. I know you got a 4 or 5 in the SATs but I'll be truthful, I'll always be truthful, I don't work on what the exam tells me. What I need to know is that you can cope. We set so the brightest can get on and the slow ones can work at their pace. I don't mind if someone finds something difficult but I do mind if you don't try. Now I'll give you a book. My other name is "wicked witch of the west" so don't forget one book for class-work and one book for homework.' She tells them to open the book and write their names on the inside page.

MRS REDMOND: Why not on the outside?
PUPIL: Because we are going to cover it up,
MRS REDMOND: Yes! You're right. It always surprises me the variety of ways so I'm going to explain how I want it done (demonstrates covering). No sellotape and no cuts. I personally will eat for breakfast anyone who sellotapes the cover to the book. Why?
PUPIL: Because you want us to use it (*the cover*) again.
MRS REDMOND: Good thinking. Sensible covers. We don't need expensive paper. Any questions?

PUPILS: Should we put our tutor group or 7.9?

MRS REDMOND: Both if you like. Oh! We have a maths shop where we sell covers for 37p so if you plan to have these you don't have to do the homework. Now we've a few minutes left so we are going to chant the nine times tables. (Pupils appear to be pleased and chorus 'Yes'.)

Afterwards, Mrs Redmond says, 'That's the best nine times tables I've heard for a long while. Why? Everyone was willing. I don't mind the wrong answer or how many times I have to explain. Never be afraid to say "I don't know." If you knew everything I'd be out of a job.'

The bell rings and Mrs Redmond tells the class, 'Every day we put the chairs up so the cleaners can do their job. We put the chairs up for them and they put them down for us. That's the way it works here.'

Mrs Redmond was not an isolated example of what the observers encountered at Channings. The geography teacher, Mrs McDougal, put a list of suggestions on the board for helping the class to learn. Working in groups, pupils had to decide what to bid from their allocation of £100 for each suggestion. One group bought *working quietly* for £9. *Listening carefully* and *spelling correctly* were each judged worth £40 while the top bids of over £60 went on *remembering facts* and *being able to work with others*. The whole class then discussed whether these choices were necessarily the best ones.

What we can discern in the above accounts, particularly the episode with Mrs Redmond in mathematics, was the subtle way in which the teacher reinforced the messages contained in the headteacher, Mrs Morris's assembly address. Mrs Redmond tells pupils that it is not so much succeeding and doing well, that counts but trying and not being afraid to question or ask for help from others. She encourages pupils to find sensible reasons for her rules although insisting that they must be followed. The notion of community is further reinforced with reference to the cleaners where 'we put the chairs up for them and they take them down for us'. Perhaps the philosophy was best expressed by the Deputy Head, Mr Burrows, who told the observer, 'We don't anticipate trouble here. If it happens we deal with it.'

We do not claim that there were not similar incidents at Channings to those described in other transfer schools. Pupils were to be found in detention for fighting and other misbehaviours. Generally, however, the observers felt the atmosphere to be more relaxed, whereas at both Guy Mannering and at Maid Marion, the behaviour of pupils like Seymour and Wayne seemed designed to test out the system, to see how far they could go before the threatened retribution would result. Teachers like Mrs Whistler, who attempted to operate in the same way as Mrs McDougal at Channings, and set up groups on the second day of term in an attempt to involve pupils in decisions about how the classroom could operate effectively, were regarded by some colleagues as weak.[16]

This less aggressive implementation and constant repetition of rules, coupled with strong messages about the school as a 'learning community' for both staff and students also appeared to influence the behaviour of the children who were quite prepared to share materials, such as colouring pencils and erasers and who would seek on several occasions to prevent a classmate from breaking a rule by reminding him or her to bring games kit or not to use a particular route into the library area. Unlike Sammy at Guy Mannering, Rebecca, who had also just moved into the area from somewhere in the North of England, was immediately included in a group at dinner and break time. This, despite the fact that in lessons she often had to sit by herself because there were an unequal number of girls in the class and the others paired up with partners from their feeder schools. For our final comparison we provide an account of the first PE lesson at Channings with Mr Hewitt. Previously, we have seen how Mr Pike at Maid Marion had started with a long list of rules and how Wayne had been told off for shuffling out of line and drumming his feet, something he had been told in one of the rules that you didn't do. Another rule was that when pupils arrived for games or PE they had to line up outside the changing rooms on the paved area. On the first day, Mr Pike made each pupil stand on a separate paving stone and then went down the line giving him or her each a number. Each child then had to remember the number of their paving stone so that they could line up and stand on it on future occasions. At Guy Mannering, Mr Richards, who with Mr Hudd took swimming and PE, also began with a long list of rules about behaviour and what to wear and Seymour, who when asked, says that he 'went swimming two years ago on holiday' is told off three times in the space of minutes for whispering and touching equipment.

Mr Hewitt, on the other hand, begins his first lesson with a question, "Why do we do PE?" Pupils respond with a number of suggestions:

GIRL: To keep fit.
MR HEWITT: Excellent.
BOY: To learn sports rules.
MR HEWITT: Good.
ANOTHER BOY: It's in the National Curriculum.
MR HEWITT: Very much (and after several other suggestions) OK! Who said, 'keeping fit'? Let's have a quick go at checking our fitness.

The pupils are then taught how to check their pulse and then do various exercises to check heart rates. There is some laughter when

Tracey claims her pulse rate is 3 per minute and Mr Hewitt says, 'Two things. Either you're dead or not using the right place.' Only at the end of the lesson when everyone is changed into school uniform does he start on the rules, but as with the other teachers he tries to elicit answers from the pupils and often gives reasons why the rule is needed.

'We start when I say start. Stop when told to stop. Usually we use a whistle. Let's start with that. What does a whistle mean to you?' (A boy answers, 'Be quiet' and Mr H continues) 'Yeh! Lots of noise carries in this room so I might use it to get quiet.'

Perhaps nothing illustrates the differences in approach better than the attitude of senior staff in schools towards school dinners. This, as we have seen earlier, is an important issue for new pupils. On the one hand it is exciting because there is much greater variety than at primary school and one can make choices and 'have chips each day if I want'. On the other hand, pupils have to manage their own money and make sure they have not chosen more items than they can pay for. This can be particularly embarrassing for children on free school meals since they have less flexibility. Having to be told by the dinner lady to put an item back or to take something extra often drew attention to their situation.

For all these reasons, over the first few days, long queues were likely at the dinner counter as pupils pondered about whether they could afford some item and attempted to keep track of the total. At Maid Marion, the system had been streamlined by introducing a smart card. Children could check on the amount left on the card before joining the dinner queue and add extra money if needed. In this way the need to give change was avoided. By day two the procedure was working smoothly and Mr Sheffer, the headteacher, expressed his satisfaction to one of the observers remarking that 'Year 6 have really settled in well. Dinner took only three minutes longer than normal.' At Guy Mannering there was heavier supervision. Pupils' trays were scrutinised and some children were sent back to change an item because 'these don't go together' (i.e. a plate of chips, a beefburger, a synthetic cream cake and a fizzy drink were thought an unhealthy combination). After lunch on the second day the observer recorded that:

> Some older children have been 'getting at' Carl because he is slow to choose and sort out his money. He asks Mrs Staunton if he could go on second dinner because of the long queues but is told there would still be queues then. She asks him 'Aren't the teachers there to help?' and he replies 'Yes! They ask you if you would eat like that at home.'

At Channings pupils were advised to join the dinner queue whenever they saw it begin to decline in length. On the first dinner time, some of Miss

Fielder's form came to look several times and go away again. The net result of this apparent lack of a system was that in the first few days dinnertime usually ran into the afternoon period. Both the headteacher and the deputy head took a very philosophical view. Mr Burrows told an observer, 'If we are lucky they will get the hang of it by next week.'

In these ways pupils learn to adapt to the system, familiarise themselves with the rules and the ways of different teachers. They come to know things about each other such that while Seymour has only been swimming once, Jane has done 50 metres and has a certificate to prove it. They learn about the danger areas in the school and which pupils to avoid if they don't want to be labelled troublemakers like Wayne. To the observers there seemed to be clear differences in the ways that some of the schools in the study went about this process of induction and acclimatisation. How far these differences are reflected in pupils' attitudes towards school we shall explore in a later chapter.

Cross-phase continuity

The typical secondary classroom is, then, a very different learning environment compared to its primary counterpart, both in terms of its appearance and in terms of the teaching and learning strategies which go on there. But as we shall see, in the present study it was clear that it was neither the place nor the delivery of the curriculum which lacked familiarity for pupils. There were also many instances of a lack of constancy in the curriculum itself, so that there was a disjunction between the content and language of, say, the science of the primary classroom and that of the secondary laboratory. Alternatively, continuity was disrupted where teachers took pupils back to an earlier phase of learning, involving the repetition of already familiar skills and knowledge, often justified as 'starting afresh' or providing a 'level playing field'. At Channings, Mrs Salter set them the task of deciding 'what is Science?' Although now a National Curriculum core subject in primary school, pupils were then sent to cupboards to find pieces of equipment and asked to name them. At Maid Marion, Miss Mowbray had the apparatus out on the front laboratory bench and pupils made drawings in their books and were sent away to find the names for homework. Most children wrote in the names as they drew. The observer in the same school saw a similar lesson during the original ORACLE transfer study two decades previously. In mathematics, as we saw earlier in the chapter, Mrs Redmond said she did not base her judgements on the pupils' Key Stage 2 National Curriculum Test scores. Most of the teachers began on the first page of the mathematics book which they used as the standard text. In some cases the same book was distributed to all sets and as term progressed the 'top' set was expected to work through the examples at a faster pace. English presented more variation, partly because as argued by Marshall and Brindley (1998) secondary teachers approach it through literature. In Miss Welch's class at Channings, pupils made a list of likes and dislikes in the first lesson and in the second they are told to write the title 'Myself' at the top of the page. Miss Welch said to the class:

> 'Hands up! What do you need when you go abroad? (answers her own question). 'A passport, why?' Several children give answers. 'So you can get back on the flight again' (Ben). 'You can clear through customs' (Pete). Miss Welch asks, 'Why do you have customs?' Pete responds, 'To stop people smuggling things.' Ignoring this answer, Miss Welch then tells the class, 'To say who you are. So we are looking at your Channings' passport.'

Other English teachers began in similar ways including writing accounts of 'My holidays', 'My pets'. There were sessions on comprehension and grammar and descriptive writing, similar to those experienced by pupils in primary schools. For example children had to choose characters and describe their personality, the clothes they wore, what they did and then give them a name.

We do not intend, therefore, to suggest that all these new experiences come as a complete shock to children when they first arrive at secondary school. We know that they expect things to be different, and we have already discussed in Chapter 2 pupils' often-expressed excitement about the prospect of the new as much as they show anxiety about it. Equally some pupils may be put off by a lack of challenge, particularly in science, where following the pyrotechnic displays on induction day they may have harboured high expectations. But as Stillman and Maychell (1982) argue, the impact of sudden change can be much softened by acknowledging the past. Their call, in response to what they saw then as an atmosphere of 'mutual mistrust', was for the kind of liaison procedures that schools now routinely deploy. Yet despite these efforts to reassure and inform pupils about their new school, this would seem to be an almost entirely forward-looking exercise. While both primary and secondary teachers busily prepare pupils for what is to come, once they actually arrive there is much less effort to find out about, or take account of what has gone before.

Gorwood (1991), as we saw in the first chapter, regards this situation as the natural outcome of fundamentally different philosophies of primary and secondary schooling which appear to have changed little in recent years. This was routinely demonstrated by comments which began 'I don't know what you did at primary school' almost inevitably followed by something like 'but this is how we do it here' and this applied equally to the syllabus as it did to pupil behaviour. In other words, there was little or no attempt to find out what pupils actually did at primary school since it was to have no bearing on what was to follow. Some teachers did begin by asking pupils what they had done at the previous school. A history teacher, for example, asked pupils. 'What do you know about the Tudors?' while one French teacher expressed his surprise when 'half the class put up their hands in response to his question, "How many of you can count up to ten?"' However, to the observers, these enquiries served at best as a mild form of reassurance for those pupils who had already covered the topic, since it rarely impinged on the planned activity whether they had or not. Such attitudes can suggest what is at best a lack of understanding or interest in, and at worst plain mistrust of, what goes on in primary schools, and correspondingly the knowledge and experience that children bring with them.

In a number of cases, teachers went beyond a simple lack of knowledge of or interest in the pupil's former educational experience, revealing a stereotyped view of the primary classroom which belied claims to a greater communication and understanding between the two phases. The implication behind this was that the teacher in question did know what they did in primary school and, what is more, disapproved of it. This applied equally to behaviour as it did to subject knowledge or expertise, as if the children had never been taught how to walk down a corridor, knew they should be quiet when a teacher asks for attention, or that they were expected to get on with work independently. This was demonstrated in the use of such phrases as not 'getting up and walking about', or 'chatting as you did at your old school'. In Galton and Willcocks (1983), Delamont argues that one of the main ways that secondary teachers distance themselves from what went on in primary feeder schools is through the use of different terminology. Delamont reported that teachers spent considerable time teaching children new terms during these early encounters. Terms like 'evaporation' in science, 'erosion' in geography and replacing 'sharing' with 'dividing' in mathematics served to demonstrate that 'every subject had its own language' (ibid.: 114). In the present study there were fewer such examples, partly because the National Curriculum at Key Stage Two has gone 'specialist' and already introduced many of the terms, particularly in English. However, Mrs Staunton at Guy Mannering took a slightly different approach. She introduced the different terms but also attempted to point to the similarities:

> 'When I was at a village school it was called sums. When I got home my dad asked, "What are you doing at school?" I replied "Same as before but there is a new subject called Maths. We don't do sums any more." Then my dad laughed and said, "You're in for a shock. Get a dictionary and look up Mathematics."'

What many teachers seemed to see in front of them was not a group of children who arrived with several years of education already behind them, who already had considerable knowledge and expertise, but a series of 'blank slates' on which to write afresh. This was presented as being a virtue by a number of teachers who argued that the fairest approach, given that pupils came with different levels and kinds of knowledge and expertise, was simply to start from scratch on a 'level playing field'. Given the difficulty of achieving this with players with such different starting points, this often meant beginning with the lowest common denominator. Perhaps the most overt example of this was the French teacher at Maid Marion who informed the observer that she was delighted to find that few children had any previous knowledge of the language. Although it might be argued that this is an unrepresentative example, since modern languages is not on the primary curriculum, there were numerous instances in other curriculum areas where pupils spent this first period of their secondary education going over previously learned material, or using skills which were often well below those which they had developed at their former schools. This seems an experience common to most first year secondary pupils to judge by surveys such as SCAA (1996) and Suffolk LEA (1997).

Sorting pupils out: the use of tests

This approach was also exemplified in some schools by the administration of a variety of tests during the early days of secondary school. We have already provided one account of testing in Mrs Staunton's class at Guy Mannering. Some of these assessments were the kind of routine class-based testing with which the children would have been familiar from their primary school days, for example, short mental arithmetic or spelling tests. Others were school- or department-based tests to enable teachers to determine ability groupings or 'sets' or to ascertain differential needs in at least one of the core subject of English, maths or science. Although not all schools used these more formal assessments during the first week, all but one (which we will examine in more detail shortly) did so at some time early on in the term. In those which were observed, teachers generally sought to reassure pupils about the process, for example, presenting tests as 'a little quiz' or as 'nothing to worry about', and explaining that:

> 'We just want to find out what you can do.'
> 'It would be awful to give you work you would be worried about.'
> 'We don't want you to get in the wrong maths group.'

In only one instance, at Kenilworth, where children were told (rather sternly according to the observer's account) that they were to work under 'strict test conditions', was there anything resembling a formal examination.

While such reassurances and explanations were helpful, they also said something about the school's attitudes towards the information that they had received from the feeder schools. Feeder schools provide a great deal of information, which will usually include teacher assessments of achievement levels, various measures of literacy and numeracy and topics or areas covered in each curriculum area. In addition, information about individual children with special educational needs and/or emotional or behavioural difficulties, friendship groups, attitudes to school and work and so on will also be passed on. In some cases further material was made available including pupils' records of achievement folders and examples of children's work. Because children going to Channings and Danesbury transferred at the end of Y6, these schools also received KS2 National Curriculum test results from all their feeder schools. When first assigning pupils to forms or tutor groups, secondary schools often devote considerable effort in striving for balance. The schools aim to ensure that there is a roughly equal spread of ability, that no one form has a preponderance of pupils with a learning or behavioural difficulty, or of children from one feeder school. All these factors must be considered while at the same time trying to ensure that some elements of friendship groups survive transfer. As McCallum (1996) also found, excepting for this initial grouping process, and despite the wealth of valuable information available, little use was actually made of it, beyond perhaps making it accessible to other members of staff who were at liberty to use it or, more often, not. This did not go unnoticed by some primary school-teachers, who understood that much of their efforts were largely wasted.

Seemingly sound reasons might be advanced for this approach. For example, in the absence of equivalent measures of, say, reading ability across all feeder schools, it becomes difficult to make comparative judgements about children based on different sources of data. This is particularly true in some cases where under the present 'market-driven system' schools accept pupils from perhaps as many as twenty different feeders, although in the present study this was not the case. It might also be argued that lack of standardisation of other sources of information such as teachers' assessments could also create problems when attempting to set or band using these kinds of criteria. In such circumstances, the administration of a uniform test for all children on entry would seem to make sense. However, the practice continued even where feeder schools had used identical assessment procedures, for example, in the case of Channings and Danesbury schools who had National Curriculum test data for English, science and maths for every incoming pupil. Moreover, even where teachers' assessments were collected on a standard form provided by the receiving school, the information thus gathered was rarely used in any systematic way. Some schools argued that early testing provided a form of 'cross-checking' of primary school information, or as one teacher put it, 'seeing if what your primary school told us about you is true'. Implicit in this approach, as argued earlier, is at best scepticism towards the data that the primary schools had supplied and at worst mistrust of it, since accepting its accuracy would by definition eliminate the need to 'check'. Certainly this interpretation is borne out by the findings from the survey carried out by Worcester LEA (1997) where the majority of headteachers said that lack of confidence in the tests was the main reason they placed little reliance on the results from feeder schools. In some respects, their views may be an accurate reflection of the finding that over the summer vacation pupils' test performance does decline, particularly, one might speculate in Year 6, where in the last term of the primary school they have been prepared for a 'high stakes' examination. Whatever the truth of such claims, however, it remains a fact that the considerable effort primary school teachers devote to collecting and collating such information seems to be largely wasted, rendering one of the central features of cross-phase liaison little more than a time-consuming ritual.

What makes this situation all the more worrying is that many of the tests which schools or departments depended upon to provide them with 'setting' data were far from thorough assessments of children's existing knowledge and skill, and were often inconsistently administered. We have already cited the case of the English test used at Guy Mannering. At the other (9–13) school, Gryll Grange, pupils were given a test during their first history lesson which they were told was 'to do with Romans' in order to help the teacher know 'what level I'm going to pitch the work for you'. When, at the end of the session some 40 minutes later, a clearly concerned boy complained that he 'hadn't done the Romans before' he was told 'Martin, this isn't to see whether you've done the Romans, it's to see whether you can write sentences . . .'. This relatively crude kind of assessment of basic abilities was a fairly common feature of these first few days. It was repeated in subject after subject, even though a simple examination at the data provided by Martin's former teacher may have been a better guide to this pupil's writing ability than this particular 'history' test. In another school, a science test (which despite teacher's reassurances to the contrary was labelled 'Year 6 exam') made no attempt to assess pupils' knowledge of scientific process, an important element of National Curriculum primary science, instead focusing entirely on factual knowledge. Moreover, a number of the questions were ambiguously phrased. For example, one question concerned the effects of heat on a range of materials, which included requiring the students to classify, from a given list, those materials which 'melt when warmed', 'do not change when they are warmed' or 'burn when heated in a flame'. Each material could be assigned to one of these three categories only. Among the listed materials were butter and sand. While the correct response was presumably that butter melts when warmed, while sand does not change, it could equally be argued that butter burns if exposed to strong heat, or indeed that all materials (including sand) change when warmed (for example, by expanding). Moreover, the issue of 'how warm is warm' was not addressed. Sand which is heated sufficiently will melt, as any child who had studied the properties of glass would have known. Since there was no requirement (or space) to offer any reasoning behind the answers, the child who 'thought things through', rather than gave the 'obvious' answer might actually have been penalised, not only in his or her final score, but also, in this strictly timed test, in lost minutes.

The major exceptions to this general rule would seem to be information about learning difficulties and/or behavioural problems. Liaison between Special Educational Needs Coordinators (SENCOs) before transfer was generally given a high priority, as was accommodating the particular needs of children with special needs, or who had emotional or social difficulties on arrival. An example of this difference in attitude was seen in Kenilworth, where all children were tested in English on the third day of the new term, in order to place them in ability sets. However, children designated as having reading difficulties were tested as a separate group. Although the school was not fully prepared to accept primary school data for the majority (hence, as we have already argued, the decision to proceed with further testing), it had taken note of information about children with special needs. In a similar way, information concerning children who had displayed challenging behaviour in primary school was also disseminated, although receiving schools (or individual teachers) adopted different strategies in dealing with such pupils, in some cases making explicit disciplinary procedures from the beginning, while others opted for the 'clean slate' approach.

We have said that one school took a rather different approach which involved a good deal of collaboration and consultation with teachers in the primary feeders. This was Maid Marion, which, as we have seen, provided a more primary-type environment for the new pupils, including a Year 6 base and recreation space. Just as in other schools, children were to be assigned to different ability sets in maths (but not English), but rather than testing the new intake on arrival, the schools worked together to construct suitable assessment materials which were given to the children before transfer. All involved benefited from this arrangement. The primary teachers knew that their expertise and knowledge were valued, and that their involvement actually influenced the outcome. The transfer school had standardised and reliable information to work with well before the new pupils arrived. Because the tests were taken in a familiar environment with their regular teacher, the children were spared much of the anxiety which testing provokes, and were assigned to their subject groups from the beginning, rather than having to change after a few days or weeks.

We have so far examined what was common to the schools in general terms. As we have been at pains to point out more than once, not all schools (and certainly not all teachers) conducted affairs in an identical fashion. There were many, often notable, exceptions to these general rules, which we will examine in the following section. In conclusion, however, we feel reasonably confident in saying that, in terms of content, the picture we have presented is a pretty true reflection of what goes on during the first few days at secondary school. As we have also mentioned more than once, however, the context in which these events occurred was rather different from school to school. These differences reflect each school's underlying ethos or culture, and it is to these differences to which we now turn.

School culture: 'The way we do things round here'

In the previous chapter we discussed the different ways in which schools went about the business of introducing prospective pupils to the ways of the school children during their transfer or induction day visit. These different approaches fell into three broad models or approaches, the broad characteristics of which are presented in Figure 3.1. In general terms, the first approach emphasised the differences between primary and secondary school cultures and sought to impress the transfer school's regulatory procedures; the second approach acknowledged the difference between the two phases, but aimed to reassure and to support pupils during the change process; and the third approach was designed to provided a measure of continuity by providing a familiar learning environment. In this final section, we intend to explore in greater detail some of the issues we have already identified earlier in this chapter, as well as introducing one or two additional themes, in the context of these different models. In considering this, the reader should bear in mind that we use as our unit of analysis these three generic models, not particular schools, since it is clear from Figure 3.1 that no single school fitted these categories in every particular, although some are clearly more closely matched than others.

In addition to the general point that while the content may be similar, the context will often differ, we have so far introduced two further basic arguments concerning the ways schools attempts to assimilate new pupils into the unfamiliar environment. First, we would suggest that these different contexts

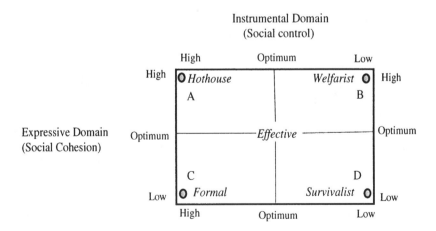

Figure 3.1 A typology of school cultures.

reflect the underlying philosophy or guiding principles of each school, around which their various policies and practices are organised. We shall henceforth refer to this as the school's culture. Second, that the culture which is revealed to would-be pupils during the various activities which comprise induction day is a good predictor of what children may expect once they have gained membership of the school community after the summer vacation.

Schools, like other organisations, need a regulatory framework, or to put it more simply, a set of rules and procedures, if they are to operate effectively. If they are to be more than merely efficient, however, there is also a need for a social framework which determines the nature of human relationships within the school (both between management and staff and between teacher and pupil). Together, these two systems combine to shape and define the way in which a school operates, and to create a culture which is unique to each institution. D. H. Hargreaves (1995) proposes a typology of school cultures which emerges from the tension between the instrumental (regulation and maintenance of order) and the expressive (promotion of social harmony) functions. A school where both social control and academic expectation were high would have what Hargreaves calls the hothouse culture, characterised by a 'frenetic' and anxiety-ridden atmosphere where both staff and pupils feel 'under surveillance'. The survivalist culture, meanwhile is typical of an 'at risk' school, where academic achievement is very poor and effective control has broken down. In a *formal* culture, considerable emphasis is placed on social control mechanisms but little is offered in the way of social support. Such a school would be characterised by a strong work ethic, with an emphasis on academic achievement within a rigidly enforced regulatory framework. Pupils are largely socially isolated from teachers, and therefore seek support through informal peer-groupings rather than institutional structures. At the opposite extreme is the school with a *welfarist* culture, where social controls are low, pupil–teacher relationships are informal, and there is an emphasis on personal development rather than academic performance.

As Hargreaves points out, relatively few schools occupy these extreme positions, and the majority fall somewhere in-between, and nearer to the mid-point. This represents the effective school culture, in which discipline and support are balanced at an optimum level for both domains. Within a firm, rather than a strict regulatory structure, expectations of academic progress are high, but social development is equally valued.

These four basic cultures bear considerable similarity to the four parenting styles identified by Maccoby and Martin (1983), which are also located in terms of the interrelationship between two 'functions', demand/control and acceptance/responsiveness. A parent who exercises a high level of control coupled with a low level of acceptance (rejection) would be defined as authoritarian, while those who take the opposite approach would be defined as permissive (the equivalent of formal and welfarist respectively). A parent

93

who had little control and rejected the child is described as neglectful (high-risk). All three of these styles were found to be associated with negative behaviour or attitudes in children. The most consistently positive outcomes – 'well adjusted' children – tended to be associated with authoritative parents, who exercised optimal levels of both control and acceptance, the equivalent of the formal school culture.

In fact, the schools in our sample tended to fall mainly between the formal and welfarist cultures. The differences between the schools were reflected both in their different approaches to inducting pupils into the life of the school, and in their relationship to the outside world. Schools which tended towards the (collegial/welfarist/permissive) culture were characterised by what we call an internal orientation. In internally oriented schools, there is a clear distinction between rules (laws which must be followed, e.g. the forbidding of chewing gum) and procedures (ways of doing things, such as being required to always underline in pencil). Rules are in place mainly to ensure that the system runs smoothly or for reasons of safety, rather than to regulate the pupil. Procedures are sometimes school- or department-wide to ensure a degree of coherence or order or the preferences of the individual teacher. While rules are normally not negotiable, certain procedures might be, for example, if a more efficient way is suggested. Within a school adopting a welfarist approach, in the case of both rules and procedures, there is usually no censure for children who question their purpose, and explanations for their existence are usually given. While appearance, behaviour, level of attainment and so on are all considered important, as in any school, the emphasis is on a partnership between teacher and pupil, so that the child fulfils his or her potential.

In externally oriented schools, on the other hand, such attributes are seen as markers of the school's excellence, so that the pupil becomes a public representative of the school. There is, accordingly, great store placed on the importance of upholding tradition and reputation, with rhetoric often about not 'letting down' the school (year, house, form, etc.). To do so may attract public censure and/or punishment. Here the distinction between rules and procedures is less clear, both are often negatively expressed ('don'ts' featuring much more frequently than 'do's') and may take the form of military-type commands in the sense that they may not be challenged (which can sometimes lead to the perpetuation of 'arcane' rules which have no apparent purpose or rationale) and which foreground issues about uniform and uniformity, with explicit rules about silence, lining up, moving around the school in single files, walking correctly and due deference to those higher up the chain of authority.

The most formal (and therefore least welfarist) school, Kenilworth, had a strong external orientation. The emphasis on appearance and behaviour, rules and regulations which was evident on induction day (for example the 'fashion show') continued to be a major constituent of introductory activities during the first few days. Rules were typically accompanied by warnings and injunctions, with the threat of firm and swift sanctions for any infringements. Silence was the order of the day, reinforced regularly by various versions of the teacher's rule 'I talk, you don't'. Public example was often made of pupils who did not conform to the school's 'way of doing things', particularly during assemblies. Teachers had a habit of referring to unnamed children who were 'letting the school down' in some way, with the implication that they either knew who they were or could find out. In this respect there was something of Hargreaves' 'hothouse' culture in which pupils are (or are encouraged to believe that they are) under constant surveillance, even when out of school.

In the most 'liberal' or welfarist of the six schools, Channings, rules, as we have seen, were rarely mentioned. The school operated on the principle that children already knew how to behave appropriately. For example, silence was not enforced in the recognition that children, particularly during these first days, needed to talk. Rather, it was assumed (correctly) that the children knew when it was appropriate to work quietly or to fall silent during an assembly, that they could walk down corridors without the aid of 'corridor monitors' and that they understood when to be quiet.

Despite our misgivings, the majority of pupils seemed to settle in remarkably quickly, regardless of the nature of the school regime that they encountered. We will consider evidence to support this assertion in Chapter 5 when we look at the changes in pupils' attitudes before and after transfer. It may be, of course, that teachers understand this, and therefore see little need to fix something which isn't broken. But in the original transfer study (Galton and Willcocks 1983) we saw that this approach appeared to lead to a hiatus in progress and that there were some vulnerable pupils, rather like Sammy and Carl in the present study who did not adjust well to elements of the more formal culture while others like Seymour and Wayne reacted strongly against it and were immediately labelled 'troublemakers'. How far these cultural differences impact on the behaviour of teachers in the classroom once the introductory period comes to an end and they assume their specialist roles is an interesting question. In the next chapter, therefore, we will explore this issue, in a more systematic way, and also compare the teaching that pupils received with their previous experience of primary school.

Notes

1 The sequence of events we describe above is a composite, drawn from observations of the first 20 minutes or so in all six of the schools we observed, but we hope one which captures something of the essence of this moment of transition.
2 A reference to James Elroy Flecker's poem, 'Gates of Damascus'. Travellers en route for Baghdad left by the East Gate of Damascus and entered the desert where many perished. The parallel is with passing through the New School Gates to face the uncertainties of life in the secondary school.

3 As we saw in Chapter 1 (p. 15), improving continuity between primary and secondary schools was one rationale for introducing the National Curriculum according to the then Education Minister, Kenneth Baker's account of these events.

4 The different researchers used different procedures for recording observations. In the case of this particular observer, extensive notes were made throughout the school day and a fuller, more coherent version, including background information about, for example, content of any worksheets, text books, etc. was then dictated into an audiotape recorder the same day. Also included were verbatim accounts of any conversational exchanges where recorded. The tapes were then transcribed and used for subsequent analysis. This procedure was used in the original ORACLE transfer study by the same observer.

5 Chapter 7 of Galton and Willcocks (1983) briefly addresses the issue of the pupils' first few days in their new school. Chapter 3 of Delamont and Galton (1986) while going into much greater detail, nevertheless serves mainly to set up the 5 major analytic themes which (define) the remaining sections of the book, and which deals with the whole first year at secondary school. While we shall make such comparisons as are possible between the findings presented in these accounts and those of the present study, we do not intend, in this chapter, to pursue Delamont and Galton's thematic structure, but will instead explore issues which seem, to us, to be particularly important.

6 Kenilworth was the only school to hold both first-year and whole-school assemblies on the first day.

7 Observers' field notes confirm that the range of activities was very similar for the parallel group in each school.

8 Having said this, teachers did routinely assess children at an early stage of the term in most curriculum areas, regardless of primary-school data, an issue we will pick up again later in the chapter.

9 Observers' field notes confirm that the diet was very similar for the parallel group in each school.

10 This school opted to hold over the first whole-school meeting until the second day.

11 Ashburton was local authority A in Galton and Willcocks (1983).

12 In metalwork at Merlin Court Mr Steele's way was to draw a margin, a ruler wide, on the left-hand side of the page plus a similar margin across the top of the page. This gave a square in the left-hand corner of the paper where the date was to be put. In English, Mr Evans, at Kenilworth insisted on a similar sized margin drawn with a sharp pencil. Pupils put their name on the left, date on the right and began the title or heading 5 cm. in from the margin. All titles had to be underlined twice with a red ballpoint. Interestingly, Mrs Staunton, who was a colleague of Mr Evans, before he retired, used the same system twenty years later. The only difference was that the margins were now printed on the paper so didn't need to be drawn.

13 Based on *post-hoc* information from teachers and pupils (no observation data available).

14 As we shall later see, while this 'primary model' was the major means of delivering the curriculum, for certain subjects these pupils also went to specialist teachers and rooms (for example, art, music or technology), or less commonly teachers came to them for, say, maths.

15 The heading is taken from a chapter by Sara Delamont in Galton and Willcocks (1983).

16 Mrs Whistler confessed as much to one of the observers.

4

TEACHING IN THE TRANSFER SCHOOLS

Maurice Galton and Tony Pell

In the previous chapter we saw that during the first few days in the transfer school the teachers' main preoccupation was to establish rules for working in the classroom and for setting out work, to sort pupils into appropriate groups and to identify particular children who caused problems. These problem children included those with learning or behavioural difficulties but more generally involved those who either worked too slowly or too quickly, making it difficult to pace the lesson.

Two months[1] into the new school year, when a second round of visits were made, the atmosphere was more settled. Lunch queues at Channings, for example, were no longer a problem while at Maid Marion and Guy Mannering most children came to school with the right books and the right equipment for the day's lessons. During these second and later series of visits in the following two terms observers carried out systematic observation during English, mathematics and science lessons but also followed pupils into other classes during the rest of the day. At Channings the day started with assembly followed by English:

> Miss Welch tells the class to go to the drama studio. Pupils make a circle and are told to fall down and die with screams. They all do this. They then get into pairs and are told to mime walking on a tightrope. During this exercise Miss Welch either silently walks up and down or stares out of the window and bites her nails. They then come back into a circle and each pair performs the mime.
>
> The bell goes and it's Mr Price for Design. He has changed groups at half-term and proceeds to give the same lesson I saw on day two of the term. The pupils are to make a box. For homework they are to decide what to put in their box and make a note of the measurements. For the rest of the period they will do an exercise. Mr Price draws a picture of a man in a lorry whose job is to take tree trunks to a paper mill. The class is put in groups and each is given two pieces of cardboard and some straws. The task is to make the strongest lorry which Mr Price will test by seeing how many blocks he can load before it bends.

Mathematics at Maid Marion is taught by the Head of First Year, Mr Baines:

He begins the lesson returning the books with the homework marked and then hands out squared paper with a table of numbers. Mr B gets pupils to add up the rows and columns which all total 34.

13	8	12	1
2	11	7	14
3	10	6	15
16	5	9	4

They are to find as many ways as possible of making different combinations of this number. After twenty minutes of this activity they are told to open the textbooks on page 32 and do exercise 1 and 2 on factors in their rough books.

Mrs Staunton at Gryll Grange tells the pupils to 'get their maths brains working'. She then begins a quiz:

10 add 4 units?
How many tens in 104?
If I say 7 how many do I need to make it 10?
That's better! Fingers are out.

The questions gradually get more difficult.
Add the numbers 8, 3, 5 and 7
How many ways are there of adding the numbers in 1997?
    Then pupils are given a worksheet with the heading Number Bonds. They are to work on their own, silently, and complete the 20 questions by the end of the lesson

At Maid Marion in science:

The lesson begins five minutes late because teachers in the various maths sets have not kept to time. Some pupils have stopped at their lockers to pack their bags so that they can go straight home after the laboratory period ends. The bags are dumped in a huge pile in the corner of the room.
    Miss Mowbray reminds pupils that unless they arrive on time they will not be able to do exciting experiments. Today they are going to learn about filtration. She begins by asking them for examples of filtration in the home. She mentions the word coffee but either the children all drink instant brands, use plungers, or amuse themselves

by only talking about tea bags much to Ms Mowbray's frustration. 'Oh, you are asleep today,' she tells them. 'Too much dinner.'

She produces a filter funnel, demonstrates how to fold the paper, and then sends them to a cupboard to get similar apparatus and a retort stand to hold the funnel. She then points to a bottle of dirty water, tells them to fill half a beaker with it and to pour it into the filter collecting the clear liquid in a conical flask. All these objects are on the front bench clearly labelled.

The filtration experiment takes five minutes. For the rest of the lesson the class has to write up the experiment. Miss Mowbray puts up an overhead with a labelled diagram and paragraphs which pupils have to copy and fill in the missing words from the list provided. One paragraph reads 'We took a filter f—— and a filter p—— and stood it in the r—— stand. Then we poured the dirty l—— into the f—— and collected the r—— in a c—— flask. It was clear etc. (at the bottom of the overhead the words *conical, funnel, liquid, paper, residue, retort* are displayed).

At one point during the experimenting there is a slight altercation with a boy who has not put on his safety glasses.

MISS MOWBRAY: What have I been telling you these past weeks?
BOY PUPIL: But it's only water. That's not dangerous.
MISS MOWBRAY: Doesn't matter. Wear them always.
BOY PUPIL (mutters as Miss Mowbray moves away): Stupid old bag.
MISS MOWBRAY (turning): What did you say?
BOY: I've got to get something from my bag Miss.

Elsewhere, similar kinds of worksheets, in which pupils filled in the missing words, were a common feature of many science lessons. For example at Channings during the second term with Mrs Savoury, a colleague of Mrs Salter whom we met in the previous chapter, pupils had to look at a table of data in their textbooks. This listed a range of common foods and their calorific values. The worksheet listed the food consumed by a girl called Susan. Pupils then had to answer the following questions:

Susan's total energy for the day is . . .
Susan did (did not) get enough energy
The five foods that gave Susan most energy were. . . .
If Susan's energy intake for the day was lower than 9700 kJ when she needed to be active she would . . .

The second part of the worksheet asked pupils to make a list of everything they ate on the previous day and to use the table to work out their energy intake. For homework they had to complete the following tasks:

99

A 12-year-old girl needs about 9,700 kJ per day and 12-year old boy needs about 11,700 kJ. I ate . . . food yesterday so my energy intake was . . . On squared paper, draw a bar chart to show the energy needed per minute to carry out the activity shown in Question 1 of page 41 of the textbook.

Pupils were required to work on their own in silence, with no opportunity for sharing ideas or raising questions such as, for example, why boys and girls had different calorific requirements.

The pupils then moved on to history where they were doing the Battle of Hastings. In the previous lesson they held a debate with pupils taking sides to argue whether Harold the Saxon, Harold Hardrada, the Viking, or William Duke of Normandy should have the throne.

Mrs Diepers takes them through the story explaining the soldiers were mostly local peasants who worked the land for their living. She asks the class why they would be worried while waiting for William to come. Pupils offer various answers.

'They'd be frightened.'

'They'd be worried that their buildings were misused.'

Eventually after some prompting by the teacher a boy offers, 'There would be weeds in the crops.'

Mrs Diepers tells them Harold let them go home but then had to go North to fight his half-brother Tostig and Harold Hardrada, the Viking, at Stamford Bridge near York. Rebecca volunteers the information that it takes her father 4 hours to drive to Newcastle. Meanwhile William lands and Harold rushes back to do battle with him.

MRS D: Where did they meet?

STACEY: Colchester.

MRS D: No. You're mixing it up with the Romans we did earlier.

CLARE: Hastings.

MRS D: Yes, it's called the Battle of Hastings but it took place at Senlach Hill. We know a lot about it. Why?

Only Rebecca knows about the Bayeux tapestry and has seen it. After this brief question and answer session, the pupils are told to open their books and look at pictures from the tapestry. They have to look at the sentences written below which are jumbled up and match each picture with an appropriate sentence. When they have finished Mrs Diepers tells them for homework they must say who they think will win the Battle of Hastings basing their case on the following facts. She begins to dictate:

January – Harold crowned King.

July – William prepares fleet.

September 8 –No supplies for Harold's army. He sends the troops home.

September 18 – Harold Hardrada, the Viking, lands in Yorkshire.

September 20 – Harold defeats English Earls at Fulford.

September 25 – Harold defeats Harold Hardrada and Tostig at Stamford Bridge

September 28 – William lands at Pevensey.

Stacey says she is confused and asks, 'What happened on the 25 September?'

Mrs D decides to change tack and to get pupils to make a chart putting in the dates showing what Harold, Harold Hardrada and William did. However, the bell goes so Mrs S tells them the home-work will be set on Friday instead of today.

The pupils then move onto French.

Mr Glass shows them an overhead with four names and four houses. Phillip has no front garden; Karren lives in a detached house while Jean lives in a terrace. Marie lives in an apartment. Mr Glass sees a pupil fiddling with her pencil case and shouts out in English,

'Pencil case alert! Pencil Case Alert!'

The lesson continues in French, Marie has gaz, Karen mazout and Philip charbon central heating. Pupils have to work in pairs, each pupil acting out the parts of one of the French children. He tells them off for speaking English:

'Look I'm in charge of this lesson (he says this in English). I want you to listen to me speaking French. I don't want you to talk English among yourselves.'

After about fifteen minutes pupils are told to open their rough books. Another overhead is displayed showing various objects inside a detached house. The class are given a worksheet with a list of sen-tences in pairs. The task is to copy the drawing and then choose the appropriate sentence from each pair. This is also to be copied into their book.

Chez Amanda il y a un jardin devant la maison

Or

Chez Amanda il y a un jardin derrière la maison

Il y a le chauffage central au mazout

Or

Il y a le chauffage central au charbon

Mr Glass checks the SEN pupils and tells them they need only do a drawing. He then asks who was not tested with cue cards during the last lesson and begins to test those with their hands up. The other pupils get on with colouring in the pictures in their drawing and at one point Mr Glass complains that 'You're hardly making any progress.'

Finally he tells the class that if they are not writing down sentences because they are not sure which one to choose they can do it in pencil. There are seven pairs of sentences and the class works slowly. Mr G tells them he will come round to check their answers but the bell goes for lunch and he is still occupied testing pupils on the cue cards.

This lengthy description of a morning's schoolwork, half way into the second term of the first year in one of the transfer schools provides a not untypical description of the daily experience of these first year secondary pupils. In all the lessons, despite spurts of innovative activity, the main teaching strategy consisted of setting pupils to carry out exercises based either on the textbook or specially constructed worksheets. In Mrs Dieper's class they spend part of the lesson taking down dictated notes. In Mr Glass's French class pupils copied pictures from an overhead and colour them in. Mrs Savoury adopted a similar strategy in science with pupils manipulating data from a textbook and then filling in worksheets. Apart from the brief episode in Mr Glass's lesson when pupils worked in pairs, there were few opportunities for group discussion or 'hands on' experimentation. For most of the day pupils entered into their 'rough' books information displayed on the blackboard, overhead projector or worksheet only to reproduce the same material by making a fair copy in their homework books. In coping with these demands pupils often adopted the strategy identified in Galton and Willcocks (1983: 53–55) as *easy riding*. Thus in the French lesson, the pupils took as much time as possible to colour in the pictures of the various objects contained in the house in the picture. In this way they were able to delay the moment when they were forced to address the main demand of the task, which was to select the appropriate French sentences from the various pairs and copy them into their books. In the history lesson, setting the homework had to be put back for several days because a lesson planned to take one period had to be extended into a second session.

In commenting upon the above episodes the observer remarked on, what to him, appeared to be the relative slow pace of the lessons in these Year 7 classrooms compared to those seen previously in the primary schools. In the latter classes, as described in Galton *et al.* (1999b) levels of teacher–pupil interaction have increased. Compared to the same classrooms twenty years ago, about 20 per cent less time is now spent on monitoring pupil activity and listening to children report on the work. Consequently the impression conveyed to the outsider was one of 'extreme busyness' with the teacher, when not addressing the class, rapidly moving from pupil to pupil. In contrast with the secondary approach it is as if the video recording of a lesson was played with the 'fast forward' button depressed.

However, the opposite was true of transitions between lessons. In the primary classes, because pupils generally stayed in their own base with the same teacher, the shift from, say, English to mathematics was gradual. At transition time while chosen pupils gave back books that have been marked since the previous mathematics lesson, other children might continue to work on their previous English task until the teacher called them to attention and began to introduce the new topic. In the secondary school, however, once pupils have been dismissed at the end of a lesson, everything is rushed. In the examples describing a morning at Channings, pupils leaving the science laboratory had to go to the other end of the main building for history and up two flights of narrow stairs to where their French lesson took place. In the process of moving classes pupils had to confront other children moving in the opposite direction, make a detour to their lockers to get out relevant books and, perhaps where necessary, visit the lavatory. For all these reasons lessons rarely began on time but often finished early, because teachers did not wish to have a colleague complain to them during break or lunch-time about late arrivals.

Not all lessons which were observed fitted the above descriptions. In Mrs Staunton's class at Gryll Grange, pupils in a science lesson studied differences between gases, liquids and solids. The lesson began with Mrs Staunton opening a bottle of ammonia at one end of the classroom with pupils at various distances putting up their hands when they first smelt the vapours. Having established that gases move rapidly, the pupils were told they were to move around as if they were molecules with arms outstretched. If two pupils' arms accidentally touched they should link together and thus cease to operate independently. As more pupils joined together their movements slowed. Eventually the whole class formed a writhing, immobile mass in the centre of the room, with their arms entwined, thus imitating the movement within a solid. Pupils were then asked to work in groups using this model to predict as many differences as possible between the three states of matter.

There is a danger, as pointed out by Delamont (1981) that accounts of lessons, such as those describe here, tend to focus on the unusual, because it is more difficult to find words to describe the more mundane transactions that go to make up a large part of most lessons. The 'stupid old bag' rejoinder of one boy in Miss Mowbray's lesson might convey an impression, for example, that events in her classroom were moving beyond the teacher's control. In reality, this was a relatively isolated case and for most of the session pupils were 'on task'. In the remaining sections of this chapter, therefore, we examine the systematic observation data collected during English, mathematics and science lessons. It is precisely this kind of quantitative measure which best describes typical practice and so allows us to see how far the above impressionistic accounts are fair representations of the curriculum experienced by pupils in their first year after transfer.

Twenty years of primary classroom practice

Since the previous transfer study over two decades ago, considerable change has taken place in primary school classroom practice. The main features of this change were described in some detail in Chapter 3 of *Inside the Primary Classroom: 20 years On*. First and foremost there was a shift away from individualised teaching towards greater use of whole class instruction. Whereas in the original ORACLE study 19 per cent of instruction took place in class, by 1996 the figure had risen to just over 35 per cent (Galton *et al.* 1999b: 59). This shift towards greater use of class instruction was mainly achieved by decreasing the amount of time when teachers listened to pupils either reporting on their work or reading out loud what they had written. Another prominent feature of these 'silent interactions' in primary classrooms twenty years ago was silent marking. In this latter instance, teachers would sit alongside individual pupils reading and marking work while occasionally giving instant feedback concerning a correct spelling or an appropriate use of grammar. In general, therefore, as remarked in an earlier paragraph, primary teachers in the 1990s were working harder in the sense that they were actively engaged in conversations with pupils for most of the day with little time left for monitoring pupils' work.

A feature of whole class teaching in the 1976 primary classrooms was that it was identified with high use of more challenging questions, particularly those which were of an open-ended kind (i.e. offering the possibility of more than one acceptable answer). It might be assumed, therefore, that with an increase use of whole class teaching the level of such questioning would have increased. This proved to be so but it also transpired that the use of statements, particular statements of fact and those concerned with issuing of directions also rose. When the ratio of questions to statements was calculated it was found that over the two decades there was little difference. In 1976 an ORACLE teacher typically made use of 3.7 times as many statements as questions. By 1996 the ratio was 3.6, a change well within errors of measurement. It would seem therefore that although the overall strategies, in terms of organisation, had changed dramatically, the nature of the moment by moment interactions had remained remarkably stable. Under the various pressures exerted on them to promote whole class teaching, primary teachers had, indeed, modified their former organisational strategy but had then simply 'bolted' existing classroom practice onto these changes. There was, it was true, an increase in the amount of group work undertaken. This had risen from 9.8 per cent in 1976 to around 16.4 per cent in 1996. Moreover, more of this group work activity was now task orientated unlike the earlier ORACLE survey where most talk between pupils was off task. In some respects, therefore, the 1996 primary classroom somewhat resembled the 1976 secondary one. For the most part it was dominated by teacher talk and most of this talk was of a cognitively low level.

Classroom interaction in the transfer schools

It is of interest, therefore, to see how far today's primary classroom compares with its secondary counterpart in terms of the target of the teachers' attention.[2] Unfortunately figures for the 1977–78 transfer study are no longer available so shifts in practice over the twenty years in the transfer schools cannot be determined. Figure 4.1, however, shows the differences between pre-transfer and transfer schools in the present study. As might be expected, the figures represent an even greater level of whole class teaching (52.2 per cent). In the transfer schools, therefore, pupils interacted with the teacher for over half of the time as a class, compared to around a third of the time in the pre-transfer schools. There were corresponding decreases in the amount of group interaction (down by just over a third from 16.4 per cent to 10.2 per cent) and in the proportion of individual interactions. The latter dropped from 48.4 per cent before transfer to 37.6 per cent after the pupils moved to their middle or secondary schools. Thus the pattern of classroom interaction was reversed, in that there was approximately 1.4 times more class than individual teacher–pupil interaction at secondary level, whereas in the pre-transfer schools pupils, typically, received 1.4 times more teacher attention as individuals than they did as members of the class.

Table 4.1 examines the overall patterns of interactions consequent on this shift in this teaching strategy. As Table 4.1 shows, there appeared to be only slight changes to the overall pattern. Whereas, it will be remembered, in the primary feeder schools there were around 3.6 as many statements as questions, this figure had now fallen to 3.1. More interesting were the differences in the silent and no interaction categories. In the primary schools the percentage of interactions in each category was almost the same (12.2 per cent compared to 12.4 per cent). Now, however, in the transfer schools there were

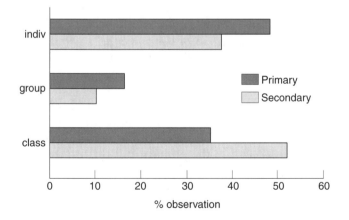

Figure 4.1 Secondary vs. primary classroom interaction.

one and half times as many silent interactions (14.7 per cent compared to 9.5 per cent). Class teaching in the transfer schools therefore involved slightly more questions and, it would seem, more demonstrations, more use of the blackboard or overhead projector, more marking and possibly more listening to children report or read an extract from their work. All these latter one-way exchanges between teachers and pupils were coded under the *silent interaction* category.

Table 4.1 Patterns of interaction in secondary vs. primary classrooms

	Secondary	Primary
Questions	18.5	16.2
Statements	57.3	59.2
Silent interaction	14.7	12.2
No interaction	9.5	12.4
Total	100.0	100.0

Questioning in the transfer schools

To pursue this analysis further it is necessary to examine in more detail the nature of the questioning taking place. For readers familiar with the previous ORACLE studies it will be remembered that questions were of five kinds. There were *task* questions where pupils could be asked either to recall *facts* or respond to problems posed by the teacher who required either a single correct answer (*closed*) or a more speculative response (*open*). The remaining questions could either deal with *task supervision* (as when a teacher asked a pupil 'What are you going to measure the volume with?') or of *routine* ('Who gave you permission to leave your place?'). Table 4.2 represents questions in two ways. First, various categories are expressed as a percentage of all questions and, second, as a percentage of all observations. Corresponding figures for the primary schools are taken from *Inside the Primary Classroom: 20 Years On* (Galton *et al.* 1999b: 63). It will be seen that there were only minor differences between the situation before and after transfer. The biggest difference concerned the use of closed questions (up 2.7 per cent from 34.6 per cent to 37.3 per cent). This change was compensated for by the slight decline in task supervision (down 2.3 per cent from 18.5 per cent to 16.2 per cent) and in routine questioning (down 1.5 per cent from 12.3 per cent to 10.8 per cent). The relative similarities of the two patterns of questioning in the primary and the transfer schools can more readily be discerned if the analysis concentrates on the use of task questions.

Figure 4.2 expresses the three types of questions (of fact, closed, open) as a percentage of all task questions. The bar chart shows that while factual questions were almost identical, there was a slight shift towards the use of

Table 4.2 Questioning in secondary and primary classrooms

	% of all questions		% of all observations	
	Secondary	Primary	Secondary	Primary
Of fact	26.0	24.7	4.8	4.0
Closed	37.3	34.6	6.9	5.6
Open	9.7	9.9	1.8	1.6
Task supervision	16.2	18.5	3.0	3.0
Routine	10.8	12.3	2.0	2.0
Total	100.0	100.0	18.5	16.2

more closed questions in the transfer classrooms at the expense of more open-ended ones. Overall, however, these changes were relatively slight and lead to the conclusion that although there was slightly more questioning taking place in the transfer schools, it operated at a fairly low level in terms of cognitive challenge. This analysis therefore supports the proposition that the earlier descriptions of lessons at the beginning of this chapter were not untypical of the experience of pupils, in general, when they moved to secondary school. This finding is of some significance when the expectations of pupils prior to the move to the new school are taken into account. Some pupils were concerned that the work would be more demanding. More able pupils relished the challenge, particularly in subjects such as science. In reality, although the way that lessons were organised may have made different demands on pupils, if the types of questions that were asked of them by teachers are taken as a yardstick, the intellectual challenge remained

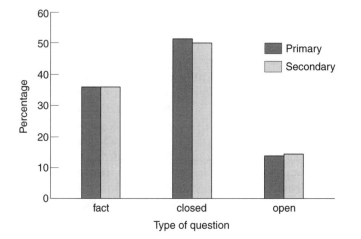

Figure 4.2 Percentage of task questions (secondary vs. primary).

somewhat similar. How far this was also true of teacher statements, which form the large proportion of all teacher interventions, will now be considered.

The use of statements in the transfer school

Table 4.3 conducts a similar analysis in relation to the statements made by teachers in the transfer classes. Again, these interactions are expressed first as a percentage of all statements and, second as a percentage of all possible observations. If we examine differences of greater than 1 per cent we see that in the transfer schools there were more task statements (up 4.1 per cent from 13.7 per cent to 17.8 per cent), more statements telling pupils what to do (up 5 per cent from 22.1 to 27.1 per cent), less feedback on work (down 2.5 per cent from 18.7 per cent to 16.2 per cent) less routine directions, as for example when teachers placed particular children to work with others in a group (down 3.8 per cent from 17.4 per cent to 13.6 per cent), and less neutral feedback as when pupils were asked to work quietly or to tidy up their table (down 2.9 per cent from 7.6 per cent to 4.7 per cent). Thus the transfer classroom generally contained more adult-dominated teacher–pupil exchanges with the emphasis on giving information. For example, if only task interactions are considered, there were 1.9 times as many statements giving information as there were statements concerning ideas (65.8 per cent as against 34.2 per cent). In the pre-transfer classrooms this ratio was 1.4 (59.1 per cent to 40.9 per cent). These differences were, however, relatively insignificant when the overall proportion of teacher statements as a percentage of all observations is examined in the last two columns of Table 4.3. Teachers talked *at pupils* for approximately the same amount of time, irrespective of the age group. Secondary pupils were given more information and more task directions. Primary pupils received more feedback on the work, presumably as a consequence of the increased emphasis on individual attention. However, this same emphasis required more time to be spent on matters of a routine nature such as giving directions about movement in and around the classroom or instructions about the use of equipment. Primary teachers also gave feedback more frequently on routine activities such as, telling pupils they had done well in tidying up the base or perhaps needed to do better on a subsequent occasion. As in *Inside the Primary Classroom: 20 Years On*, most teachers, irrespective of the age range taught, appeared to regard the main purpose of whole class teaching as transmission. The notions of 'interactive teaching' as a means of developing ideas and concepts did not occupy a significant amount of time either at primary or secondary level. Differences that arose appear to be a consequence in the shift in the proportions of individual and class teaching within each phase. For the pupils, therefore, it is not so much the different levels of cognitive demand that faced them when they moved schools but rather the different ways in which teachers posed these intellectual challenges. For those pupils who had come to

Table 4.3 Teacher statements in secondary and primary classrooms

	% of all statements		% of all observations	
	Secondary	Primary	Secondary	Primary
Fact	17.8	13.7	10.2	8.1
Ideas	9.3	9.4	5.3	5.6
Telling what to do	27.1	22.1	15.5	13.1
Praise/criticism of work	5.9	5.0	3.4	3.0
Feedback on work	16.2	18.7	9.3	11.1
Routine directions	13.6	17.4	7.8	10.3
Routine feedback	4.7	7.6	2.7	4.5
Critical control	3.8	3.7	2 .2	2.2
Small talk	1.6	2.4	0.9	1.4
Total	100.0	100.0	57.3	59.3

regard transfer as an important status passage between childhood and adolescence, this degree of similarity may have come as a disappointment. How
such feelings, if they do exist, should manifest themselves in changes of attitude towards schooling which will be examined in the following chapter.

Other interactions in the transfer classroom

Table 4.4 carries out a similar analysis for the remaining two major categories of the observation schedule concerning silent interactions and cases
where no interaction took place. Again, the corresponding figures for the
pre-transfer classrooms are taken from *Inside the Primary Classroom: 20
Years On* (Galton *et al.* 1999b: 68). The figures are again reported both as
a percentage of all observations and percentage of silent and non-interaction
categories. Looking at differences of greater than 1 per cent we see that
there was more demonstration (showing) in the transfer classrooms (up 1.9
per cent from 12.2 per cent to 14.1 per cent), less marking with the pupil present (down 2.6 per cent from 10.1 per cent to 7.5 per cent) but greater use
of telling stories (up 7.1 per cent from 4.9 per cent to 12 per cent). There was
also greater amounts of time spent listening to children either read or report
on their work (both up 2.1 per cent from 4.5 per cent to 6.6 per cent). The
increased use of demonstration and showing presumably came about from
the availability of equipment in science laboratories and specialised craft
rooms. Teachers in the transfer classroom, however, had less interactions
with other adults (down 3.9 per cent from 10.1 per cent to 6.2 per cent) or
in housekeeping (down 6.7 per cent from 23.6 per cent to 16.9 per cent).
These latter figures were again not altogether unexpected. Secondary schools
unlike their primary counterparts do not attract visiting adults, such as parents, who come in to help with reading and other practical activities such as

Table 4.4 Silent interactions (secondary vs. primary)

	% of silent interaction		% of all observations	
	Secondary	Primary	Secondary	Primary
Gesture	5.8	5.7	1.4	1.4
Showing	14.1	12.2	3.4	3.0
Marking	7.5	10.1	1.8	2.5
Waiting	2.5	3.3	0.6	0.8
Story	12.0	4.9	2.9	1.2
Listening to report	6.6	4.5	1.6	1.1
Listening to reading	6.6	4.5	1.6	1.1
Watching	5.0	4.5	1.2	1.1
Not observed	0.4	0.4	0.1	0.1
Adult interaction	6.2	10.1	1.5	2.5
Visiting pupil	1.2	2.0	0.3	0.5
Housekeeping	16.9	23.6	4.1	5.8
Monitoring	14.0	8.5	3.4	2.1
Out of room	1.2	5.7	0.3	1.4
Total	100.0	100.0	24.2	24.6

cooking and sewing. The fact that primary teachers stay with the whole class for all subjects inevitably means that there will be an additional degree of housekeeping when books are collected and exchanged at the end of one subject session and new materials made available for the next. On the other hand, spending time silently monitoring pupils' activities increased in the transfer classrooms (up 5.5 per cent from 8.5 per cent to 14.0 per cent). This suggests that pupils perhaps spend more time working silently while the teacher either sat at the desk or walked around the classroom making sure pupils were fully engaged on their tasks.

The increase in the amount of time devoted to reading stories in secondary school compared to that which was allocated by teachers in pre-transfer classes is an intriguing result and not one that might readily have been anticipated. However, the clue may come in the research reported earlier in the first chapter (p. 8) suggesting that one of the main differences between primary and secondary schools is the manner in which English is taught. While in the primary school the emphasis, particularly since the advent of the Literacy Hour, has been placed on teaching skills in comprehension and grammar, a more typical strategy in secondary schools has been to approach English through literature (Marshall and Brindley 1998). An example of this kind of lesson took place at the beginning of the transfer year in Channings in Miss Welch's class. Children took turns to read extracts from a story about a boy who was always getting into mischief. The class read for about 20 minutes but, because she wanted to get to the end of the chapter, Miss Welch then took over the story, reading expressively and creating different voices for the various characters. The pupils were extremely attentive and appeared to enjoy the performance, laughing aloud on several occasions. The class then had to write down their own individual suggestions about how they thought the story might continue. In the next English lesson Miss Welch took the class to the drama studio where they were encouraged to act out their stories. During the whole of this dramatic activity Miss Welch rarely intervened but, instead, watched silently with very little comment. In these two lessons, therefore, there would have been high incidences of Miss Welch listening to children read, reading a story to the children and also monitoring their work. To see just how far Miss Welch's approach is typical of English lessons in general, however, we need to explore in greater detail the systematic analysis that we have already carried out by examining differences between the core subject areas.

Comparison of classroom practice across subjects areas

The 1976 ORACLE study did not look at subject differences in any great detail in the primary school. However, this was not the case in the 1996 replication study. In terms of the primary level analysis, perhaps the most surprising finding was the heavy reliance by teachers on whole class teaching during science lessons. Whereas for both mathematics and English the amount of time spent on whole class teaching was very similar to the overall figure of 35 per cent, in science the figure was almost 50 per cent (Galton et al. 1999b: 71). This increase in whole class teaching was largely at the expense of individualised interaction since the pattern for group interaction was only marginally higher than that for either English or mathematics (16.9 per cent as against 13.4 per cent and 13.2 per cent respectively). Furthermore, when the level of *sustained* interaction was examined, a category which was recorded if the teacher was engaged in conversation with the same group or the same individual pupil on the next time signal 25 seconds later, then science had the lowest level of the three core subject (10 per cent in contrast to 23.3 per cent and 26.7 per cent for mathematics and English respectively). The kind of teacher–pupil conversation which one would have expected to accompany an enquiry approach to science teaching appeared to be largely absent from these lessons in the primary classroom.

A similar analysis was carried out for art, geography and history but these are not relevant to the present comparisons because in the transfer schools only the three core subjects were observed using systematic analysis. Table 4.5 therefore shows the differences in classroom organisation in each of the three core subject areas. The figures for English offer some support for the earlier description of Miss Welch's lessons. Whereas in the primary classroom, teachers spent nearly half their time interacting with individual pupils and a third of the time on whole class activity, at secondary level this ratio was reversed. This fits into a pattern where in the primary classroom

111

Table 4.5 Differences in classroom interactions between core subjects

	English		Maths		Science	
	Secondary	Primary	Secondary	Primary	Secondary	Primary
Class	57.7	34.6	48.4	34.1	51.5	49.6
Group	10.0	13.4	7.4	13.2	13.5	16.9
Individual	32.3	52.0	44.2	52.7	35.0	33.5
Total	100.0	100.0	100.0	100.0	100.0	100.0

language exercises or extended writing were done individually. In contrast, activities in the secondary classroom, such as a teacher reading to the class, while pausing occasionally to discuss the plot or a character in the story, involved all the pupils. How far the Literacy Hour activities at Key Stage 2 and the more recent initiatives at Key Stage 3 have affected these interaction patterns will be discussed in the final chapter.

In mathematics there was an increase in whole class teaching of 14.3 per cent in the secondary classrooms and this was compensated by a decline in both group and individual interactions. Science, however, had a similar pattern both before and after transfer. At secondary level, for example, teachers were interacting with the whole class for up to half the time during the average lesson. There was even less interactions with group of pupils after transfer (down from 16.9 per cent to 13.5 per cent). This category could include working in pairs, which in the laboratory setting might have appeared to be a useful strategy when a limited amount of apparatus was available. However, the description of both Miss Mowbray's lesson on filtration and Mrs Savory's exercise, where pupils wrote down what they ate in a day and then estimated their 'energy intake', had very little extended practical activity which would have required pupils to work in pairs or small groups for most of the lesson. The same was true of Mrs Staunton's lesson on 'states of matter' at Ghyll Grange where the curriculum tended to be organised in ways similar to a typical primary school.

Within these patterns of interaction, therefore, there may be variations in the types of pupil exchanges across the different subjects. This issue is examined in Table 4.6 where comparative data taken from Table 3.10 of *Inside the Primary Classroom: 20 Years On* (Galton *et al.* 1999b: 74) are also included. In Table 4.6 the figures in each of the columns represent the proportion of a particular category as a percentage of questions, statements or silent interactions. Turning first to the English data and examining questions, in each case there were nearly twice as many questions of ideas as there were of fact in both the transfer and the pre-transfer schools. This may be contrasted with the more typical finding that factual questions generally predominated. However, the major difference lay in the make-up of these

Table 4.6 Interaction patterns between core subjects before and after transfer

	English		Maths		Science	
	Secondary	Primary	Secondary	Primary	Secondary	Primary
A. Questions						
fact	23.4	22.4	29.2	31.3	24.0	27.4
closed	26.6	35.2	45.8	46.8	38.0	43.3
open	19.6	12.8	3.2	4.5	8.4	20.0
supervision	19.0	21.2	13.4	14.7	16.8	7.4
routine	11.4	6.4	8.4	2.7	12.8	1.9
sub-total	100.0	100.0	100.0	100.0	100.0	100.0
% of all observations	15.8	15.6	21.6	26.5	17.9	21.5
B. Statements						
fact	10.9	17.6	20.0	19.9	21.4	21.8
ideas	8.2	10.5	10.5	15.4	8.9	11.7
task directions	29.5	23.7	26.0	27.7	25.9	24.8
praising	7.2	5.6	6.0	5.4	4.6	5.3
task feedback	20.7	27.1	15.8	19.6	12.6	15.5
routine directions	12.7	7.6	12.8	6.6	15.5	11.0
routine feedback	4.1	3.7	4.5	2.3	5.7	6.5
critical control	4.9	2.5	3.3	2.5	3.6	2.7
small talk	1.8	1.7	1.1	0.8	1.8	0.7
sub-total	100.0	100.0	100.0	100.0	100.0	100.0
% of all observations	51.2	59.0	60.1	64.8	61.0	60.0
Ratio of B to A	3.24	3.78	2.78	2.46	3.40	2.79
C. Silent interact						
show	9.7	9.1	14.2	19.5	20.9	23.6
mark	3.9	22.4	16.4	31.0	4.7	14.8
listen read	13.9	24.4	0.0	2.2	0.5	0.0
listen report	7.9	9.4	7.1	7.7	4.3	7.7
other	64.6	34.7	62.3	39.6	69.6	53.9
sub-total	100.0	100.0	100.0	100.0	100.0	100.0
% of all observations	33.0	25.4	18.3	8.7	21.1	18.2

questions. In the transfer schools there were a far greater number of open-ended, challenging questions, whereas in the pre-transfer schools there were three times as many closed questions as open ones. After transfer this ratio had dropped to around 1.4. Furthermore, there were also differences in the proportions of routine questioning where teachers asked almost twice as many questions after transfer compared to before.

This pattern again fits with the earlier descriptions of post-transfer English lessons. In the pre-transfer primary classrooms the dominance of closed questioning can be directly related to the teaching of language skills. When pupils were engaged in composition, for example, the teacher was likely to have asked questions such as, 'Do you need speech marks here?' or 'When do you use a capital letter?' After transfer, however, during lessons like Miss Welch's, a higher proportion of questions tended to seek pupils' opinions. For example, during the class discussion of the story Miss Welch asked pupils to make suggestions as to how they thought the plot would develop in the subsequent chapters. Nearly half the class was encouraged to offer ideas before the teacher made any comment. Thus although the proportions of questioning, as a percentage of all observations, were almost identical before and after transfer, the above differences in types of questioning do appear to indicate a shift in teaching approach.

For the statement categories, the proportion concerned with tasks (facts plus ideas), as a percentage of all statements were higher in the pre-transfer schools (28.1 per cent as against 19.1 per cent). Again, this fits with the notion that a higher proportion of the lesson was devoted to the use of direct instruction to teach skills of comprehension, grammar and spelling. Pre-transfer schools also gave more immediate task feedback, presumably in response to pupils' queries when working individually on an exercise or a piece of writing. Transfer teachers gave more task and routine directions (41.5 per cent compared to 31.3 per cent in the pre-transfer schools) and appeared to exercise greater efforts in maintaining control (4.9 per cent compared to 2.5 per cent respectively). This could have arisen because when pupils worked by themselves during English in most of the transfer schools they were more often expected to work in total silence. This was different from the pre-transfer situation where a reasonable level of conversation between pupils was often tolerated. Consequently, after transfer teachers often found themselves rebuking pupils for talking to their neighbours. Generally, however, the trend across all three subjects was for greater use of the *critical control* category after transfer.

In the silent and non-interaction categories the differences were quite marked. In the pre-transfer classrooms, compared to the post-transfer ones, there was more marking of the child's work in the child's presence (22.4 per cent and 3.9 per cent) although in the two decades since the original ORACLE study, the proportion of so-called silent marking of pupils' books in class has decreased considerably. Before transfer the teachers listened to the children reading almost twice as often as they did after transfer. This despite the fact that the observers frequently saw episodes such as the one in Miss Welch's lesson where pupils were invited to read out aloud to the rest of the class. In primary classrooms, however, guidelines were often in place that required the teacher to hear every child read on a number of occasions each week and this would help boost the totals. Most of the remaining silent and non-interaction categories are grouped under 'other'. They include reading stories, silently monitoring class activity and carrying out various housekeeping duties. The descriptions of Miss Welch's lesson afford several reasons why in post-transfer English lessons nearly twice as much use was made of these other categories compared to classes in primary schools. Indeed, looking at all three core subjects, it was the case that monitoring and similar activities occurred more often in the post-transfer classes. This finding goes some way to supporting the earlier claim that pre-transfer classrooms were busier places, in the sense that teachers more frequently engaged in verbal interaction with their pupils.

Turning to the patterns of interactions for mathematics, here, except in one important aspect, the patterns of questioning were fairly similar in both the transfer and pre-transfer classrooms. In both cases closed questioning predominated largely because pupils spent most of their time during the lesson solving mathematical problems with specific, unique answers. There were nearly 5 per cent more questions, overall, in the pre-primary classes but the percentages across different categories were remarkably close, except in respect of *routine* where three times as many questions in this category were asked after transfer (8.4 per cent compared to 2.7 per cent). Turning to statements, again, the overall patterns were remarkably similar, although there were slightly greater amounts of statements of ideas and of task feedback in the pre-transfer classes. This, in turn, was compensated by the increase in routine interactions including, no doubt, directing pupils where to sit, what books to use, how to set out work, etc. A feature of the transfer classrooms in the 1976 ORACLE study was the increased dependency of pupils and their attempts to slow down the rate of working by spending as much time as possible on routine activity (Galton and Willcocks 1983: 57). At the time, this was adjudged to be the pupils' way of avoiding having to engage in rather repetitive practice exercises, since the reward for completing one set of questions would be to receive a further set of similar, if slightly more difficult, numerical problems to solve.

The major differences between the two sets of observations for mathematics lay in the use of silent and non-interaction categories. In transfer schools there was less showing, demonstrating, less marking, no occasion when children were heard reading and again, as with English, it was the other categories including the monitoring and housekeeping which more frequently occurred. The overall pattern described here suggests that teachers employed similar strategies in both pre-transfer and post-transfer mathematics lessons. Teachers taught mainly from the textbook or, as in the example from Mrs Staunton's class, produced their own worksheets. When starting new topics teachers first presented a number of worked examples on the blackboard or overhead projector. They then required the pupils to work through a series of graded questions during the remainder of the lesson. After transfer, in contrast to the pre-transfer lessons there were, however, fewer interactions during this period of what American researchers call 'seat work'. Whereas in most primary classrooms teachers moved round the class inspecting pupils' work and asking them for explanations as to how they got particular answers, the tendency in the secondary classroom was to let pupils 'get on with it' by themselves. Any necessary corrections were then worked through with the whole class at the beginning of the next lesson after the books had been marked and returned. The relative slight increases in routine statements relating to neutral feedback and control would suggest that the levels of pupil distraction, particularly in the lower sets, tended to increase under these conditions.

Finally, we turn to the science categories. Here the main overall difference lay in the pattern of questions and silent and non-interaction categories. Pre-transfer science involved greater amounts of questioning (21.5 per cent) and less silent interactions (18.2 per cent) compared to post-transfer lessons (17.9 per cent and 21.1 per cent respectively). Interestingly, the proportion of questions requiring pupils to offer closed or open solutions was higher in the pre-transfer classrooms, particularly the latter category. In transfer class-rooms only 8.4 per cent questions were open-ended compared to 20 per cent before transfer. This imbalance is compensated for by the greater use in transfer classes of questions to do with both supervision and routine (29.6 per cent compared to 9.3 per cent). This disproportion is clearly related to the increase in laboratory work after transfer. If, as discussed in Galton *et al.* (1999b), science in the primary classroom tended to have little to do with enquiry approaches, it would seem that after transfer this was even more the case.

Moving to the next major category in the observation schedule, the pro-portions of various statements during science lessons both before and after transfer were very similar. At both primary and secondary levels statements took up around three-fifths of all observed interactions. Statements of *fact* were roughly in the same proportion in each case but there were slightly more statements of *ideas* in the pre-transfer schools and greater amounts of *feedback* on work (difference equal to 2.8 per cent and 2.9 per cent respec-tively). In the post-transfer classes there were more *routine* directions (15.5 per cent as against 11.0 per cent) again, presumably, because these lessons usually took place in a laboratory setting. Turning to the silent and non inter-action categories there was less *demonstrating* and considerably less *marking* in the post-transfer classrooms. In neither case did pupils spend significant amounts of times reading or *reporting* on their work during lessons, although the latter activity was more frequent in the pre-transfer classrooms. Again in keeping with the use in English and mathematics of the other silent and non-interaction categories, science teachers in the post-transfer class-rooms would appear to have engaged more often in monitoring pupil's work and in housekeeping (21.1 per cent compared to 18.2 per cent). This differ-ence was less marked than for either English or mathematics although the trend was in the same direction. In science the use of these categories could have arisen when pupils, having done an experiment, were then required to write up a report in their books along the lines described at the beginning of the chapter when Miss Mowbray set pupils the task of filtering dirty water.

In another similar lesson seen at Channings pupils were taught how to use a thermometer. The experiment consisted of filling a beaker with water, first from the cold tap and then from the hot one. On this occasion pupils, working in pairs, were asked to note the temperatures and record them in their rough books. They then were required to write up this experiment in their science homework books and to paste in a worksheet containing a drawing of a thermometer in which the temperatures of ice, boiling water and steam, as well as the typical body temperature were marked. The task for homework was to insert the temperatures of hot and cold tap water in the appropriate place in the diagram.

It can be seen from these descriptions that, typically, post-transfer science lessons involved short periods of practical activity followed by extensive periods of writing up experiments during which there was little interaction between pupils and the teacher. In mathematics there would usually be intense periods of interaction whenever the teacher began a fresh topic. During such times the teacher would present worked examples on the board or on the OHP after which pupils were sometimes required to take part in a class question and answer session. When this interactive session was over, pupils would work through further examples from the textbook. Pupils who failed to complete this task would then add on the remaining questions to any extra ones set for homework. In many ways, therefore, science and mathematics lessons had similar characteristics with short bursts of either teacher–pupil or pupil–pupil activity followed by longer periods where children engaged in solitary working. As with science lessons described in the Suffolk LEA (1997) survey, such teaching could not be described as very demanding intellectually. Nor, to the observers, did it seem to inspire a great deal of enthusiasm among the pupils.

It should not be thought, however, that all lessons took this form. In mathematics in some of the transfer schools certain lessons would be reserved for 'investigations' outside the National Curriculum programmes of study. These activities were designed to stimulate critical thinking. Children would be set mathematical puzzles or asked to work out different ways of arriving at a solution to a particular problem. At Guy Mannering these investigations were a weekly feature taking up one whole session, while at Maid Marion they appeared to take place at the whim of Mr Baines but were restricted to the top set. In science, while at Channings pupils worked through a textbook week by week carrying out a series of brief experiments and copying much of the material from the textbook into their rough books, at other transfer schools pupils were sometimes asked to identify an 'unknown substance' or to work out the best value of a certain commercial product such as 'baking powder'. In general, however, the demands made on pupils were set at a relatively low cognitive level. This can best be seen by looking at the row in Table 4.6 that records the ratio of teacher statements (B) to teacher questions (A). The figures in this column come closest to measuring what in the earliest classroom observation research by Anderson (1939) and later Flanders (1964) was known as the i/d ratio. These researchers classified teachers as *indirect* when they spent a higher proportion of the lesson *asking* questions rather than either *telling* pupils what to do or *giving directions*. Both Anderson and Flanders produced average i/d ratios of 0.40 indicating that there were around two and a half times as much telling as asking in these mid-twentieth-century American classrooms. In Table 4.6 only the primary mathematics ratio approached this figure while in the remaining columns it was exceeded. After transfer there were 3.40 times as many statements as questions in science followed by English (3.24) and then mathematics (2.78). In the latter case this result comes about because of the high proportion of closed questions associated with the frequent use of worksheets or textbooks containing various numerical exercises. Furthermore, within the statement category in both mathematics and science it was statements of *fact* and *task supervision* that were most frequently used.

The analysis carried out in the 1976 ORACLE study (Galton and Willcocks 1983) reported similar findings in respect of teaching offered in these same transfer schools. Gage (1985) has also noted the persistence of teacher-centred classroom teaching and refers to the work of Cuban (1984) who documents 'a seemingly stubborn continuity in the character of instruction'. Certainly the evidence presented here suggests that in so far that the National Curriculum was designed to promote continuity of teaching methods, it can claim some success. In the 1970s the aim was to encourage teachers in the first year in the transfer school to adopt the practice of their primary colleagues. The data presented in Table 4.6 would suggest that primary and lower secondary classroom practice now shares much in common, in the sense that teachers in the latter years of Key Stage 2 have become more like their secondary counterparts. The preferred teaching styles are now largely dominated by teacher talk with even less intellectual challenge than two decades previously. Further evidence on this point will now be considered.

Teaching styles in the transfer classrooms

In *Inside the Primary Classroom: 20 Years On* a detailed analysis was made of the teaching styles employed in the primary classrooms in comparison to those used two decades previously. Readers interested in the technique of cluster analysis that was used to create these styles are referred to Galton *et al.* (1999b: 109–111) where descriptions of the various styles identified in the original ORACLE analysis are represented. However, the increased emphasis on the use of whole class instruction over the two decades from 1976 has inevitably meant that there have been changes in the styles of teaching. In 1996 by far the largest group consisted of teachers who mainly used a combination of class and group organisation, to provide direct instruction. This approach laid the main emphasis on stating facts and giving directions, interspersed with low-level cognitive questions. A small group of teachers could still be identified with the practice of *individual monitoring* which was so prevalent in 1976 and was characterised by the more frequent use of silent interactions such as marking and listening to pupils report on their work. However, even within the 1996 individual monitor style, with the highest levels of individual teacher–pupil interaction, there was a marked increase in the use of low-level questioning and statements of fact in a whole class setting compared to the 1976 profile. In general, therefore, it was concluded that teaching styles in the 1996 upper primary classrooms now most closely resembled those that were found in the 1976 post-transfer schools.

The notion of a teaching style has been criticised by researchers concerned with teacher effectiveness. This is because when average pupils' gains in attainment have been compared across different styles, it is generally the case that the variation of performance within any given style has usually been greater than that between the styles. This suggests that teaching style itself is not a major determinant of pupil progress, at least when it is defined in the cluster analysis by the classroom variables used to determine the various styles. Part of the reason for this reduced between-cluster variation is that, overall, there are only a limited number of categories where variations exist in the use of different interactions across the styles. Some aspects of teacher–pupil interaction are common to all styles. *Class enquirers*, for example, although distinguished from *individual monitors* because they tended to ask more open-ended questions, nevertheless did this relatively infrequently in comparison to the use of categories such as making factual statements or giving directions to pupils on how best to perform the set tasks. These latter interactions dominated all styles. It could be argued, therefore, that if there were bigger differences between the various teaching styles on variables, such as open-ended questioning and giving non-critical feedback, etc., then this would also be reflected in significant differences in patterns of pupil's attainment. This is because challenging questioning and feedback are both highly correlated with academic progress (Brophy and Good 1986). Nevertheless, as Galton and Croll (1980) were able to show even where small differences in attainment are found, these trends appear to be remarkably consistent on a year-by-year basis.

In the 1976 study, for example, it was found that a group of pupils, with low scores, who were taught by individual monitors in the first year, but who then moved to a teacher using a class enquiry approach in the following year, improved their performance relative to other pupils. Another group of pupils with high scores in the first year, moved in the opposite way and their progress declined. By seeking to maximise the characteristics that distinguish the more successful styles, it should therefore be possible to build up pupil performance from small beginnings year by year. Nevertheless, even if this were not the case, the notion of a teaching style can still be of some value, in that it can point to the different patterns of interaction that tend to occur when different forms of organisation are used. For example, there are large differences in the amounts of time pupils spend on task during individualised instruction as against whole class teaching. Similar differences have also been found across subject areas and between different phases of schooling during transfer from primary to secondary school. These differences, in turn, may reflect a change in styles of teaching.

When this kind of analysis was carried out during the 1977–78 ORACLE transfer study only two clusters emerged (Galton and Willcocks 1983: 50–51). This came about because of the relatively low use of whole class teaching in the primary school and the dominance of this form of organisation in the secondary transfer schools. The teacher–pupil interaction patterns associated with these two types of organisation were such that the clustering resulted in two broad groupings representing primary and secondary styles of teaching.

In order to avoid a similar result on this occasion, and bearing in mind the present-day shift within the pre-transfer schools towards greater use of whole class teaching, the cluster analysis was carried out using broader interaction categories. These were chosen because they were thought to reflect important differences between the two phases and between effective and ineffective teaching. Some of the categories were constructed by combining those variables where the analysis reported in the previous paragraphs showed there was the biggest variation in use before and after transfer. Others were created by combining the frequencies of several interaction categories that were related to key variables in the school effectiveness literature (Sammons *et al.* 1995). For example, a measure of greater intellectual challenge was constructed by combining the frequencies of both open and closed questions with statements of ideas. In this manner, it was hoped to reduce the *within group* and increase the *between-group* variation across the clusters. Six other composite variables were created, in addition to the *cognitive challenge* variable. These consisted of *low-level tasks* (either questions of fact or statements of fact), matters of *routine* (either routine questions or statements), *task supervision* (either questions or statements dealing with task supervision), all *silent* and all *non-interaction* categories and *sustained interaction* (the proportion of interactions which were sustained over more than two 25 second sampling time units). The remaining categories were obtained from *teacher's audience* (the proportion of teacher utterances directed at an individual, group or class).

As in the 1977–78 transfer study, values for each of these composite variables were calculated for all teachers both in the pre-transfer and post-transfer phases and then combined into a single cluster analysis. In the original ORACLE transfer study this was done irrespective of whether the teacher in the transfer school was only observed teaching his or her specialist subject. For this present analysis, however, subject differences were taken into account. In the pre-transfer classes each set of lesson observations for a teacher was aggregated by subject to create what was termed a teacher's *sub-*

ject profile. This provided 181 such pre-transfer profiles for the analysis. These were then combined with the specific subject profiles of the specialist teachers in the transfer schools although there were some teachers in this group who had also taught more than one subject. This latter sub-group of teachers was dealt with in a similar manner to the pre-transfer sample. In all, 281 profiles were included in the analysis.

The initial analysis yielded eight clusters but some of these clearly offered partial descriptions of previously identified styles in both the 1976 and 1996 primary samples. For example, the *individual monitor* style was divided between a cluster representing individual task supervision, including high proportions of task directions and feedback (76 profiles) and another representing individual silent interaction, especially marking (14 profiles). These interactions were all key characteristics of the 1976 individual monitor. In the same way, the original *class enquirer* style was now sub-divided into low and high level cognitive tasks, particularly questioning and statements of ideas (77 and 51 profiles respectively). This was also a feature of the analysis in *Inside the Primary Classroom: 20 Years On* (Galton *et al.* 1999b: 120) where the style linked to class teaching could be split into two sub-groups. The first of these was closely related to *direct instruction*, with the emphasis on factual and closed questions, while the second pattern of interactions more closely resembled *interactive* whole class teaching with more use of open questions. The remaining clusters in the present analysis represented group activity, mainly to do with routine organisation (26 profiles) and supplying routine information to the class (10 profiles). Two other clusters described mainly exchanges involving either time spent in monitoring and housekeeping (16 profiles) or story telling (7 profiles) or routine management (10 profiles).

In representing the various profiles the procedure developed for *Inside the Primary Classroom* (Galton and Simon 1980: 129) and repeated in *Inside the Primary Classroom: 20 Years On* (Galton *et al.* 1999b) was again used. In the earlier analysis, to indicate the trends in the data, the values for a particular observation category within each cluster were placed in rank order and the range for that category was divided by 4. By way of illustration, let us take a category of teacher behaviour where one cluster had the highest proportion of observations (14 per cent) and another the lowest (6 per cent) while the average value for all teachers was, say, 10 per cent. The range between the highest and lowest cluster would, therefore be 8 per cent so that a quarter of this range would equal 2. For this particular category of teacher behaviour, any cluster value greater than 12 per cent would be classified relatively 'high' while one which was less than 8 per cent would be classified relatively 'low'. This allowed the value of each category in every cluster profile to be described either as '*above average*' if located in the top quartile, '*below average*' if in the bottom quartile, or '*average*' if located in between these two extremes. What is gained is a simple pictorial representation of the

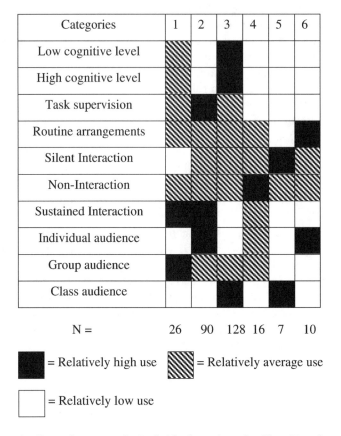

Categories	1	2	3	4	5	6
Low cognitive level						
High cognitive level						
Task supervision						
Routine arrangements						
Silent Interaction						
Non-Interaction						
Sustained Interaction						
Individual audience						
Group audience						
Class audience						

N =   26   90   128   16   7   10

■ = Relatively high use   ▨ = Relatively average use

☐ = Relatively low use

1= Group instructor 2= Individual monitors 3= Class Enquirers
4= Housekeepers 5= StoryTellers 6= Classroom Managers.

Figure 4.3 Teaching style profiles in pre- and post-transfer classes.

trends across the clusters, but what is lost is any indication of the range or the relative use of a particular category compared to the others. In Figure 4.3 therefore, this representation is provided for combined pre- and post-transfer profiles.

All but four of the 281 teacher profiles could be accommodated within this analysis. The group cluster appears to be a less extreme version of the *group instructors* of the earlier primary analysis (Galton *et al.* 1999b: 115). In terms of individual interaction categories within this cluster most lie close to the average with the emphasis mainly on statements to do with *task, task supervision* and *routine management*. The *housekeeper* profile, as its name suggests, reflects the fact that for nearly 50 per cent of the observations no interaction took place other than housekeeping or monitoring. In the *storytelling* cluster 53 per cent of time involved the category 'story' and 83 per cent of these recorded observations took place with a class audience. This therefore described episodes where the reading was interspersed with comments and questions to the class. The final set of profiles had the highest value for providing *routine information* and *feedback* and recorded zero instances of questions (both closed and open) as well as statement of ideas. The bulk of these interactions took place with individual pupils and appeared to be related to aspects of classroom management.

Teacher profiles across subjects

The numbers of any given profile from Figure 4.3 do therefore indicate, to some extent, the relative proportions of lessons given over to, say, instruction as opposed to routine management, monitoring and housekeeping. Clearly, this cluster solution also represents partial descriptions of lessons because the profiles of teachers were based on their use of the composite categories when teaching English, mathematics or science. An English lesson, such as the one described earlier, might mainly involve drama based on characters in a story with the teacher monitoring the pupils' performance and perhaps engaging in some interventions of a disciplinary nature. This would have been included in either the storytellers or classroom manager clusters depending on the relative frequencies of the various composite categories. Another English lesson might emphasise certain aspects of written composition and be included in either the class enquiry or individual monitor cluster depending on whether the lesson was mainly a class discussion or consisted of individual work. Examining the proportion of the different clusters with respect to each subject therefore provides a description of how English, mathematics or science was typically taught. In Table 4.7, therefore, the percentage number of the various profiles in each cluster is presented by subject. For this analysis there is the possibility of an in-built bias in favour of the secondary teachers since, except in a few instances where a teacher taught, say, maths and science, all recorded observations were subject specific. In the case of a primary teacher, their profile in science, for example, might have

Table 4.7 Percentage teaching profiles in English, mathematics and science

Teacher persona	Subject English (N=76)	Maths (N=77)	Science (N=61)
Group instructor	10.5	9.1	8.2
Individual monitor	31.6	29.9	27.9
Class enquirer	40.8	58.4	59.0
Other	17.1	2.6	4.9
Total	100.0	100.0	100.0

constituted only a small proportion of the total observations because of the emphasis given to English and mathematics at Key Stage 2. In constructing Table 4.7, therefore, only profiles of primary teachers where approximately 50 per cent of observations were in a particular core subject were included. In this way it was hoped a more balanced picture between the primary and secondary lessons in each of the core subjects might emerge.

Table 4.7 displays considerable similarity between typical mathematics and science lessons. In each case just under 60 per cent of the lesson was taken up by whole class teaching (58.4 per cent and 59 per cent respectively) with approximately a further 30 per cent devoted to interaction with individual pupils. In science the amount of group interaction was slightly less than in mathematics. Since, in general, pupils worked at least in pairs when carrying out experiments, because of the limited amounts of apparatus available, this finding supports the earlier conclusion that such activities often took up a small proportion of the lesson. Investigating the Bunsen burner flame cones, filtering dirty water, or evaporating a salt solution were typical of many such experiments in the autumn term following transfer. The relatively small amount of activity in the 'other' profile categories was composed entirely of 'housekeeping'. As might be expected, there was more housekeeping in science because of the need to collect and put away apparatus.

The major difference between English and the other core subjects lay in the drop in the proportion of whole class interaction (40.8 per cent) and the considerable use of the 'other' or combined profile categories (17.1 per cent). In the case of this latter figure over 58 per cent consisted of the teacher reading the class a story and of these storytelling profiles, 93 per cent occurred in secondary classrooms. Again, therefore, these figures support the earlier descriptions of English lessons and particularly the differences between the way in which primary and secondary English was typically taught (Marshall and Brindley 1998). It remains something of a paradox that in the subject where there is a supposed emphasis on the development of communication skills, there were the fewest verbal exchanges between teachers and pupils. This was illustrated not only in the relatively high proportion of 'other' profiles in English but also in the breakdown of the individual monitor category.[3] This was made up of a combination of two profiles consisting of individual task supervision and individual silent interaction. In the case of English, silent interaction made up a third of the profile whereas in both mathematics and science task supervision contributed around 95 per cent of the profile.

The same kind of analysis can be done for the class enquirers. Here again, the latter style was made up of a combination of two profiles, low level and deep level class questioning. This distinction related to the relative frequency of use of closed and open questions respectively and was identified in the case of primary classrooms in Galton *et al.* (1999a: 63). In the case of English there were 1.2 times as many low-level questioning profiles, as there were deep-level questioning ones. For mathematics the corresponding figure is 1.6 while in science it was 1.25. While none of these differences were statistically significant, they do match the description of lessons presented at the beginning of the chapter. Mathematics had the highest ratio in favour of low-level closed questioning in which the whole class participated. This reflected the emphasis in most mathematics lessons that required pupils to solve problems from exercises in their textbook either as an introduction to a new lesson or as part of consolidation or revision. The fact that in science there did not appear to be any great emphasis on deep-level class questioning confirmed the earlier conclusion that many of the lessons in the post-transfer year did not sufficiently challenge pupils.

In general, however, although there were these differences between subjects, it is the similarities in the overall patterns which were the more striking. None of the differences between subjects in Table 4.7 reach significance level. Furthermore, if a similar comparison is made between pre- and post-transfer lessons, only in the case of low-level class questioning did a significant difference emerge. In the pre-transfer classes this profile represented around 20 per cent of the 137 profiles recorded. In the post-transfer classes the corresponding figure was 34 per cent out of 144 profiles. Increasingly, therefore, the evidence presented suggests that the pressures experienced by primary teachers to 'change the way they teach' and, in particular, to increase the amount of whole class teaching, have produced a degree of uniformity across the different phases. This can be seen even more clearly in Figure 4.4 where the distribution of teacher profiles is recorded for Y4, Y5, Y6 and Y7 separately.

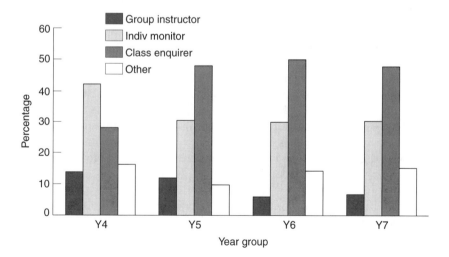

Figure 4.4 Teacher profiles by year group.

The most striking feature of the above representation is the close similarity of the patterns in Y6 and Y7 classrooms. Group instructor profiles represented 6 per cent and 6.5 per cent of the total respectively. The corresponding figures for individual monitors were 30 per cent and 30.4 per cent while class enquirers accounted for 50 per cent and 47.9 per cent of the totals. Although Y5 classes, like Y4, had a higher percentage of group instructors (12 per cent and 14 per cent respectively), the figures for individual monitors (30.4 per cent) and class enquirers (47.8 per cent) were much closer to those for Y6 and Y7. It is clear that earlier suggestion that classroom practice in pre- and post-transfer classrooms has, in most respects, become identical is supported by this further analysis. Of the 281 profiles, 218 (77.6 per cent) fell into the individual monitor or class enquirer clusters. This suggests and is confirmed in Figure 4.4 that these styles were to be found in every age range. In Figure 4.4 the proportion of class enquirers and individual monitors remained much the same in the three oldest year groups (Y5 to Y7). Only in Y4 was the overall pattern dissimilar with a more reasonable balance between the different cluster profiles and this difference was highly significant, statistically ($p < 0.002$). The highest proportion of class enquirers was in Y6, the year in which pupils take the Key Stage 2 National Curriculum Tests. The evidence deduced from *Inside the Primary Classroom: 20 Years On* that much of this year was spent in coaching pupils for this 'high stakes' test is confirmed by these figures.

Teaching 20 years on

Using the above analysis as a guide it is not difficult to review the field notes of the different observers and select lessons which illustrate the cluster patterns depicted in the previous paragraphs. For example, in English:

> Miss McP gives out the books and pupils have to pass them back. Pupils call out 'Are we going to finish that story?' and 'What page?' She goes over what has happened in the story so far. The story is about a boy with tuberculosis, a trolley and a secret love, who does not go to school. Miss McP starts them reading around the room . . . She stops Peggy reading because she hasn't paid attention to the punctuation. She makes her examine the question mark and read it like a question. At one point she stops for some time to go over the meaning of the words 'optimistic' and 'pessimistic'.

Here, the bulk of the lesson was given over to hearing pupils read (silent interaction) interspersed with individual monitoring of readers such as Peggy and class discussion of various points in the story as they arise (e.g. the difference in meaning between optimistic and pessimistic). In mathematics, however:

Mrs McO checks that they have met the word equation and says that today they will do substitution. She gives the whole class an explanation using a football analogy. Glen gives a bad explanation of substitution in football. Mrs McO then uses a good analogy in cooking. She demonstrates how to do substitution, replace one thing by another.

Doing $2 \times a = 2a$
$2 \times a \times b = 2ab$

The class is told to rule off fractions and put page 73 Algebra and copy what she has put on the board. The class then settles down to work on substitution problems from the book until the bell goes for break.

Again, the main vehicle for instruction was whole class teaching incorporating relatively low-level cognitive challenge. The teacher explained a new concept; the pupils copied her work from the board and then practised similar calculations using worked examples from the textbook. During the latter part of the lesson Mrs McO engaged in individual monitoring of pupils' work:

She says they can talk about their work but if it's a big difficulty they should go to her . . . She moves to mark Petula's work, then Norman's, then his neighbour's. She then bases herself at her desk and is marking rapidly.

These two extracts, however, are not descriptions of typical English and mathematics lessons that were recorded by the observers taking part in the ORACLE replication study. They were, in fact, the field notes used by Delamont in a chapter entitled, 'Teachers and their Specialist Subjects' which formed part of her ethnography of transfer in Galton and Willcock's (1983: 131–136) portrait of transfer two decades earlier. However, perhaps it is in science that it is easiest to demonstrate the extent of the similarity between today's lessons and those observed twenty years ago. If we compare Miss Mowbray's lesson on evaporation at the beginning of this chapter with the following extracts from Delamont's accounts, it provides convincing evidence that, despite the introduction of the National Curriculum, little has changed. The particular field notes offer the following descriptions:

Science with Mrs McK where again presentation was the key purpose of the lesson. Pupils[4] were reminded that they were to draw a diagram of a Bunsen burner (not a picture) and that the margins had to be 2 cm wide and the title written in ink. The diagram was to take up a page and be drawn in pencil. The labelling was to be done on the right of the diagram in ink. And the lines showing which part of the Bunsen they were labelling were to be drawn in pencil. Never on any account were diagrams in science to be coloured.

(Galton and Willcocks 1983: 130)

In Mr McL's class they were evaporating a salt solution to obtain the salt which had been dissolved in it. Mr McL warned the children in a rather casual way not to lean too close over the evaporating basin because it might spit and he did not want them to get splashed with boiling salt solution. At the end of the practical lesson he said he did not want the children to taste the salt.

The children put the apparatus away and their task was to write up the experiment. Mr McL said, 'At the end of each experiment we write down what we have discovered.' In this case the conclusion was that rock salt could be purified if we grind, dissolve, filter and evaporate. He told the children to write down a conclusion at the end. This was another science word and the conclusion was the most important part of the experiment.

(Galton and Willcocks 1983: 130)

Mr McL's lesson, which as it happens also took place in Maid Marion (10–14) school, is almost an exact replica of Miss Mowbray's attempts to instruct pupils on the process of filtration. Apart from greater emphasis on aspects of safety, the results of more recent legislation, any former pupil, perhaps now a parent, would, no doubt, have experienced feelings of nostalgia on observing Miss Mowbray's science lessons. Despite the introduction of science as a core subject in the National Curriculum at Key Stage 2, and the vast sums of money spent on in-service training for primary teachers to improve their scientific knowledge, little appears to have changed regarding both the content and teaching in the first year at secondary school. Indeed, a recent survey of secondary teachers in one LEA[5] found that less than half of those who taught science to Year 7 pupils had ever seen the Key Stage 2 science programmes of study.

As discussed in the opening chapter, one of the aims of those promoting the National Curriculum in the 1980s was to improve continuity between pre- and post-transfer. The notion of curriculum continuity embodied not only the idea of progression in matters of content but also the idea of developments in pedagogy to reflect the more complex knowledge demands of more advanced work. In the final chapter of *Inside the Primary Classroom: 20 Years On,* it was argued that the shift from Key Stage 1 to Key Stage 2 should be marked by a greater emphasis on teaching for understanding rather than for transmission (Good and Brophy 1994). This is because much of early primary teaching has to do with the acquisition of factual and procedural knowledge, to do with the use of spoken and written language or the application of the basic algorithms in mathematics. Research evidence points to the fact that these procedures are best taught by direct instruction (Rosenshine and Meister 1994). At Key Stage 2, however, there should be an increased emphasis on helping pupils manage their own learning. To do this, pupils must become 'metacognitively wise' (Galton 2001) in the sense that they must be able to regulate their own learning. To accomplish this in science, for example, means that they can understand the reasoning behind the design of 'fair' experiments and in history they are capable of making valid judgements about evidence from the past. Again, research emphasises the importance of helping children construct their own thinking frameworks through cooperative learning with peers (Webb and Palincsar 1996) or approaches such as reciprocal teaching involving the use of challenging questions (Rosenshine *et al.* 1996). Moving to Key Stage 3 one might, therefore, expect pupils to encounter a greater variety of knowledge demands representing much wider variations in the different teaching profiles, particularly in areas such as science where the availability of laboratories allows much greater emphasis to be placed on 'learning by doing'.

Yet the results displayed in Figure 4.4, and the observers' description of lessons, suggest that while there is, indeed, a degree of continuity in teaching approaches between Y6 and Y7 classes, this represents a regression rather than an expansion in the learning opportunities provided for these pupils. Class teaching that was mainly concerned with giving information or engaging in low-level cognitive questioning now appears to be the staple diet of pupils in both the pre- and post-transfer classrooms. How far this motivates pupils is a question to be considered in the next chapter. There the attitudes of pupils will also be examined as well as the effects of transfer on pupils' self-esteem. This will lead on to an examination of pupil performance on standardised tests of attainment. Writing about transfer two decades ago, Galton and Willcocks (1983) argued that pupils' lack of progress in attainment and the dips in attitude and motivation were the result of the lack of curriculum continuity and progression, a consequence of the considerable amount of repetition of work already done at primary school. At the time, however, there were significant differences between the styles of teaching experienced by pupils before and after transfer. In the late 1990s this is no longer true, partly it would seem because of the emphasis on content rather than process in the Key Stage 2 National curriculum and the pressures of the 'high stakes' tests at the end of Y6. Whether this degree of uniformity in teaching methods reassures pupils or increases levels of dissatisfaction is an important question that we will endeavour to answer in the next chapter.

Notes

1 Some of the schools began the new term in the last week in August. The second round of visits were made early in November immediately after the half-term break.
2 In this chapter the terms class, group and individual refer to the teacher's audience. This differs from Chapter 6 where it refers to the classroom organisation concerning how pupils are expected to sit (*base*) and how they were expected to work (*team*). For a fuller explanation of these terms see Galton *et al.* (1998).
3 These figures are not presented in Table 4.7 but subsequent analysis explored the relationship between the core subjects, the contributing clusters and the categories that best described their determining characteristics.
4 The original field notes have been slightly amended in order to clarify their meaning in the present context. For example, the pseudonym of the particular teacher or a specific reference to pupils or children has been substituted for 'they, he or she' in the original text to remove any ambiguity about the subject or object of a sentence.
5 This LEA is taking part in phase 2 of the DfEE-funded study, *The Impact of Transitions and Transfers on Pupil Progress and Attainment* (Galton *et al.* 1999a).

5

THE CONSEQUENCES OF TRANSFER FOR PUPILS

Attitudes and attainment

Maurice Galton, Chris Comber and Tony Pell

In the previous chapter, we have seen that the reality of teaching before and after transfer at Key Stage 3 is that it does provide a certain kind of continuity. It would appear to be the case that the tendency at primary level for Year 6 pupils to experience a style of teaching traditionally associated with secondary school is now well established. More recent initiatives such as the Literacy Hour and Numeracy Hour might be expected to exacerbate this trend in certain respects. In the 1970s when the first ORACLE study took place, the recipe for overcoming the problems of transfer, particularly the lack of pupil's motivation in Year 7 was to make that year more like primary school. We now appear to have reversed this trend whereby Y6 teaching has become more similar to that found in secondary schools because of various pressures, such as the 'high stakes' National Curriculum tests. In this context, therefore, it is important to examine the consequent effects on pupils' attitudes and attainment.

The most and least attractive features of the transfer school

Perhaps an appropriate point to begin this investigation is to examine the views of pupils about moving up to the new school shortly before the end of their final term in the pre-transfer school. Pupils were asked to name three things that they were most looking forward to in the following year. Table 5.1 displays the choice pupils made in rank order as well as breaking down these choices for boys and girls. The rank orders were obtained by adding together the number of times a particular topic or theme was mentioned by pupils in the feeder schools. For example, in Table 5.1 the highest ranked statement, that *pupils were looking forward to making new friends*, was recorded by 217 pupils (numbers in brackets) out of a total of 609. The next most frequently used comment concerned either physical education or sport, totalling 204 comments. Overall, the traditional subjects, science, mathematics and English were not given a high priority in contrast to comments about friendships, school dinners and meeting new teachers. The increased size of the new school, compared to the feeders, as might be expected, was not something that appeared particularly attractive to these pupils. In Table 5.1 the four top ranked choices are presented but in column one, there are five entries because there was a tie for fourth place. The sixth highest ranked topic, art, received only 86 nominations (14.1 per cent). For boys, the fifth ranked choice, mathematics, was mentioned by only 54 boys (17 per cent) while 52 girls said they were looking forward to art, their fifth choice.

There were some small differences between boys and girls. For girls, making new friends was most important whereas it was only ranked third in the boys' choices. Sport and PE were the firm favourites for boys but were only ranked fourth by girls. Both boys and girls gave a high priority to school dinners but boys were less enthusiastic about new teachers. The differences concerned with meeting new friends and new teachers were significant at the 1 per cent level. There were also differences in relation to the core subjects.

Boys, for example, ranked science fourth as something to look forward to, but girls placed it sixth. Even more striking is the difference between mathematics where it was ranked fifth for boys and ninth for girls. Design and technology received particularly low ratings from girls and did not do much better with boys. The differences between mathematics and science were again significant, this time at the 5 per cent level. In the top rankings differences between boys and girls with respect to PE and sport, new teachers and new friends were all statistically significant at the 1 per cent level.

As might be expected when pupils were asked what they were least looking forward to, the ranking of some of the themes and topics was reversed. In Table 5.2 pupils, overall, were least looking forward to doing mathematics. This was followed by homework, English, detention and bullying. Science appeared to be one of the least attractive of all the subjects for these particular pupils. There was now much less agreement among pupils about the worst aspects of transfer. Mathematics was mentioned by only 25 per cent of the sample while science, the bottom ranked, was referred to by 10

Table 5.1 What pupils look forward to on transfer

All pupils (N = 609)	All boys (N = 302)	All girls (N = 305)
new or more friends (217)	PE/sport (125)**	new or more friends (132)**
PE/sport (204)	school dinners (108)	school dinners (91)
school dinners (201)	new or more friends (84)	new teachers (83)**
new teachers (124)	science (76)	PE/sport (79)
science (124)		

Note: **$p < 0.01$ (chi-square).

per cent of pupils. In Table 5.2, therefore the five highest ranked aspects of transfer are listed since differences in frequency of choices were small. Again there were variations between boys and girls. Particularly noteworthy was English which boys were least looking forward to, whereas for girls it was ranked sixth. On the other hand, the prospect of bullying and coping with the increased size of the school was of much greater concern to girls than to boys. The differences with regard to English were significant at the 1 per cent level and those concerning size at the 5 per cent significance level.

In both cases the various choices were correlated to see if there were any combination of topics where boys and girls differed markedly. In general, the subject pairings went in similar directions so that, for example, if boys were looking forward to maths then they would also be looking forward to English and vice versa. This was also true of girls' choices. However, boys were likely not to link science with this combination while the girls did. Furthermore, those girls or boys who were looking forward to PE and sport were unlikely to mention making new friends as equally important and vice versa. With regard to the features that pupils were least looking forward to, then the core subjects, particularly mathematics and English were closely linked with homework, and detention. School size had a much more negative effect influence for girls, while boys worried more about doing English. School size was associated with bullying for boys but not for girls. Girls therefore would appear to have assumed that bullying would take place irrespective of the size of the school. For all pupils, concern about new teachers was linked with having to do harder work. The most likely explanation for the wider variation of topics in Table 5.2 compared to Table 5.1 is that different choices were made by pupils of high and low academic ability. It might be assumed that those pupils who were finding it difficult to make progress in the core subjects would be more apprehensive about continuing their studies in the secondary school. Accordingly, the choices were again examined but this time dividing children into high and low ability groups. This was done by taking the scores from the first administration of the Richmond Tests during the final term in the pre-transfer schools and identifying two groups of pupils who scored either below the 25 percentile

Table 5.2 What pupils are not looking forward to on transfer

All pupils (N = 609)	All boys (N = 302)	All girls (N = 305)
mathematics (151)	English (70)**	mathematics (85)
homework (126)	mathematics (66)	homework (71)
English (110)	detention (63)	being bullied (51)
detention (108)	homework (55)	size (51)*
being bullied (105)	being bullied (54)	detention (45)

Notes: *$p < 0.05$ (chi-square) and **$p < 0.01$.

(low attaining pupils) or above 75 percentile (high attaining pupils). Table 5.3 examines the rankings for those aspects that pupils were most looking forward to and also for those that they were least looking forward to.

There were significant differences (5 per cent level) between high-attaining and low attaining boys. For high-attaining boys it was school dinners, new friends followed by PE, sport and science that were among the most attractive features of the new school. For low-attaining boys it was PE and sport, science, school dinners and then mathematics that they most looked forward to. There was, however, less difference in the choices of girls. Irrespective of whether they were in the high-achieving or low-achieving groups, all girls were mostly looking forward to meeting new friends, having school dinners, meeting new teachers and doing PE and sport. Although the rankings differed, these differences did not reach a statistically significant level. Turning to those consequences of transfer which pupils were least looking forward to, there were small differences in choices between high- and low-attaining pupils but none of these reached a significant level. For high-attaining boys, it was the homework, detention, English, new teachers and mathematics which were of concern. For low-achieving boys it was all three core subjects (mathematics, English, science) being bullied and detention. High-achieving girls worried about the size of the new school, homework, mathematics, English and humanities. Low-achieving girls were more concerned about mathematics, bullying and detention, and having to work hard.

It should also be remembered, however, that the sample consisted of three age groups. There were pupils in Year 4 and Year 5 about to transfer to 9–13 and 10–14 middle schools, as well as Year 6 children who were about to

Table 5.3 High- and low-attaining pupils' views on transfer

High-attaining boys (N = 60)	Low-attaining boys (N = 59)	High-attaining girls (N = 57)	Low-attaining girls (N = 54)
Most looking forward to			
school dinners (29)	PE/sport (28)	new or more friends (23)	new or more friends (24)
new or more friends (25)*	science (21)	school dinners (15)	PE/sport (16)
PE/sport (23)	school dinners (17)	new teachers (13)	new teachers (16)**
science (14)	mathematics (15)	PE/sport (12)	school dinners
Least looking forward to			
homework (16)	mathematics (17)	school size (16)*	mathematics (16)
detention (13)	English (14)	mathematics (13)	being bullied (13)
English (12)	science (11)	homework (12)	detention (13)
new teachers (12)	being bullied (10)	English (9)	homework (13)

Notes: $*p < 0.05$: $** p < 0.01$ (chi-square).

transfer to secondary schools. Table 5.4, therefore, shows the differences in respect of these age groups. In examining the topics which pupils most looked forward to, there were similarities across all three age groups. In each case the top choices concerned sport, meeting new friends, school dinners and having new teachers. Only for Year 6 was having new teachers replaced by doing science. These differences were significant at the 1 per cent level. Across the three age groups there was not the same degree of agreement with regard to those aspects that pupils were least looking forward to after transfer. For Year 4 pupils it was mathematics and English followed by new teachers and homework. Year 5 pupils agreed about homework and mathematics but listed detention and bullying as their other priorities. Year 6 pupils also mentioned mathematics and homework as areas for concern but then prioritised different aspects such as the size of the school and humanities. All these differences were statistically significant. Within these choices therefore mathematics emerged as an area of concern and anxiety for all pupils irrespective of the age of transfer while science was seen as particularly attractive for Year 6 pupils about to move to secondary school. However, as was seen in the previous chapter science at secondary school appears, in particular, to be one of the subjects where the teaching has remained relatively unchanged over the two decades since the original ORACLE study. English was also perceived to be a particular problem area for boys.

It would appear, therefore, that prior to transfer it is the social aspects which dominate pupils' thoughts when they are asked about their positive feelings towards the move. School dinners, having the opportunity to make more friends, engaging with new teachers are all things that are mentioned frequently. Pupils, when asked what they are not looking forward to, focus on the academic demands, with concerns expressed about homework, being put into detention and having to cope with harder work. For all pupils mathematics is seen as the subject where they are most likely to meet these difficulties. For boys these mathematical concerns are closely linked with

Table 5.4 Views on transfer: differences between year groups

	Y4 pupils (N = 244)	Y5 pupils (N = 183)	Y6 pupils (N = 182)
Most looking forward to	PE/sport (89) new friends (75) school dinners (68) new teachers (59)	school dinners (82)* new friends (70) PE/sport (56) new teachers (37)	new friends (72) science (70)** PE/sport (59) school dinners (50)*
Least looking forward to	mathematics (76)* English (59) * new teachers (49)* homework (44)	detention (51)* homework (42) being bullied (37) mathematics (29)	mathematics (46) size of school (42)* humanities (40)* homework (38)

Note: * = $p < 0.01$ (chi-square).

similar feelings about English while for girls it is worries about science which are linked with the mathematics.

Pupil attitudes towards school both before and after transfer

The degree to which the above concerns were realised will be explored by looking at the pupils' attitudes and comparing differences before and after the move to the new school. The attitudes of pupils towards school were measured on three occasions. First in June before transfer, then in the November after the move and finally again in the following June after the children had been one year in the new school. The November administration reflected the fact that within earlier research on transfer it has been argued that most pupils have settled down in their new school by middle of the first term.

All items on the questionnaire were rated on a four-point scale. For ease of analysis the items were subjected to factor analysis and this procedure yielded three stable scales across all three administrations. The first of these was the *enjoyment* scale with a reliability of 0.79 (Cronbach alpha). Pupils with high scores on this scale *looked forward to going to school*, *liked their teachers* and generally *found them friendly*. The second scale emphasised the pupils' inability to adjust *socially* to the new situation and was characterised by feelings of loneliness and isolation. Pupils *felt lost and alone*, *did not belong to many friendship groups*, *felt they did not have much luck* and *were afraid of being regarded by others as a fool*. This scale also had a reliability of 0.79. The third scale represented general satisfaction with the pupils' own situation and was an indicator of *self-confidence* and of being *well motivated*. Pupils scoring highly on this scale *were relaxed*, *were pleased with the work they were doing*, *felt confident about tests* and *had little trouble keeping up with the work*. The reliability coefficient for the third scale was 0.70. Each scale contained eight items so that the maximum possible score was 32 and the minimum score 8. For the second score measuring social adjustment, the scores were reversed so that a high score indicated greater *social isolation*. Table 5.5 shows the means and standard deviations (in brackets) for the three scales with respect to boys and girls across the three administrations. For the enjoyment of school scale it will be seen that in general, girls appeared to enjoy schools more than boys. However, both the boys' and the girls' results followed a similar trend. Between the first administration in June, prior to transfer and the second in the November, following the move to the new school there is hardly any change in attitude. However, by the time the third administration took place in the June, one year after transfer, there has been a decline in enjoyment for both boys and girls. For the former group this difference was significant at the 1 per cent level whereas for girls it occurred at the 5 per cent.

With the second scale registering the extent to which children have problems in adjusting socially to the move, the trend for both boys and girls was in keeping with what might have been predicted following the increase in levels of liaison activities as reported in Chapter 2. Feelings of isolation and concern about adjusting and making friends were highest prior to transfer in the case of both boys and girls. By November these concerns had declined and in the case of the boys this drop was significant at the 1 per cent level. Thereafter from the period of November to the following June there is a further, if slight, decline. The patterns for both boys and girls were very similar. (Kvalsund 2000 and Demetriou *et al.* 2000) both comment on the importance of friendships and on the fact that these have to be continually renegotiated from day to day according to events that take place either in school or elsewhere. Thus pupils' anxieties about isolation and friendship cannot be expected to decline to a point where they may be regarded as insignificant even though the initial traumas of transfer have been successfully negotiated. These circumstances are reflected in the data in Table 5.5.

Table 5.5 Pupils' attitudes before and after transfer

Scale	Gender	June pre-transfer	Nov. post-transfer	June post-transfer
Enjoyment	Boys	22.67 (4.99)	22.65 (4.87)	21.52 (5.62)**
	Girls	24.20 (4.81)	24.44 (4.19)	23.63 (4.45)*
Social isolation	Boys	18.64 (5.47)	17.78 (6.09)**	17.08 (5.56)
	Girls	18.41 (5.37)	17.88 (5.50)	17.46 (5.61)
Motivation and	Boys	21.75 (4.47)	22.26 (4.03)	22.44 (3.64)
confidence	Girls	22.19 (3.36)	22.58 (5.90)	22.65 (3.34)

Notes: *= $p < 0.05$: **= $p < 0.01$.

For the third scale measuring pupils' confidence in their capacity to cope with the work and their intrinsic motivation there were relatively small changes across all three administrations. There was a slight increase in the mean scores following transfer and then a very small further increase by the time the first year in the new school has been completed. In no case, either for boys or girls did these differences reach a statistically significant level.

Table 5.6 takes this analysis a stage further and examines the relationship between pupil attainment and the scores on the three scales in the November and June after transfer. Pupils were grouped into three attainment bands on the basis of their standardised test scores on the Richmond Tests of Basic Skills (France and Fraser 1975). Low attainers scored below the 25th percentile, high attainers above the 75th percentile and average attainers in-between these two levels. For the November data these categories were derived using the standardised test scores obtained during the final term in the feeder school. However, for the third administration of the attitude measures in the following June the attainment scores obtained at the end of the first year after transfer were used. An analysis of variance across the three levels of attainment showed that while enjoyment of school remained independent of pupils' attainment immediately after transfer, by the end of the first full year in the new school this was no longer the case. While for low attainers liking of school remained unaltered (in terms of statistical significance) the most able pupils' enjoyment of school had declined significantly (at the 1 per cent level).

Examining Table 5.6 it can be seen that, after transfer, the mean score of the high attainers declined from 24.55 in the November to 21.28 in the following June. By the end of their first year in the transfer school, therefore, the most able pupils were likely to see teachers *as less friendly*, be less sure that the work they were required to do *was not just set to keep them busy*, were less happy *at being told what to do* and *liked their teachers less*. If we disaggregate this data further and calculate correlations separately for boys and girls across the three ages of transfer (Year 5, Year 6 and Year 7) then, from the third administration of the attitude tests, small but significant negative correlations between enjoyment and attainment were found for boys, but not for girls. Year 5 boys had a significant positive correlation ($r = 0.33$) suggesting that those who begin by doing well academically were enjoying school at the time of the November administration. However, by the following June the correlation was just negative ($r = -0.05$). For Year 6 boys there were negative correlations between enjoyment and attainment both in the November and in June ($r = -0.12$ and -0.13 respectively) but these were not significant. For Year 7 boys a positive correlation in November ($r = 0.18$) had become a negative one by the time the test was again administered in the following June ($r = -0.16$). There was a trend, therefore, pointing to high-attaining boys, in particular, as the source of the general dissatisfaction with school that emerged at the end of the first year after transfer as displayed in Table 5.5.

This, in itself provides an interesting perspective on the issue of *pupils at risk* during the transfer process. In general, when primary teachers were asked to identify pupils at risk in the new school they tended to concentrate on the factors reflected in the second scale which dealt with pupils' feelings of isolation and loneliness. Pupils who found it difficult to make friends or to integrated easily were generally seen as being 'as risk' as a consequence of transferring to the bigger school. When, however, a similar question was put about pupils in the secondary school at the end of the first year and teachers were asked to identify pupils who had not settled, then the tendency was to identify pupils who had not done well academically. But the data from Table 5.6 suggest that there may be a group of pupils who do well academically but who are not enjoying school to the same extent as they did before transfer. It is likely, therefore that these pupils will not be picked out as requiring special attention.

Table 5.6 Pupils' attitudes and attainment after transfer

Scale	Period	Mean scores (standard deviation in brackets)		
		Low attainers	Average attainers	High attainers
Enjoyment	November	23.22 (5.22)	23.60 (5.13)	24.55 (4.59)
	June	23.03 (4.86)	22.48(4.97)	21.28 (4.80)*
Social isolation	November	20.02 (6.32)	17.16 ((5.68)	14.78 (4.91)**
	June	19.26 (6.26)	17.62 (5.52)	15.21 (4.54)**
Motivation	November	21.53 (4.01)	22.18 (4.02)	23.55 (2.67)**
	June	20.97 (3.90)	22.36 (3.34)	23.43 (2.74)**

Notes: * = $p < 0.05$: ** = $p < 0.01$ for attainment levels.

Turning to the second scale concerning the pupils' feelings of isolation and loneliness, Table 5.6 shows, as might have been expected, that it was the low-attaining pupils who had the greatest problems. Analysis of variance shows that there were significant variations across the three levels of attainment at the 1 per cent significance both in the November and June administrations. In the case of the low-attaining pupils these feelings declined during the course of the first year after transfer while for average attainers they remained relatively unchanged. In the case of the high attainers there was a slight increase although none of these differences reached significance level. Again examining the correlations between the degree of isolation and the level of attainment there was little difference either between the year of transfer or between boys and girls. Year 5 girls in the November administration and Year 6 girls in the subsequent June administration both showed smaller insignificant negative relationships between feelings of isolation and levels of attainment. This suggests that these pupils' concerns about friendships and fears of being isolated from one's peers were common across the whole year group. This was also true of Year 7 boys at the time of the November administration. In most cases, therefore, irrespective of the year and gender it is the low achievers who were more likely to experience greater concern about being isolated in the new school and lacking friends.

On the third scale indicating the confidence which pupils feel about engaging with the work, the trend was again in the expected direction. High attainers exhibited more confidence and were more motivated than average attainers who, in turn, displayed more confidence than the lower attaining group. This was true in the case of both the November and subsequent June administrations of the attitude test. The differences across attainment levels were all significant at the 1 per cent level based on an analysis of variance. Across the two administrations there were slight although insignificant variations between the different attainment groups. Low attainers became less confident in their ability to handle the work over the year in the transfer school (down from 21.53 to 20.97) while average attainers were slightly more confident (up from 22.18 to 22.36) and high attainers' confidence also declined slightly over time (down 23.55 to 23.43). Examining the differences in confidence levels across the years of transfer and also by gender, there were insignificant correlations between attainment and confidence in the November apart from Year 7 girls which was significant at the 5 per cent level ($r = +0.37$). By June following transfer, however, Year 5 boys and girls, Year 6 girls, and Year 7 boys all demonstrated strong links between feeling positive about work and academic performance. As the year progressed boys at all levels appeared to become more confident in coping with the work, although as we have seen earlier, less satisfied with the school and its teachers.

Pupils' self-image and the effects of transfer

Pupils were also given items from an inventory designed by Maines and Robinson (1996) which measures pupils' self-image. The terms self-image, self-concept, self-esteem, etc. are sometimes used interchangeably by writers. For Bernard and Joyce (1984) an individual's self-concept is a person's understanding of 'who they are'. The self-image is an individual's description of themselves and refers to the picture a person builds up about themselves in respect to their *physical self*, their *cognitive abilities* and their *social, emotional and behavioural attributes*. Self-esteem is the value that a person then places on this image. Self-concept is therefore a global term encompassing aspects of both a person's self-image and self-esteem which are also clearly interdependent. A person's self-concept will be highly influenced by the way that 'significant others' (family, friends, etc.) respond to him or her. Unsurprisingly, in the school context it is teachers and other pupils who often play a crucial role as described by Kvalsund (2000). Most although not all the items on the Maines and Robinson (1996) scale generally relate to these three aspects of self-image. Pupils, for example, were asked about aspects of their physical self with questions such as *'are you a fast runner?'* or *'are you strong and healthy?'*. However, in the main the items refer to cognitive attributes. Pupils were asked to say whether they *'are as clever as other children'*, whether the teacher is *'pleased with your work'* and whether they *'need a lot of help'*. There were also questions on social, emotional and behavioural aspects such as *'are you good at looking after yourself?'*, *'Do you like being a boy/girl?'* and *'Do other children like playing with you?'*.

A subsequent factor analysis of the pupils' responses to the questionnaire produced four scales. The first relating to academic self-image contained items such as good at reading, clever, was able to do work without a lot of help, etc. and had an internal reliability co-efficient of 0.59. Two items related to progress in school, had a reliability of 0.55 and referred to school work being good and the teacher being pleased with the work. This then appears to be a sub-scale of the academic self-image. Two further scales could be identified although the reliability was low. The first of these related to the pupils' physical perceptions of themselves. Pupils were asked whether they were strong and healthy, good looking, or fast runners. The other scale was concerned with social and emotional characteristics such as liking being a boy or a girl or having other children play with you, being good at looking after yourself, having a best friend, etc. The scales themselves appeared to be distinct, having very low inter-scale correlations. Selecting the items with the highest inter-correlations produced a 16-item scale that could be said to measure a general self-image. Overall, therefore, the scale, as used in this study, corresponds reasonably well with the original Maines and Robertson (1996) analysis with regard to academic self-image but measures relating to both physical, social and emotional characteristics were found to be relatively unreliable. They were therefore not used further in the present study. All items were answered on a dichotomous scale so that the measure of general self-image had a maximum score of sixteen and the academic self-image a maximum of five. The inventory was administered along with the attitude measures in the June before transfer and then in the November and June following the move to the new school. Table 5.7 shows separate analysis for boys and girls respectively. There was an increase in the general self-image following transfer. For boys, the difference between the pre-transfer and November post-transfer scores of 9.07 and 9.46 respectively was significant at the 1 per cent level and the difference between the June administrations before and after transfer at the 5 per cent level. For girls, however, there were no statistically significant differences.

Table 5.7 Pupils' self-image and transfer

Scale	Pupils	June pre-transfer	November post-transfer	June post-transfer
General self-image	Boys (N = 138)	9.07 (1.67)	9.46 (1.78)**	9.43 (1.63)*
	Girls (N = 143)	9.28 (1.58)	9.47 (1.45)	9.31 (1.29)
Academic self-image	Boys (N = 138)	2.25 (1.00)	2.37 (0.85)	2.40 (0.85)
	Girls (N = 143)	2.12 (0.88)	2.41 (0.84)	2.41 (0.85)

Note: $*= p < 0.05$ $**= p < 0.01$ between pre- and post-transfer mean scores.

In contrast, however, academic self-image hardly changed over the three administrations. In the case of girls there were no significant differences across the three administrations either for their general of self-image or academic self-image. Residual gains were also calculated for each of the different transfer groups. Again there were no significant differences between the first administration prior to transfer and the second occasion in November after the move to the new school. Across the different attainment groupings the gain in self-image appeared to be greatest amongst low-attaining pupils and this increase tended to be greatest with boys than girls. This was particularly true with the group of pupils who were below the 25 percentile on the pre-transfer attainment tests and remained in that band in the follow-up test one year later. They showed significant increases both in general self-image and in academic self-image at the 5 per cent level across all three administrations. Those pupils who were in the 75 percentile both before and after transfer, made gains both in general self-image and academic self-image between the June administration prior to transfer and the November administration, but this progress was not maintained in the third administration one year after transfer. This adds support to the earlier finding that there was an increasing sense that 'all was not as they might have wished it to be' among pupils of higher ability whose enjoyment of school and the teaching has also dipped in the period between November and the following June.

These relationships between the pupils' academic self-image and their attainment are not unexpected in that most teachers are aware that low self-esteem and lack of confidence often accompany academic failure. However, the increasing emphasis on the notion of multiple intelligences developed by Howard Gardner (1983) and particularly the importance given to those aspects of intelligence lying in the emotional domains (the intra-personal and the inter-personal) have led to a growing awareness amongst schools of the importance of what has come to be known as 'emotional literacy'. Schools are now attempting to develop a range of emotional and social skills in young adults including the motivation to learn and the ability to form meaningful relationships, but much of this work is done through non-academic activities such as circle time, citizenship and special pro-grammes such as peer-mediation where older children in Year 10 act as mediators for pupils in years 7 and 8. However, it is less usual to see the need for helping pupils to cope with the emotional climate within the classroom which may result in failure to answer questions or of pupils' lack of confidence in being able to offer correct solutions to problems. The data from this study show that factors such as general and academic self-image have a high predictive validity. Pupils with below average self-image scores both before and after transfer will inevitably have a high probability of ending up in the bottom 25 percentile on attainment by the end of their first year in the new school. In general as the self-image score declines, then so does attainment. The Maines and Robinson (1996) scale was not altogether successful in this context, since less than 50 per cent of the variation in attainment scores could be attributed to specific measures of self-image, either academic or general, despite the considerable predictability for pupils with low attainment. Within the limits of the measure used it can be tentatively deduced that transfer was accompanied by an increased score for pupils on both general and academic self-image with the greatest increase occurring for boys.

Transfer from Year 5 to Year 6 was more likely to enhance general self-image than transfer at Year 6 to Year 7. The major change took place in the first few months of the new school year, thereafter from the November administration to the following June the scores for both boys and girls showed no overall change.

There were, however, some puzzling features. First, it was pupils in the lowest attainment band in the primary school that make the greatest gains in self-image in the year after transfer, although as we have already seen, there was a sub-group within this band who consistently scored below average. Boys in this low-attaining band, in particular, made the largest gains. Part of the explanation must be that they find ways of maintaining their self-image by becoming part of the 'counter-culture' in ways described by Demetriou *et al.* (2000) These researchers argue that these friendships have a major impact on attainment and describe the difficulty pupils experience when seeking to escape from what is sometimes called the 'dosser' group. Rudduck[1] cites the case of one boy who wished to 'mend his ways' and to begin working harder in Year 8. However, to be seen doing so would have destroyed his relationship with his friends on which his general self-image has been built. This particular boy therefore decided to behave badly in class, gaining the approval of his friends, while earning the disapproval of his teacher with the result that he was placed in detention. While in detention he was able to work without having losing face among his valued peers.

There are also interesting differences with girls in both Year 6 and Year 7. The relationship between improved attainment and increased self-image no longer holds for girls beyond the November administration in first year of the transfer school. This in part seems to be associated with concerns about personal attributes and also whether the effort they are making is noticed by the teacher. Both items (*are you nice looking?* and *does the teacher notice when you work hard?*) showed positive correlations for girls with increased attainment in Year 5, but then became negative in Year 6 and by Year 7. This trend was significant at the 1 per cent level ($r = -0.41$ and -0.38 respectively). Concern about how others see them appeared to dominate girls' thinking irrespective of their attainment level. We shall return to a discussion of this issue in the final chapter but the area is certainly under-researched and the data here support the arguments by Demetriou *et al.* (2000), that the study of friendships in Years 7 and 8 should receive much greater attention in any attempt to improve standards and performance at Key Stage 3.

Attainment gains and losses at transfer

As described in detail in *Inside the Primary Classroom: 20 Years On* (Galton *et al.* 1999b) the measures of attainment used in this study were the Richmond Tests basic skills (France and Fraser 1975). This was because one of the aims of the project was to compare the performance over two decades and this required us to use the same tests on each occasion. Chapter 6 of *Inside the Primary Classroom: 20 Years On* describes the modifications to the Richmond Tests which were designed to put them in a format which would be familiar to today's pupils taking the National Curriculum Tests of Attainment at Key Stage 2. The tests covered language use, reading comprehension and vocabulary and mathematics.

In monitoring transfer from Year 4 to Year 5 there was a particular difficulty. This was because in Year 4 prior to transfer a shortened form of the test was used with these younger pupils. In Year 5, however, the full form was administered. This gives rise to an in-built probability that most Y4 pupils will make gains when re-tested after transfer, since even if pupils were merely to guess the answers, rather than attempting to work them out, they would be advantaged on the second administration. This is because the longer the test, the greater the chance of getting more items correct by guessing. Indeed, when raw test scores are used, 85 per cent of pupils transferring into Year 5 made gains in the Language test and over 90 per cent for mathematics and for reading.

An alternative procedure is to represent a pupil's score as the percentage of the total number of items in the test which were answered correctly. For Year 4 pupils transferring into Year 5, however, this is a more demanding criterion, in that to record an improvement they must increase their *proportion* of correct answers. Suppose, for example, a pupil got 10 out of 20 items correct on the first administration, thus scoring 50 per cent. If the number of items were increased to 30 for the second administration the same pupil would need to get 16 correct to register a gain. In the case of pupils who took the longer 30-item test on both occasions an individual getting 10 correct on the first administration would only need to get one additional item correct on the re-test to show improvement. When, therefore, comparing results of transfer from Year 4 with those for Year 6 and Year 7 using percentage scores this fact should be taken into account.

A further possible way of making these comparisons is to express the difference in scores before and after transfer as a proportion of the standard deviations of the test. Table 5.8 displays the data for all three years in terms of this measure of gain or loss. In the case of transfer from Y4 to Y5 only the common items on the shorter and longer version of the test were included. In all comparisons the measure of standard deviation used was that obtained for the pre-test. For language use 59 per cent of pupils transferring into Year 5 failed to make gains and of these 16 per cent record losses greater than 1 standard deviation. This compares with transfer into Year 6 where only 26 per cent of pupils failed to make gains and only 5.6 per cent record losses of more than 1 standard deviation. Corresponding figures for transfer into Year 7 were 42.1 per cent with 7.1 per cent making losses greater than 1 standard deviation.

Table 5.8 Percentage change in attainment scores at transfer (proportion of sd)

Test	Transfer	N (sd)	Loss > 1 sd	Loss < 1 sd	No change	Gain < 1 sd	Gain > 1 sd
Language	Y4–Y5	144 (20.8)	16.0	40.2	2.8	29.9	11.1
	Y5–Y6	54 (16.6)	5.6	14.8	5.6	35.2	38.8
	Y6–Y7	154 (17.2)	7.2	24.0	11.0	45.5	12.3
Maths	Y4–Y5	142 (19.8)	10.6	35.2	0	43.7	10.5
	Y5–Y6	51 (18.0)	2.0	13.7	5.9	43.1	35.3
	Y6–Y7	156 (17.0)	3.8	19.9	10.9	50.0	15.4
Reading	Y4–Y5	144 (18.9)	9.7	34.0	2.1	43.1	11.1
	Y5–Y6	54 (18.0)	7.4	25.9	5.6	37.0	24.1
	Y6–Y7	160 (15.2)	5.6	22.5	11.2	43.8	16.9

In mathematics the corresponding percentages are 45.8 for transfer into Year 5, 21.6 per cent for transfer into Year 6 and 34.6 per cent for transfer into Year 7. Of these pupils, 10.6 per cent in Year 5, 2 per cent in Year 6 and 3.8 per cent in Year 7 made losses greater than 1 standard deviation.

The data for reading follows the same pattern as mathematics, 45.8 per cent of pupils in Year 5, 38.9 per cent in Year 6 and 39.4 per cent in Year 7 failed to make progress. Of these pupils 9.7 per cent in Year 5, 7.4 per cent in Year 6 and 5.6 per cent in Year 7 made losses greater than 1 standard deviation.

These results suggest that overall performance on all three tests results from a greater hiatus in Year 5 followed by Year 7 with the least effect in Year 6 except in the case of reading where more Y7 pupils make gains than in Y6. One obvious explanation for these differences is that the testing took place shortly after pupils in Year 6 had completed the National Curriculum tests. Given the importance of these high stake assessments because of the impact of the league tables, it could certainly be the case that during the summer term, in particular, teachers had concentrated on preparation of children for this examination and part of this preparation had then influenced the pupils' performance on the Richmond Tests which covered similar areas. In Year 7 it could be argued that less attention was paid to the specific areas covered in the tests throughout the year and as a consequence the test had less curriculum validity. Nevertheless the descriptions of lessons contained in the previous chapter do suggest that for mathematics, in particular, there was considerable overlap. Although, therefore, the existence of a hiatus in progress would appear to be a continuing feature of transfer, the proportion of pupils doing less well, compared to those in the original ORACLE study two decades ago, was now slightly less in the case of mathematics in Year 6 and Year 7 and in language usage for Year 6. As the summary set out in Figure 5.1 shows, for reading, overall, around 40 per cent of pupils failed to make progress after transfer to Years 6 and 7, for mathematics the average over the two year groups was around 25 per cent while for language it was approximately 32 per cent. In the original ORACLE study the figures were between 40 and 45 per cent in each case.

As pointed out earlier, the Year 5 results need to be interpreted with some caution because of the shift from the shorter to the longer version of the Richmond Tests from Year 4 to Year 5. A conservative estimate might argue that the figures for Year 5, taking into account this difference is probably not too dissimilar to those for the other two transfer years. The figures suggesting that at least 35 per cent of pupils failed to make progress after transfer are close to those reported by American studies for transfer to Junior High and High Schools (Roderick 1993; Scott *et al.* 1995; Ward *et al.* 1982). Table 5.9 shows a breakdown of the data on which Figure 5.1 was based for boys and girls separately but this time as a percentage of pupils who made progress. Although there were no significant differences (using the non-parametric sign test) the figures for transfer at Year 6 are interesting in that they demonstrated a considerable improvement among the boys where, for example, in the language tests 91.3 per cent improved their scores compared to the previous year before transfer. For mathematics the corresponding figures were 85.7 and 70.7 per cent respectively. This suggests that a considerable part of the effort of Year 6 teachers was directed at improving the boys' performance. Given that the issue of boys' underachievement has received considerable attention in recent years, particularly when linked to ethnicity (Sammons 1995; Strand 1999), it is clear that if a school is to do well in the league tables then boys' performance must improve significantly, relative to that of girls and this appeared to be the case in these transfer schools.

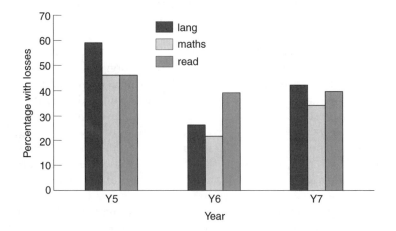

Figure 5.1 Hiatus in pupil progress after transfer

Table 5.9 Progress at transfer (per cent of boys and girls making gains)

Test	Y4–Y5		Y5–Y6		Y6–Y7	
	Boys	*Girls*	*Boys*	*Girls*	*Boys*	*Girls*
Language	46.6	35.2	91.3	61.3	58.7	57.0
Maths	50.0	58.6	85.7	73.3	65.3	65.4
Reading	58.9	49.3	70.8	53.3	57.3	63.5

Language skills after transfer[2]

Looking at the specific language skills, the language usage test was sub-divided into four areas, spelling, capitals, punctuation and usage. This is shown in Table 5.10 which displays the mean scores (as a percentage of the total score). For the transfer from Year 4 to Year 5 spelling declined from an average of 49.9 per cent to 40.3 per cent while use of capitals improved (up from 39.0 per cent to 42.2 per cent). Punctuation also declined from 47.6 per cent to 40.6 per cent while usage rose slightly from 46.3 per cent to 48.1 per cent. Analysis by gender showed there to be no significant difference between the scores of the boys and the girls among this age group. For Year 5 to Year 6 transfer resulted in significant gains in spelling up from 34.2 per cent to 52.8 per cent, a decline in use of capitals (45.2 per cent to 41.8 per cent) and

Table 5.10 Mean percentage scores before and after transfer

Test	Y4–Y5		Y5–Y6		Y6–Y7	
	Pre-trans	*Post-trans*	*Pre-trans*	*Post-trans*	*Pre-trans*	*Post-trans*
English language						
spelling	49.9 (2.2)	40.3 (1.7)	34.2 (2.2)	52.8 (2.4)	48.6 (1.7)	54.7 (1.4)
capitals	39.0 (1.8)	42.2 (1.2)	45.2 (1.5)	41.8 (2.4)	46.6 (1.5)	49.8 (1.3)
punctuation	47.6 (1.6)	40.6 (1.2)	39.7 (1.3)	47.5 (2.4)	42.0 (1.5)	46.0 (1.1)
usage	46.3 (2.1)	48.1 (1.8)	45.4 (2.1)	53.0 (2.9)	51.7 (1.9)	53.5 (1.6)
N	238	258	194	96	200	302
Reading						
vocabulary	59.1 (1.4)	57.9 (1.5)	56.0 (1.4)	62.5 (2.0)	63.4 (1.3)	67.6 (1.2)
comprehension	51.6 (1.4)	56.0 (1.4)	51.2 (1.5)	57.7 (2.0)	59.4 (1.3)	61.1 (1.1)
N	242	255	189	96	198	317
Maths						
concepts	57.2 (1.4)	57.1 (1.5)	58.0 (1.4)	69.9 (1.8)	63.9 (1.3)	69.0 (0.9)
problem solving	50.2 (1.5)	54.2 (1.2)	49.7 (1.7)	58.5 (2.3)	59.4 (1.6)	66.5 (1.1)
N	235	259	193	100	196	308

Note: Standard error of mean in parentheses.

an increase in both punctuation and usage up 7.8 per cent from 39.7 per cent and up 7.6 per cent from 45.4 per cent respectively. In this case there were significant gender differences with girls outscoring boys on both the use of capitals, punctuation and in language use. In transfer from Year 6 to Year 7, gains were recorded for spelling, use of capitals and punctuation but there was a decline in language use proficiency. Spelling rose by 6.1 per cent from 48.6 per cent, capitals by 3.2 per cent from 46.6 per cent, punctuation by 4 per cent from 42 per cent while usage declined by 4.2 per cent with a mean of 51.7 per cent for Year 6. Again, there were differences between boys and girls, this time on all four language skills. The biggest differences recorded were in spelling where the mean score for girls was 10 per cent greater both before and after transfer. The overall gain for girls in spelling was significant at the 1 per cent level ($t = 2.94$).

Reading performance after transfer

Reading scores were divided into two sub-totals for vocabulary and comprehension (see Table 5.10). For Year 4 to Year 5 transfer, vocabulary use declined from 59.1 per cent to 57.9 per cent, while comprehension increased from 51.6 per cent to 56 per cent. There were no significant differences between boys and girls. In transfer from Year 5 to Year 6 both sub-test scores increased. Vocabulary improved from 56 per cent to 62.5 per cent, while comprehension moved from 51.2 per cent to 57.7 per cent. Here, there was a difference in favour of the girls in vocabulary pre-transfer but not one year later in Year 6. With transfer from Year 6 to Year 7 there were again increases in both sub-tests.

Vocabulary improved by 4.2 per cent from 63.4 per cent, while comprehension increased by 1.7 per cent from 59.4 per cent. Again it was the girls who out-performed the boys. In vocabulary girls scored significantly higher on both the pre- and post-transfer test administrations. For comprehension the difference in favour of girls was only significant after transfer (60.8 compared to 66.7; $p < 0.01$)

Mathematics performance after transfer

Finally in mathematics the full test score was divided into two sub-tests, mastery of concepts and problem solving (see Table 5.10). For transfer at Year 4 there were no significant differences overall on either of the two sub-tests but in Y4 boys out-performed girls both at mastery of mathematical concepts (61.0 compared to 53.5) and problem solving (55.2 compared to 45.4). Both differences reached the 1 per cent significance level. After transfer, however, boys maintained their advantage only in problem solving but at the 5 per cent level (56.8 compared to 51.4). In transferring from Y5 to Y6 girls were able to reduce the differences further to the point where there were no statistically significant results on either sub-test. For the move from Y6 to Y7 girls were now matching boys on concept mastery after transfer (69.4 compared to 68.6) and problem solving (66.5 to 66.4) so that over the three stages of transfer gender differences had disappeared. Sammons' re-analysis of the Mortimore *et al.* (1988) study of London schools suggests that although on entry to Key Stage 2 girls are not out-performing boys, they have done so by Year 5 (Sammons 1995: 470–472). However, as pointed out by Strand (1999) who cites the support of Plewis (1991) the effects of interactions between gender and ethnicity can have major effects on overall results from different studies because of the variations in sample composition. In contrast to Mortimore *et al.*'s (1988) London sample schools, the present ORACLE replication study had few Asian and even fewer Afro-Caribbean children and it is in this latter ethnic group where the gender disparity in favour of girls is most marked (Gillborne and Gipps 1996).

Another possible explanation lies in the selection of the samples before and after transfer. In every case some of the pupils who were included in the above analysis had not taken both the pre- or post-transfer tests. This was because not all schools feeding into the transfer schools were tested and even in these feeders some pupils did not move on to the designated school in their pyramid. The analysis was therefore repeated using a reduced sample of pupils who sat both the pre- and post-transfer tests. For language at Y5 to Y6 transfer the gender differences disappeared although this could be due to the reduction in the size of the sample to only 23 boys and 31 girls. At Y6 to Y7 transfer all gender differences were maintained and extended after transfer to include the *use of capital letters* scale. Again, with reading a similar pattern occurred for both analyses and girls in the reduced sample consistently out-performed boys on all aspects of reading after transfer to Year 7. In mathematics, however, the advantage of boys in Y4 was maintained but disappeared after transfer to Year 5. Otherwise the pattern within both the larger and reduced samples was similar.

Pupil performance and transfer: twenty years on

It is not easy to make comparisons between the present analysis of pupils' attainment and attitude after transfer and the results presented in Galton and Willcocks (1983) from the original 1977–78 ORACLE transfer study. In Chapter 5 of that book Paul Croll, for the most part, presented results for the combined scores of all three tests. It is also not always clear whether what might be termed the combined *basic skill* scores for the pupils who transferred from Year 4 to Year 5 were calculated from the actual scores, irrespective of the length of the test, or made use of proportionate scores as in the present analysis. The sample sizes in the 1977–78 study were much smaller because only the scores of the eight target pupils in each class were used and some among this reduced sample did not record both pre- and post-transfer scores.

Nevertheless, it is possible to make some interesting comparisons. To begin with, there is the question of what Croll in Galton and Willcocks (1983: 78–79) termed the continuities in relative class status. In the original ORACLE study, target pupils were placed in four quartiles depending on their academic achievement within their particular class. Thus depending on the overall level of achievement within a class in a given school, a pupil with a particular score in one class might find him or herself in the top quartile while another pupil with the same score in another class might be placed in either of the middle quartiles. After transfer pupils from different schools would be mixed to form new classes where perhaps the two mythical pupils with the same scores in their different primary schools could now find themselves together. Croll used the post-transfer test data to explore whether the new class arrangements altered pupils' relative class positions. The figures displayed in Tables 5.1 and 5.2 in *Moving from the Primary Classroom* are here reproduced in Table 5.11. Compare Table 5.11 with Table 5.12.

Table 5.11 Relative class position before and after transfer (ORACLE)

| | | End of first year after transfer | | | |
		Top quartile	Middle	Bottom	Total
end of first	top quartile	16	3	1	20
observed	middle	8	33	9	50
year	bottom	1	6	12	19
in primary	total	25	42	22	89

Table 5.12 Relative class position before and after transfer (ORACLE replication)

| | | End of first year after transfer | | | |
		Top quartile	Middle	Bottom	Total
end of last	top quartile	33	19		52
year in	middle	24	76	19	119
feeder	bottom		19	21	40
school	total	57	114	40	211

In the ORACLE study the relative positions of pupils in the pre-transfer schools were measured one year before transfer except in the case of Gryll Grange and Guy Mannering. This was because in the other schools pupils were observed for two years before transferring from their primary school so that the first administration of the Richmond Tests was made at the end of the beginning of the penultimate year before transfer. It is therefore somewhat remarkable that over a period of three years the relative class positions should have remained relatively stable. Combining the two original tables

150

(5.1 for Gryll Grange with Guy Mannering and 5.2 for the remainder of the schools) makes little difference, however, since the pattern was consistent. Here 16 pupils of the 20 (80 per cent) who were in the top quartile in their feeder schools remained in the top group in their class one year after transfer. In the bottom quartile 63 per cent (12 out of 19) retained their relative status after transfer. There was a small proportion of pupils who crossed over into another group. One pupil from the bottom quartile in primary school moved into the top quartile after transfer, perhaps because the classes in that school were streamed by ability and he or she was placed in the lowest stream.

The reverse case of a pupil who was in the top group at primary school but in the bottom quartile after transfer is more difficult to explain, unless it was indicative of a high degree of disengagement. There was an equal lack of movement in the middle quartile groups where 66 per cent (33 out of 50) occupied the same relative positions before and after transfer. The pattern identified here, as Croll in Galton and Willcocks (1983: 81) argues, can have important consequences for a child's 'life chances', since the opinions and consequent behaviour of teachers and other pupils have been shown to reflect a pupil's relative position within his or her class.

A similar analysis was therefore carried out with the sample used for the ORACLE replication. The results are shown in Table 5.12. Now 63 per cent (33 out of 52) remained in the top group within their class compared to 21 pupils out of 40 (52.5 per cent) in the bottom quartile. In the middle quartiles 64 per cent, that is 76 out of 119 pupils, remained within this group after transfer. Such consistent patterns help to explain findings such as Sammons (1995: 479) in which the effects of socio-economic factors 'on absolute attainment at the end of compulsory secondary education remained stable and mirrored patterns already-evident in junior school'. There were, however, interesting gender differences suggesting a greater degree of stability with girls. Whereas 71 per cent of girls remained in the same relative class position before and after transfer, the corresponding figure for boys was 57 per cent. Overall, 56 per cent of pupils retained their class position when transferring to Year 5 compared to 67 per cent for transfer to Years 6 and 7 respectively.

Mention has already been made of the reduction of the number of pupils experiencing a hiatus in progress at transfer with reference to the discussion of Figure 5.1. where the data was broken down by test domain and age of transfer. In Tables 5.3 and 5.5 in *Moving from the Primary Classroom* figures for the combined test score (on language use, mathematics and reading) were examined for differences between transfer age and gender. In the 1977–78 study, 47.5 per cent of boys and 78 per cent of girls made gains after transfer. The corresponding figures for this ORACLE replication study were 87 per cent of girls and 90 per cent of boys. These figures are based upon raw scores and therefore favour the cohort transferring to Year 5 for reasons explained earlier concerning the use of a shortened version of the tests in Year 4. If we do not include this cohort, then the corresponding figures for Year 6 and Year 7 transfer were 68 per cent (girls) and 71 per cent (boys) respectively. There has been a considerable change over the two decades with respect to boys' gains, no doubt, as we have argued, in part, a consequence of attempting to boost the school's 'league table' position at the end of Key Stage 2. This is reflected in the overall figure where 69.2 per cent of pupils who made gains on a 'combined' score of basic skills in 1977–78 compared to 73 per cent in the present study.

Pupil enjoyment and motivation: twenty years on

The measures of attitude, enjoyment and motivation were not the same in both studies. In Table 5.8 of *Moving from the Primary Classroom* the figures are reported as percentage scores and not as means as in Table 5.5 in this present chapter.

Table 5.13 Motivation and enjoyment for gainers and losers before and after transfer

Scale	Period	Gainers		Losers	
		1977–78	1997–98	1977–78	1997–98
enjoyment	before transfer	70.0	74.3	70.8	74.7
	after transfer	73.6	69.1*	61.8*	73.5
motivation and	before transfer	73.4	69.3	71.2	70.4
confidence	after transfer	71.9	69.6	63.5*	72.0
number of pupils		51	141	24	64[3]

Note: *$p < 0.05$ t-test.

Table 5.14 Differences in levels of interaction between gainers and losers

Interaction (% all observations)	Pupils making gains after transfer				Pupils making losses after transfer			
	Pre-transfer		Post-transfer		Pre-transfer		Post transfer	
	1977–	1997–	1977–	1997–	1977–	1997–	1977–	1997–
Teacher–pupil interaction	14.6	31.2	29.5	44.4	13.9	28.3	31.6	41.2
Pupil–pupil interaction	17.9	25.8	17.9	16.9	17.9	26.8	15.0	18.7
Pupil–pupil off task	13.6	8.6	10.3*	10.9*	11.5	9.0	11.1*	11.0*
Total time on task	59.9	62.7	69.6*	69.2*	58.5	71.5*	61.8*	67.6
N	51	151	51	91	24	59	24	39

Note: *$p < 0.05$ t-test.

However, since both the enjoyment and motivation scales in the present study each had eight items giving a maximum score of 32, it is possible to reproduce part of the table from Galton and Willcocks (1983: 88) as Table 5.13. This compares the enjoyment and motivation scores for pupils who made gains after transfer, the *gainers*, and those who made losses, the *losers*, in terms of their combined scores on the tests of basic skills. The scores were those recorded in the June before transfer and then one year later after the move to the new school.

In terms of the overall percentages, the scores on both occasions and in both decades were relatively high with pupils averaging 70 per cent of the maximum possible score on both enjoyment and motivation scales. The main difference over the two decades concerns the drop in enjoyment after the first year in the transfer school. Whereas in the original ORACLE study it was the pupils who failed to make progress whose enjoyment of school began to decline, it was now the pupils who improved their position, relative to performance in the feeder school who appeared to have less liking for school. This is in line with the earlier finding in Table 5.6 that it was among the 'high attainers' that most disaffection occurred. In the ORACLE replication motivation and confidence increased after transfer although the figures for the gainers or losers were not statistically significant. This contrasts with the original study, two decades earlier, where the motivation of the losers declined. Part of the explanation may lie in the changing nature of this scale since in the present study it also reflected the pupils' confidence to cope with the work. If, as described in the previous chapter, many lessons were relatively undemanding, then earlier concerns about 'not coping with the work' would have proved unfounded, irrespective of whether pupils were maintaining expected levels of progress.

Interaction and attainment twenty years on

The final comparison between the two studies concerns differences in the levels of interaction between the gainers and losers and this is displayed in Table 5.14. The most obvious differences were in the levels of teacher–pupil interaction across the two decades. As reported in *Inside the Primary Classroom: 20 Years On*, whole class teaching had increased dramatically over the two decades since the original ORACLE study (Galton *et al.* 1999b). This was reflected in the doubling of the amount of time (expressed as a percentage of the total number of observations) when the teacher was addressing pupils either by asking questions, making statements or giving directions. This pattern to a lesser extent was also evident after transfer where the increase in teacher–pupil interaction was approximately 25 per cent. Perhaps more interesting is the extent and characteristics of the pupil–pupil interaction. In 1977 group work was a 'neglected art' in most primary classrooms (Galton 1981). By the late 1990s it had increased slightly but, more importantly, less of the interactions between pupils were now off task. Here, for example, for pupils in the 1977–78 cohort who made gains in attainment after transfer, 76 per cent of pupil–pupil activity was off task (13.6 per cent out of 17.9 per cent) whereas in the present study the corresponding figure was only 33 per cent (8.6 per cent out of 25.8 per cent). It was not possible to test this difference for statistical significance because no estimate of the variation around this average level of interaction was presented with the 1977–78 data in the relevant table. However, judging by the differences in Table 5.14 which did reach significance level it can be assumed that this would have been true of the above result. After transfer the figures for both the original ORACLE and the present replication study are remarkably similar with similar proportions of time spent on group work (17.9 per cent and 16.9 per cent respectively) and similar levels of distraction (57.5 per cent and 64 per cent). Interestingly, despite the changes in approach to classroom organisation, the total time these 'gainers' spent on task was very similar both before and after transfer over the two decades. In 1977–78 there was a 14 per cent increase across transfer (from 59.9 per cent to 69.6 per cent) and two decades later the corresponding figure was 10 per cent.

Turning to the pupils who made losses after transfer, the 'losers' received similar amounts of teacher attention as their more successful peers. For example, whereas the 'gainers' in the 1977–78 cohort received 14.6 per cent of such interaction, the losers received 13.9 per cent. In the present study the corresponding figures were 31.2 per cent and 28.3 per cent respectively so that a small, although statistically insignificant trend existed suggesting that prior to transfer losers get less help from the teacher. This was also true after transfer where in the original ORACLE study the drop was from 29.5 per cent (gainers) to 28.3 per cent (losers) with an even bigger difference in the present study (from 44.4 per cent to 41.2 per cent). Since most attention, after transfer, took place in whole class settings, these small differences could have come about because 'losers' were less likely to respond to teachers' questions or because they were not the main recipients of the limited occasions when attention was given to individual pupils.

The main differences, however, concerned off task behaviour, particularly during pupil–pupil interactions. For 'gainers' the levels of time on task, as we have seen, were very similar across the two decades both before and after transfer. For the losers, however, there were significant differences before and after transfer between the two cohorts. In the 1977–78 study losers worked harder after transfer in the sense that time on task increased by 3.3 per cent (up from 58.5 per cent to 61.8 per cent). For the present sample time on task fell from 71.5 per cent before transfer to 67.6 per cent a year later, a decline of 3.9 per cent. Significantly, these losers had the highest levels of time on task before transfer among all the groups in Table 5.14. The same deterioration was seen during collaboration with other pupils. Prior to transfer the losers from the present study were the least distracted of all groups with only

154

33 per cent of these interactions with their peers off task (9 per cent out of 26.6 per cent total pupil–pupil interaction). After transfer this figure rose to 59 per cent which was less than the 1977–78 figure of 74 per cent but still relatively high. Overall, therefore, the patterns across the two decades represent an increasing trend to teach pupils as a class rather than in groups or as individuals. Within this structure, however, there has been little change in the amount of time that pupils work at the tasks set them by their teachers except in the case of the 'losers' in the present study. From being among the hardest working pupils before transfer they begin to waste increasing amounts of time in conversations with other pupils on matters not related to the work on hand. When this finding is coupled with a tendency to reduce the amount of work-related exchanges with the teacher, while at the same time maintaining a high level of enjoyment of school and increasing self-confidence, it is possible to discern in these pupils the beginnings of disaffection leading to the further dips in attitude and performance described by Rudduck *et al.* (1996) in subsequent years of schooling.

The effect of age of transfer

Ever since research into transfer began in the 1960s a recurring question has concerned the most suitable age at which pupils should make the move to the bigger school. Some have argued, particularly with regard to the continued existence of middle schools that the fewer the moves the better, if each one is accompanied by dips in academic progress and attitude. This ignores the effects of transition from one year group to another within a school which, as Rudduck *et al.* (1997) have shown, can also give rise to similar problems, particularly in Y8. Nevertheless, it is of interest to see if some of the dips in attainment attributed to transfer and shown in Figure 5.1 are 'an age of transfer' effect. To do this *'residual gain scores'* were calculated for each of the three Richmond Tests. This residual gain is obtained by subtracting a pupil's actual post-transfer score from that predicted by his or her pre-transfer score. These gain scores were then tested for statistical significance across year group, pre- and post-transfer schools respectively. For the language test

Table 5.15 Rank position of post-transfer schools (based on residual gain attainment scores)

Transfer age	School	Language	Maths	Reading	Mean rank
Y4 to Y5	Gryll Grange	1	6	5	4
	Guy Mannering	3	2	4	3
Y5 to Y6	Maid Marion	2	1	1	1.3
	Kenilworth	6	5	6	5.6
Y6 to Y7	Channings	4	3	2	3
	Danesbury	5	4	3	4

significant differences were found for both pre-and post-transfer schools but not for age of transfer. For the test of reading only pre-transfer school effects were found while for mathematics there were no significant effects. From none of these analyses, therefore, was it possible to conclude that relative to the progress pupils made, one age of transfer was better than another. Although, as we have seen, significant post-transfer differences between schools were only found for language, it is possible to examine the various trends by ranking the residual gains so that the largest positive effect was ranked first and the largest negative effect sixth. This has been done in Table 5.11 for all six transfer schools. It can be seen that across the three ages of transfer studied no consistent pattern emerged. The best and poorest performing schools, Maid Marion and Kenilworth, were both Y6 transfer schools. Guy Mannering (Y4 toY5 transfer) and Channings (Y6 toY7 transfer) have the same average rank position (3.0) as do Gryll Grange (Y5) and Danesbury (Y7) with a score of 4.0. Both Maid Marion and Kenilworth were part of the original 1976 ORACLE transfer study. At that time, as described in Chapter 1, Maid Marion sought to maintain a primary ethos throughout the first year. Although, two decades later, it still encouraged pupils to stay in a separate play area and had a distinct base area where most lessons took place, it had moved with the times and introduced more streaming and single subject teaching of history and geography rather than humanities. In Table 5.15 it is ranked first in mathematics and reading and second in language use. Not surprisingly the school, particularly the principal, put considerable emphasis on securing a high league table position in the Key Stage 2 National Curriculum Tests at the end of Year 6.

In contrast, Kenilworth, one of the most traditional schools in the 1976 study remained almost unchanged. In Table 5.11 it is ranked bottom in language and reading and last from bottom in mathematics. Since both schools were positioned on the same site that also included the senior (14–18) school to which both their pupils transferred, and served the same catchment area, various socio-cultural-economic factors could not have been a major determinant of these contrasting rankings. In the same way, although to a lesser extent, there were disparities between the mathematics progress made by pupils at Gryll Grange and Guy Mannering. Apart, therefore, from the cases of Maid Marion and Kenilworth, more variation is to be found across the three tests, suggesting that each of the remaining schools had certain strengths and weaknesses.

A similar analysis can be carried out for the attitude measures, enjoyment, social isolation and confidence (see Table 5.16). Here it is only possible to calculate the residual gains from the pre-transfer and the November administration since one of the schools (Channings) did not provide a set of results in the following June. In any case, given the differences in culture and ethos described in Chapter 3, it might be expected that some of the greatest variations between schools existed before pupils gradually adjusted to the regime over the course of the following two terms. So that the three attitudes can be combined the social isolation scale was reversed so that a positive gain represented increased social adjustment.

Table 5.16 Rank position of post-transfer schools (based on residual gain attitude scores)

Transfer age	School	Enjoyment	Social adjustment	Motivation	Mean rank
Y4 to Y5	Gryll Grange	3	3	3	3.0
	Guy Mannering	1	1	1	1.0
Y5 to Y6	Maid Marion	4	5	5	4.6
	Kenilworth	5	6	6	5.6
Y6 to Y7	Channings	2	2	4	2.6
	Danesbury	6	4	2	4.0

Here there appears to be more consistency compared to the attainment measures. Guy Mannering and Gryll Grange have the first and third lowest mean rank indicating some of the biggest gains. Kenilworth and Maid Marion do least well overall, perhaps attributable to the pressures pupils were under in preparing for the 'high stakes' examination even at this stage. Compared to Danesbury, pupils at Channings enjoy school more and are better adjusted by the end of the first half-term in the school. Danesbury pupils, however, are better motivated. Both Gryll Grange and Guy Mannering retained a primary ethos to some extent and this clearly helped the pupils. Nevertheless by the third administration in the following June, with Channings excluded, Guy Mannering had dropped to fourth place overall while Maid Marion and Kenilworth were equal first.

On balance, the evidence presented here would suggest that it is the school to which the pupil transfers rather than the age at which the transfer takes place which is the more important. It is suggested that the reason for the differences in Tables 5.15 and 5.16 between Kenilworth and Channings might, in part, be attributed to the ways that pupils were inducted into their new school as described in Chapters 2 and 3 of this book. In particular, the highly formal ethos[4] described in Kenilworth with the emphasis on social control and low levels of social cohesion (p. 67) might have been expected to have played a part in forming pupils' attitudes and motivation in ways that may have had a damaging effect upon their progress.

A fuller picture will, hopefully, emerge when we examine the changes in pupils' behaviour both before and after transfer. This aspect of our study will now be explored in the next chapter. This will make it possible in the final chapter to attempt some assessment of the impact which the various elements of the transfer process, such as the degree of continuity within the curriculum and teaching and the school's culture, have upon pupils' intellectual and social development.

Notes

1 Personal communication.
2 It should be borne in mind that this was not a longitudinal study in which the same pupils were followed from Y4 through to Y7. Comparisons are made between three different cohorts so the mean scores estimate the norms for each year group and are not indicators of year by year progress.
3 For the ORACLE replication the number of pupils with complete data for attainment and attitudes varied. The figures reported here are averages. In the case of gainers the number of pupils varied from 152 to 131, while for the losers it varied between 66 and 63.
4 Interestingly, this formal ethos was singled out for special praise in a subsequent OFSTED inspection as a positive factor contributing to pupils' academic progress.

6

PATTERNS OF PUPIL BEHAVIOUR
IN THE TRANSFER SCHOOLS

Linda Hargreaves and Tony Pell

The children who moved from the primary classrooms in 1997 were leaving a similar but busier classroom environment than their predecessors of 1977–78. By the late 1990s, primary children spent more time talking to each other both about their tasks and other interests. Their teachers spent more time interacting with them and less time maintaining the classroom and doing administrative jobs. The 1990s children appeared to be working harder, spending slightly less time waiting for the teacher and the same amount of time getting on with their tasks instead (Galton *et al.* 1999b: 90). They were also less likely to be distracted from their tasks (11.7 per cent in 1996, compared with 15.9 per cent of the observations in 1976 (ibid.: 91) but now spent more time partly distracted and partly involved, apparently with 'half a mind' on the task in hand. One reason for this might have been the doubling of the amount of whole class teaching to which they were subjected. This rose from 15 per cent of all interactions in 1976 to 31 per cent two decades later. Underlying these surface changes, however, was a fairly stable 'deep structure' of primary classroom life, in that:

> while in absolute terms the children received more of their teachers' attention as a member of the class, in relative terms, things were almost exactly as they were in 1976, that is three-quarters of all pupil–teacher interactions were still class-based.
>
> (ibid.: 105)

The absolute rise in the amount of class teaching, however, was making the upper primary classes more like secondary school classes and on this basis, regardless of any other implications of this organisational strategy, it could be that children found it easier to adapt to the secondary regime in the present study. We will look first at the overall changes in specific aspects of classroom behaviour as children move to the transfer schools. This will be followed by consideration of classroom organisation in primary and transfer schools. Finally, changes in pupils' classroom styles or 'personae' across transfer and over time, and their relationship with attainment will be reported.

159

Changes in pupil classroom behaviour on transfer

Galton and Willcocks (1983) examined children's behaviour before and after transfer in 1976 and found a significant increase in task directed behaviour, as the children moved to the transfer schools. Table 6.1 allows for comparisons between the 1977–78 and the present transfer pupil data on on-task behaviour. Data from the primary schools in the present study are also included for comparison. Figures for distracted or diverted behaviour were not given for the 1976 sample in Galton *et al.* (1980).

Table 6.1 Changes in pupil behaviour on transfer (per cent of all observation categories)

Activity	Primary 1976	Transfer 1977–78	Difference	Primary 1996[1] N = 9174	Transfer 1997 N = 7811	Difference
fully cooperating on task	59.1	67.7*	+8.6	62.2	67.1*	+4.9
cooperating on routine tasks	11.4	10.7	–0.7	11.9	12.5	+0.6
total on-task behaviour	70.5	78.4	+7.9	74.1	79.6	+5.5

Note: * $p \le 0.01$.

Table 6.1 shows a significant overall increase in the amount of time that children were observed fully engaged in their tasks once they moved into the transfer schools. The gap between primary and secondary total on-task behaviour between the two phases has narrowed, due to the primaries' increased time on task and the slight reduction in on-task behaviour in the transfer schools. Galton *et al.* (1999b) extended the definition of task directed behaviour to include half of the 'CODS' 'partly on task, partially distracted' category, as well as the 'Waiting for the teacher' category. This produced a total of 79 per cent task-directed behaviour in the primary schools and they suggested that this might be a 'ceiling' for on-task behaviour. If we follow the same procedure by adding 2.2 per cent (half the CODS) plus 2 per cent time spent waiting for the teacher to the 79.6 per cent time on task, we find that in the transfer schools total time on task-oriented behaviour might have been as high as 83.8 per cent. In Table 6.2 we look at the nature of time spent off task in the primary and transfer schools. No comparison can be made with the 1976 transfer schools because no figures are given.

Table 6.2 reveals a change in the nature of children's diverted behaviour on moving to the transfer schools. While complete distraction levels remained about the same at 10.8 per cent of all observations, as in primary schools (11.7 per cent), 'diverted' behaviour which was still partly work oriented had fallen more noticeably. For example after transfer, children were significantly

Table 6.2 Composition of pupils' diverted behaviour in primary and transfer classes (based on all observations)

Observation	Primary 1996	Transfer 1997
fully distracted from the task	11.3 *	10.3
distracted by the observer	0.3	0.3
horseplay and disruptive behaviour	0.1	0.2
Total completely off-task behaviour	*11.7*	*10.8*
waiting for the teacher	2.0	2.0
'CODS' (cooperating/distracted)	6.2 **	4.4
interested in the teacher	1.4 **	0.6
interested in another pupil	2.2 **	1.0
working on approved activity	0.6	0.6
responding to internal stimuli	1.1 **	0.6
Total partially diverted behaviour	*11.5*	*7.2*
All diverted behaviour	23.2	18.0

Notes: $*p < 0.05$, $**p < 0.01$.

less likely to be daydreaming ('responding to internal stimuli'), watching the teacher, or watching other pupils, when they were supposed to be pursuing their own tasks. There were also significantly fewer occasions when observers recorded the 'CODS' category which meant that pupils appeared to be partially on and partially off task. In other words, after transfer children were more likely to be either fully on task or completely distracted from it, suggesting that teachers were being more successful at discouraging half-hearted involvement in tasks. These results apply, however, to the mythical 'typical' child in the mythical 'typical' class, and are based in effect on cross-sectional analyses of the whole cohort. For any particular group of pupils the picture is likely to be more varied. Towards the end of the chapter, we shall identify classroom styles which pupils adopted as they transferred from primary to secondary school, and in particular, we shall consider the careers of children who were observed in both pre- and post-transfer classes, thus forming a small longitudinal sample. In other words we can study the changes in the behaviour of some actual individual children rather than dealing with the average pupil.

Changes in teacher–pupil interaction

Table 6.3 shows the differences in the types of teacher–pupil interaction which children experienced in both phases. The top section of Table 6.3 shows that, as a proportion of all observation pupils were significantly more often a part of the teacher's audience, and during such periods were more often the focus (STAR) of the teacher's attention. However, as can be seen by looking further down Table 6.3, pupils' attempts to gain attention, for

161

Table 6.3 Pupils' interaction with their teachers in the primary and transfer classes

Pupil–teacher interaction category	Primary school (N = 9174)	Transfer school (N = 6782)	Primary school (N = 2729)	Transfer school (N = 2595)
	Percentage of total observations		Percentage of all pupil–adult interactions	
pupil initiates interaction	1.8	1.8	6.0	4.8
pupil is STAR of teacher's attention	2.0	2.6 **	6.7	6.8
pupil is PART of teacher's audience	21.6	27.2 **	72.4	71.1
pupil is PART of teacher's audience but not the STAR	4.4	6.6 **	14.8	17.3 *
interacting adult is the teacher	28.0	36.2 **	94.0	94.6
interaction about task work	24.8	32.5 **	83.5	85.0
interaction about routine tasks or behaviour	4.2	4.4	14.1 **	11.4
pupil receives praise	0.3	0.2	0.9	0.5
pupil receives negative feedback	0.4	0.4	1.3	0.9
pupil's attempt to interact is ignored	0.0	0.9 **	0.1	2.2 **
individual attention from teacher	3.2	2.9	10.8 **	7.5
teacher addressing pupil's group	2.6 **	1.6	8.9 **	4.1
teacher addressing whole class	19.8	28.4 **	66.4	74.3 **
All pupil–adult interactions	29.7	38.3 **		

Note: Raw score frequencies compared by chi-square (*$p < 0.05$, **$p < 0.01$).

example by putting their hands up, were more often ignored in the transfer schools. The first two columns of Table 6.3 also show that teacher–pupil interaction increased by almost a third in the transfer schools (38.3 per cent compared to 29.7 per cent). Yet, moving to the last section of Table 6.3, in columns 3 and 4, as shown in previous studies, if we consider the pupils' experience within this apparently rich amount of attention from the teacher, we find that the vast majority of this time is still spent as part of a whole class audience, and just as it was in the original ORACLE study two decades earlier, when in the secondary classes children experienced significantly less attention as individuals or in small groups.

When transformed to show the interactions as proportions of pupil–adult interaction, some of the statistically significant differences disappear, and Table 6.3 shows that for most pupils, the major increase was the time they spent listening and watching the teacher while the teacher interacted with another child. This virtual loss of direct interaction with the teacher has particular relevance for some children, possibly as a partial explanation of those who revealed declining attitudes to school as shown in the previous chapter, and also in the rise of a new more passive forms of pupil persona as will be seen later in the chapter. In pursuing this issue further, the more 'highly interactive' or perhaps talkative children were identified and their characteristics examined in more detail and then compared with the experience of the other children in the transfer classes.

Teacher–pupil interaction with talkative children

Tables 6.1 to 6.3 apply to the mythical 'typical' child in the mythical 'typical' class. However, in order to consider more closely what was happening when teachers interacted with pupils, we isolated the 103 occasions (each of which includes ten actual observation points), about 12 per cent of the total number of observation records, when pupils were observed *simultaneously* interacting with the teacher and with other pupils. These were analysed separately. Table 6.4 compares the pupils' behaviour in these 'simultaneous' occasions, with the remaining 87 per cent of observations.

Table 6.4 Nature of situations when pupil behaviour attracted teacher attention

Pupil behaviour	Observations not involving teacher's attention (N = 6782)	Simultaneous teacher–pupil and pupil–pupil interaction (N = 103)
fully cooperating on task	68.8*	56.3
cooperating on routine tasks	12.5	12.8
fully distracted	9.1*	18.2
'CODS' part on task, part off task	4.0*	6.7
working on other activities	0.5*	1.5
other behaviour categories (a)	5.0	3.0

Notes: (a) Categories included are: distracted by the observer, disruptive behaviour, horseplay, interested in teacher, interested in other pupils, responding to internal stimuli. Separate frequencies have not been given for these infrequently used categories which showed no significant differences.
$*p < 0.01$.

The first column in Table 6.4 shows very clearly that when these 'multi-interaction' occasions are excluded, time spent fully engaged on tasks is slightly more than that shown in Table 6.1, while complete distraction levels are notably reduced. The second column in Table 6.4 shows that the occasions which attracted teacher attention involved complete distraction from the tasks in twice as many cases, and a much lower level of time fully engaged on the task. Further analysis of the nature of non-task-related teacher–pupil interaction was carried out by correlating separate activity categories with the overall non-task-related pupil–adult interaction scores and is shown in Table 6.5. This reveals quite distinct characteristics of the 'simultaneous' occasions, as well as differences between boys' and girls' behaviour which attracted teacher attention.

Table 6.5 Pupil behaviour which attracted non-task teacher attention, showing situations when pupil–pupil interaction attracted simultaneous teacher attention

Pupil activity	Correlations between pupil activity and total non-task-related teacher–pupil interaction					
	Non-task pupil–teacher interactions excluding simultaneous pupil–teacher interactions			Simultaneous pupil–pupil and pupil-teacher interactions		
	all $N = 683$	boys $N = 340$	girls $N = 343$	all $N = 103$	boys $N = 58$	girls $N = 45$
fully cooperating on task	−0.41 *	−0.40 *	−0.43 *	−0.72 *	−0.75 *	−0.67 *
cooperating on routine tasks	0.36 *	0.38 *	0.34 *	0.26 *	0.33 *	0.20 ns
fully distracted from task	0.07	0.04	0.09	0.43 *	0.40 *	0.46 *
including simultaneous codings	0.21 *	0.19 *	0.22 *			
CODS: part on- part off-task	0.39 *	0.39 *	0.39 *	0.42 *	0.45 *	0.37 *
waiting for the teacher	−0.03	−0.04	−0.03	−0.10	−0.13	−0.08
interested in the teacher	−0.04	0.00	−0.07	−0.05	0.16	−0.07
interested in other pupil/s	0.06	0.01	0.12 *	0.10	−0.15	0.51 *
working on other activity	0.20 *	0.07	0.27 *	0.20 *	0.21	0.23
responding to internal stimuli	0.05	0.07	0.04	0.32 *	0.11	0.52 *
horseplay	0.07	0.10	0.03	0.01	−0.10	–
disruptive behaviour	0.14 *	0.18 *	–	–	–	–
distracted by observer	0.10 *	0.19 *	−0.05	0.10	0.12	–

Notes: $^*p < 0.01$, ns = not statistically significant.

Table 6.5 shows that children were highly unlikely to attract non-task-related teacher attention when they were concentrating on their tasks. Routine activities such as changing pen cartridges or collecting books, however, were very likely to attract the teacher's attention, as were occasions when pupils were partially on task and partially off task (CODS). Boys, however, were also more likely to attract the teacher's attention on the rare occasions when they were disrupting other children's work, or looking at the observer. Girls, on the other hand, were more likely to be spoken to for working on unapproved activities, or watching other pupils at work. If we look at the 'simultaneous' codings, however, which involved more boys than girls, distracted behaviour was highly likely to attract the teacher's attention.

Boys were more likely than girls to be combining routine behaviours such as getting books out while talking to a neighbour, when the teacher interacted with them. This might suggest that the ruse of engaging in some legitimate routine activity while holding a conversation was unlikely to be successful. Girls, on the other hand, tended to receive teacher intervention when they were interested in another pupil's work, or when they were daydreaming. Finally, we can say more about the types of interactions involved. These pupils were twice as likely as their classmates to start the conversations with their peers (11.2 per cent of observations of the 'simultaneous' group compared with 5.2 per cent) or, at least, attempt to do so. The interactions were significantly more likely to be with same sex pupils, at the same base and doing the same task. These children were generally more talkative than their classmates (20.8 per cent compared with 14.8 per cent of all observations involved verbal interactions). They were also more likely to be exchanging materials or communicating non-verbally than others in the class, though such interactions were unusual (less than 3.5 per cent all observations). Some 54 per cent of these pupils' simultaneous interactions (compared with 27.2 per cent for the 'non-simultaneous' group) were as part of a class or larger group setting, and these pupils were significantly more often the initiator or 'star' of the teacher's attention. While 60.8 per cent of the teacher–pupil interactions were about the task, compared with 32.5 per cent in the rest of the class, they were also significantly more likely to receive comments about their behaviour as opposed to their work, to get individual attention, and though rare overall, to have strong negative feedback directed at them (1.9 per cent of all observations compared with 0.4 per cent for other pupils). This 'simultaneous' group experienced a very high level of teacher attention in this simultaneous interaction context (72.6 per cent of their entire pupil–adult interactions compared with 29.7 per cent for other pupils). These children were therefore highly visible in the class, experiencing relatively high levels of teacher attention, either as a result of very active participation in class sessions or because their attempts to have a chat or avoid work were spotted by the teacher. We shall return to consider specific groups of pupils later in the chapter, after considering how classes were organised in the transfer schools.

The nature of the transfer classrooms

Galton *et al.* (1999a) concluded that teaching in primary schools in 1996 was more like the teaching they had observed in secondary schools in the original ORACLE study. In this sense adjustment should have been easier for new entrants. However, other aspects of the transfer schools presented different adjustments for new pupils. The most visible environmental changes, apart from the size of the schools, were the classroom displays and furniture arrangements. Display, for example in the primary classrooms, was typically rich in children's work about science investigations, historical topics, etc., teachers' charts showing spellings and useful phrases to support writing, all presented in aesthetically stimulating ways. The decor of the transfer rooms by comparison was impoverished, although some schools had central 'exhibitions' including children's work and photographs of expeditions on show, but probably targeted more at parents and other visitors than at the children themselves.

The original ORACLE study represented transfer classes as either 'primary' or 'secondary' types. In the primary type, 'pupils [sat] in larger groups and [spent] far more of their time working on their own, drawing on each other almost as much as on the teacher for the interactions of the day'. In the secondary type, 'pupils [sat] in single sex pairs, either working on their own or engaged in a fairly constant whole-class dialogue with their teachers, and talking rather infrequently to each other' (Galton and Willcocks 1983: 46).

As Table 6.6 shows, the move to the transfer schools still meant that children had to get used to sitting in same sex pairs after transfer, but this now constituted only one-third, as opposed to a half of the observed lessons. The main changes in seating in the transfer schools were greater use of individual seating and mixed sex groups at the expense of same sex pairs and same sex groups. Only two transfer schools used predominantly one arrangement. These were Channings where same sex pairs were used in 56 per cent of the observations, and Gryll Grange where children sat in mixed sex groups 78.0 per cent of the time.

Table 6.6 Seating arrangements in primary and transfer schools

Base or seating	Primary 1976	Transfer 1977–78	Primary 1996	Transfer 1997
alone	4.8	5.3	4.9	12.2
same sex pair	14.0	48.6	9.8	32.8
opposite sex pair	2.1	1.1	1.5	2.3
same sex group	32.5	36.6	24.3	23.2
opposite sex group	44.2	7.3	46.3	23.5
class (a)	(2.3)	(1.1)	13.2	6.0

Note: (a) ORACLE 1976 did not report 'Class' separately. It might have been included in opposite sex group. The ORACLE 1996 primary study observed some sessions such as music and PE which did not appear in the 1976 study and which were more likely to involve 'Class' as the children's base.

These arrangements were typical of the 1970s' transfer and primary types respectively but did not necessarily include children grouped round large tables, however. Just as Galton *et al.* (1999b) had shown that the layouts of primary school classrooms had diversified since 1976, so had classroom layouts in the transfer schools. At Danesbury, for example, the following arrangements were found:

- square tables for four in art;
- a horseshoe arrangement which enclosed three short rows in English;
- an 'E' shape facing a reverse 'E' shape in modern languages;
- long continuous rows for ten or twelve facing forward in humanities;
- L-shaped benches to seat up to eight in science;
- pairs of seats at computer work stations around the edge of the room in ICT;
- conventional pairs of desks facing one way in maths;
- large primary-style tables in a large room, and small studios in music.

In other words, these children had to adjust to different work environments several times every day after transfer.

The relationships between time on task, interaction and seating are shown in Table 6.7, but this should be read in conjunction with Table 6.6 in order to keep the prevalence of the different groupings in mind. At primary school, although time on task did not vary significantly with seating, concentration was at its highest mean value in whole class settings and curiously, at its lowest when children were sitting by themselves. In the transfer schools, time on task increased in individual, paired and whole class settings, but was low, and almost the same as the primary levels for groups. While seating a boy and girl beside each other in the transfer schools would appear to have been very effective in increasing concentration levels and minimising pupil–pupil interaction, it was also a very unusual arrangement. Pupil- pupil interaction was generally less in the transfer schools when compared to the situation before the move, but this was particularly true of same sex pairs and same sex groups. That said, whereas at primary school pupil–pupil interaction was relatively high when children sat it pairs, at transfer schools the highest levels of peer interaction occurred when pupils were sat in groups. This might suggest that talk was encouraged whenever this form of seating was used. Finally, the last two columns of Table 6.7 show pupil–teacher

Table 6.7 Seating arrangements and mean levels of time on task and interaction in the primary and transfer schools (showing mean values ± standard deviations)

	Cooperating on task		Pupil–pupil interaction		Pupil–teacher interaction	
	Primary [ns]	Transfer***	Primary***	Transfer***	Primary***	Transfer*
alone	56.4 ±34.0	74.8 ± 25.2	10.5 ± 17.6	7.5 ± 13.4	18.0 ± 30.4	40.7 ± 36.7
same sex pair	58.3 ± 30.5	68.3 ± 28.1	38.4 ± 32.5	18.4 ± 21.9	14.7 ± 23.7	44.8 ± 44.4
opposite sex pair	58.6 ± 27.3	84.4 ± 18.5	28.8 ± 21.8	2.2 ± 5.5	10.0 ± 19.1	47.2 ± 44.4
same sex group	63.5 ± 28.7	64.8 ± 29.5	31.9 ± 27.3	24.2 ± 23.7	23.1 ± 31.3	40.9 ± 37.5
opposite sex group	61.5 ± 28.5	60.0 ± 27.8	26.9 ± 25.7	21.3 ± 21.7	22.1 ± 30.3	38.5 ± 37.1
class	65.4 ± 29.2	82.0 ± 19.0	10.2 ± 19.9	11.3 ± 14.9	81.9 ± 26.9	59.9 ± 38.8

Notes: ns = no significant difference between these settings, $*p < 0.05$; $**$ $p < 0.01$; $***$ $p < 0.001$.

interaction, and, at first sight, apparently mark a major change in the way the teacher's attention was distributed. It appears that at primary school 81 per cent of the time spent in whole class groupings involved teacher–pupil interaction, that is four times as much as they received when observed in any other setting. After transfer, however, teacher–pupil interaction was more evenly spread across different seating settings. This probably reflects the greater tendency for primary teachers to bring the class together for any whole class teaching and then for the children to move away to their various bases and work relatively independently. In the transfer schools, on the other hand, it was more likely that the teachers spoke to the whole class, while the pupils remained at their bases. This explanation is supported by Table 6.6 which shows that for only 6 per cent of the seating arrangements in the transfer schools were a whole class grouped together. This perhaps occurred when the whole class was grouped around the front bench in a chemistry laboratory to watch the teacher demonstrate the day's task.

A further way of investigating the distribution of the teacher's attention is to consider how it was distributed across different collaborative working groups which the ORACLE studies have referred to as 'team'.

Changes in work teams on transfer

Great interest in cooperative and collaborative group-work, or 'team', has emerged in the twenty-year interval between the two studies (Webb and Palincsar 1996), and studies of group work have become more sophisti-cated in the interim, as Vygotskian social constructivist principles have eclipsed Piagetian theory in this field (Wood 1998; Joiner et al. 2001). Galton et al. (1980: 69) did not collect 'team' data for each target child, but did iden-tify different types of groupings in primary classrooms such as 'semi-permanent groups' which were brought together for teaching pur-poses in a single subject, and 'evanescent' groups which were formed for specific purposes within a project. They observed that 'though children are typically seated in groups, for the great majority of their time they work as individuals' (Galton et al. 1980: 70). Twenty years on, Galton et al. (1999b: 87) found greater use of whole class team-work, and cooperative group work in primary classrooms, but still noted the mismatch between seating and working groups. In the transfer schools 20 years ago, any form of co-operative group work appears to have been rare. In Moving from the Primary Classroom (Galton and Willcocks 1983) it was reported that the children worked individually for most of the time in the primary-type class-rooms after transfer but engaged in 'almost continuous whole class dialogue' in the secondary-type schools. In the ORACLE transfer replication study, data on teamwork were collected and the results are shown in Table 6.8. It shows that individual work after transfer comprised 72.3 per cent of the team data, an increase of 5.8 per cent compared with the figure for the pre-transfer classrooms. This increase appears to be at the expense of collaborative group work which decreased by almost the same amount. The selection of 'class' to define the team (i.e. the way pupils were expected to work) occurred whenever the participation of the rest of the class was necessary for the target pupil to do his/her task, as in a class discussion, or a quiz, for example. Thus, watching a teacher conduct a demonstration or read a story required the observer to code the *teacher's audience* as 'class'. However, the target pupil's team could be coded as individual, group or class. In Miss Welch's class at Channings, for example, where she read a story and then engaged the pupils in speculation about what would happen in the next chapter, an observer would code *team* as individual during the reading but class during discussion.

Table 6.8 Comparison of pupil team arrangements in primary and transfer schools

Grouping	Primary[b]		Transfer	
	base	*team*	*base*	*team*
individual[a]	4.9	66.6	12.2	72.3
pair	11.3	8.4	35.1	7.6
group	70.6	11.0	46.7	5.1
class	13.2	14.0	6.0	15.0

Notes: (a) Cases coded 'individual' = team as percentage of cases coded 'individual' = base.
  (b) Number of team/base congruent cases as percentage of all cases (N primary = 879; N transfer = 786).

Table 6.8 reveals the now well-established asymmetry of seating versus working arrangements which existed in the 1970s and clearly has continued into the 1990s. The asymmetry consists, at primary level, of the high proportion of observations which showed children sitting in groups (70.6 per cent) but working on individual tasks (66.6 per cent) that is when '*team*' was individual. After transfer, this asymmetry continued though now group seating had been replaced, in part, by paired seating. Nevertheless 72.3 per cent of the tasks were done individually.

If, as the principle would imply, peer interaction and peer tutoring are taking place during group work, observers should have recorded more task-related behaviour in pair and group *team* arrangements. Table 6.9 shows the types of interaction which took place in these settings in the 1996–97 study in the transfer and primary schools. It shows an overall increase in task-related interaction and a decrease in non-task-related activities after transfer in every team setting. In terms of pupil–pupil interaction, placing children in groups rather than pairs improved the ratio of task-related to non-task-related talk among pupils. If the total on-task and non-task figures (shown in Table 6.9) are examined, task-related interactions increase with the size of team, so that 78 per cent of all interactions between the teacher and a whole class team were task-related.

Table 6.9 Task and non-task-related interaction in different work teams (as percentage frequency of within team observations)

Interaction	Individual (N = 568)	Pair (N = 60)	Group (N = 40)	Class (N = 118)
No interaction				
Task related	34.0 (38.1)	17.6 (17.6)	17.0 (16.7)	9.7 (3.7)
Off task	12.9 (18.9)	5.6 (16.1)	12.5 (13.3)	1.8 (4.9)
Pupil–adult interaction				
Task related	25.8 (13.0)	25.0 (8.9)	23.7 (20.9)	67.0 (60.2)
Off task	10.1 (6.5)	10.0 (7.1)	8.4 (6.5)	15.9 (24.1)
Pupil–pupil interaction				
Task related	5.2 (9.5)	24.7 (31.7)	29.3 (29.3)	11.4 (3.8)
Off task	12.0 (14.4)	17.1 (18.6)	9.2 (13.4)	4.2 (3.3)
Total on-task interactions	65.0 (60.6)	67.3 (58.2)	70.0 (66.9)	78.1 (67.7)
Total non-task interactions	35.0 (39.4)	32.7 (41.8)	30.0 (33.2)	21.9 (32.3)

Note: Primary figures in brackets.

Pupil–pupil talk in the transfer schools

Looking more closely at changes in pupils' interaction with one another before and after transfer, Table 6.10 contains information about children's attempts to begin, take part in, and sustain their conversations in class. The figures in Table 6.10 exclude the group of children who interacted with one another most frequently. These pupils will be looked at separately.

First of all, Table 6.10 shows that the total amount of pupil–pupil inter-action, in the last row, was considerably reduced in the transfer schools, and if we look back to Table 6.9, we can see that this applied to task-related interaction as well as to non-task-related talk. In other words, opportunities for peer learning and peer tutoring were reduced in the transfer schools. The first section (column 2) of Table 6.10 tells us a little more about the children's attempts to converse in class. When considered as a proportion of all obser-vations, there was a reduction in all stages of a conversation. Thus in the transfer schools, and as a proportion of all aspects of classroom interaction, as well as time spent not interacting, children were less likely to try to begin or succeed in beginning conversations. Their conversations were also less likely to be sustained for longer than 25 seconds. However, when pupil–pupil interaction was separated from other forms of classroom interaction behaviour (columns 3 and 4), pupils appear to have been more successful in beginning conversations. This category increased form 26.4 per cent of pupil interactions before transfer to 30.1 per cent afterwards. At first, these results in columns 2 and 4 of Table 6.10 appear somewhat contradictory, but they are determined

Table 6.10 Changes in pupil–pupil interaction across transfer

Pupil-pupil interaction	Primary (N = 9174)	Transfer (N = 6782)	Primary (N = 2394)	Transfer (N = 1148)
	Percentage of total observations		Percentage of all pupil–pupil interactions	
pupil BEGINS conversation	6.9**	5.1	26.4	30.1**
pupil RESPONDS to another child	6.1**	4.5	23.5	26.5
pupil TRIES to start conversation	0.7	0.5	2.7	2.8
pupil does not respond	0.8**	0.3	3.1	2.0
interaction lasts more than 25 secs	11.6**	6.5	44.3**	38.6
All pupil–pupil interactions	26.1**	16.9		

Note: Raw score frequencies compared by chi-square (**1%, *5%).

by the overall amounts of pupil–pupil interaction. Overall, in the transfer schools, pupil–pupil talk was reduced from 26 per cent to 16 per cent when expressed as a proportion of all observed classroom behaviour. In other words, pupils talked less among themselves after transfer but a higher proportion of these conversational beginnings were successful. When pupils did succeed in beginning an exchange these were less likely to be sustained beyond 25 seconds (SUST down from 44.3 per cent in the primary to 38.6 per cent in the secondary classroom).

Within this reduced opportunity for pupils to talk to each other, whether in the context of all classroom behaviour or simply within the 16 per cent of time when pupils did interact with each other, conversations were generally much shorter. If such conversations were task-related, then opportunities for effective peer learning in which children could rehearse their arguments and meet conflicts of understanding with their neighbours were severely reduced. On the other hand, many of these pupil conversations could have been unrelated to children's tasks. This was certainly true of pupil–pupil talk in these classrooms twenty years previously. In the 1976 pre-transfer classrooms many pupils worked *intermittently*, that is they worked when the teacher was looking in their direction but went off task if he or she was engaged elsewhere. After transfer with a decrease in individual attention there was less opportunity for this kind of behaviour. Pupils adopted a new strategy called '*easy riding*'. They gave the appearance of working but did so slowly. How far these practices have persisted in today's classrooms will now be considered.

Pupil personae in 1976

Having examined the frequencies and contexts of different types of pupil behaviour in the earlier part of this chapter we turn now to consider how these behaviours might occur together to form pupil styles or 'personae' characteristic of particular contexts or situations. This was done by carrying out cluster analyses of the pupil behaviour and interaction variables in a similar manner to that used for the teachers in Chapter 4. Twenty years ago the four main primary personae were labelled the *attention seekers*, the *intermittent workers*, the *solitary workers* and the *quiet collaborators*. They are described in detail by Galton *et al.* (1980: 144). These personae did not remain unchanged when the pupils moved to the transfer schools, however, because, although they contained 'echoes' of the primary styles, there were 'too many points of divergence for the two sets to be completely equated' (Galton and Willcocks 1983: 61). Instead the post-transfer styles of the late 1970s consisted of:

- *hard grinders*, who like the primary solitary workers, stuck to the task and had were little to do with other pupils or with the teacher except when they were part of his or her audience;
- *group toilers*, a variation of the *hard-grinder* who collaborated on task with the peers whenever instructed to do so by the teacher;
- *easy riders*, who used a pattern of intermittently working when the teacher was nearby, and chatting off task when he or she was elsewhere. They did just enough work to avoid the teacher's disapproval.
- *fuss-pots*, who were often off task, and frequently in contact with the teacher about routine matters. They indulged in a brand of *m'as-tu-vu* helpfulness as a cover for doing very little work.

As we have seen, the present project has shown that patterns of both teacher and pupil behaviour have intensified in primary classrooms, as teachers have increased the time they spend in direct interaction with pupils and become essentially more didactic. This was true even of the *individual monitor* style, which compared to the 1976 version showed average amounts of factual statements and above average amounts of giving directions and routine information to the whole class (Galton *et al.* 1999b: 120). At the same time pupils in general were spending more time on task compared to twenty years ago.

Primary pupil personae in 1996

The ORACLE 1996 replication study also identified pupil personae at primary level, and found that two of the 1976 styles, the *intermittent workers* and the *solitary workers*, were still recognisable with variations, but that two new styles had emerged. Interestingly, at the same time as teaching had

172

become more didactic, the 'attention seeker' persona had virtually disappeared, giving way to *'eager participants'* who were quick to respond to questions, and *'friendly ghosts'*, a persona characterised by high levels of task work, and minimal interaction with the teacher. Instead they spent most of their time passively watching the teacher and other pupils. Galton *et al.* (1999b: 123) give detailed descriptions of these personae.

We turn now to the pupil behaviour data to find the dominant pupil personae in the 1990s' transfer schools. By way of comparison we will go on to look for their closest relatives in the 1996 primary classes and try to find their 'parents' in the 1976 classrooms.

Pupil styles in the transfer schools

The pupil styles were derived from the pupil observations made in science, mathematics and English lessons in the transfer schools and in lessons which were predominantly one of these three curriculum areas in the primary schools. Thus it could be that one child, if observed in all six settings could appear in six different personae. If the same child appeared more than once in any *one* setting, a 'mean' profile was computed. Ultimately 181, 200 and 187 transfer personae and 212, 170 and 96 primary personae were identified in English, mathematics and science respectively. These individual personae were scored on ten major variables and submitted to cluster analysis. These ten variables concerned levels of task work, routine work and distraction, and interaction with teachers and other pupils, as listed in Table 6.11.

Table 6.11 Task-oriented pupil styles in the transfer schools

N personae	Hard grinders Boys 174 Girls 188	Passive participants Boys 128 Girls 153	Group toilers Boys 56 Girls 52
cooperating on task	71.3	84.1	78.1
cooperating on routine	7.5	6.3	9.3
distracted from task work	10.2	2.1	3.8
pupil–adult interaction			
task-related	5.7	64.9	14.1
non-task-related	2.7	9.9	2.5
pupil-pupil interaction			
task-related	6.1	4.0	48.3
non-task-related	11.5	2.2	10.5
no interaction			
task-related	59.5	16.1	16.4
non-task-related	14.6	4.2	10.5
simultaneous			
pupil–pupil and pupil–adult interaction	0.1	1.5	0.7

A nine-cluster solution was selected as making the best sense of the data. This included every persona except two observation records which could not be classified. Three of these nine personae were highly task oriented and included 70 per cent of the pupil records in the analysis. Their characteristics are shown in Table 6.11. The remaining 30 per cent appeared in six task-avoiding styles which are shown in Table 6.12. Where possible we have retained the style names used in the 1976 study providing there was a sufficient degree of correspondence between the characteristics which identified the respective personae.

The first and largest cluster of personae represents a third of the whole sample, and was typical of times when pupils were working on their individual tasks while their teachers were significantly more likely to be working with other individuals (72.8 per cent of observation records), doing administrative tasks (5.2 per cent) or simply monitoring the class (4.5 per cent).

When in this persona, pupils had little interaction with the teacher and engaged in average levels of pupil–pupil interaction. The style is very similar to the 'solitary workers' of the primary classrooms, but most resembles the 1977 'hard grinders' who appear to have proliferated from 8.3 per cent in 1976, to 34.4 per cent of the sample in 1997. The style has become much more common in both primary and transfer schools since the 1970s, but similar proportions, of just over a third of cases, of the primary 'solitary workers' and the transfer 'hard grinders' were seen in 1996.

The second task-oriented cluster included 26.7 per cent of the sample and could be described as teacher-oriented task workers. This style demonstrated the extremely high levels of time on task (84.1 per cent COOPTK), and was involved in some form of teacher–pupil interaction for 64.9 per cent of the time. This style was typical of the behaviour observed when the teachers were addressing the whole class. They showed low levels of interaction with their peers, but were more likely than other pupils to initiate interaction with the teacher although this was rare overall. Such interactions were probably short, as this group showed only average levels of being the 'star' of the teacher's attention, since if the pupil-initiated interaction had lasted more than 25 seconds, then the coding would have changed to 'STAR'. Their closest relations among the 1996 primary personae were 'eager participants' of whom there were only 22 among the primary pupils. So for most of the time this persona appears to have been a passive listener, or what might cynically be regarded as a perfect pupil, who attends to the lesson but does not interrupt. We will call them the 'passive participants', and this persona was observed significantly more often in the transfer classes than those in the primary schools.

The third task-working persona was adopted in 10.3 per cent of the observed lessons, and resembles the 1976 'group toilers' closely enough to retain the same name. In this guise, pupils showed the second highest levels of concentration at 78 per cent cooperating on task, compared with the 84 per cent in the passive participant persona. This style was mostly seen when pupils were collaborating on a task. They spent significantly more time talking about their tasks with other pupils doing the same task and at the same base, than any other persona. They were more likely to start conversations (BGNS 11.5 per cent), to respond to their friends (RSPNDS 10.1 per cent) and engage in sustained interactions lasting at least 25 seconds (SUST 34.9 per cent). Observations of this persona declined significantly across transfer, from 13 per cent of the primary personae to 8 per cent of the transfer personae.

Thus, the overall picture in 1976, was of relatively relaxed pupil types, only 34 per cent of whom were the highly task-oriented 'hard grinders' and 'group toilers', with the majority of pupils (about 60 per cent) using an *intermittent working* or *easy rider* style. By the time of the present study, however, this pattern had altered. The proportion of highly task-oriented personae had doubled, to 70 per cent. 'Hard grinders' were now the most common personae, closely followed by the 'passive participants'. In today's secondary classrooms, therefore, children are working harder although, as we saw in Chapters 3 and 4, the work on which they are engaged does not seem to be more intellectually challenging than it was two decades ago.

The characteristics of the non-task-oriented personae are shown in Table 6.12. They have been combined into three styles, one of which spent more time than most engaged on routine activities, while the second and third showed low levels of task involvement and high levels of distraction.

Table 6.12 The task-avoiding pupil personae in the transfer schools

Behaviour variable	Routine helpers		Distracted ghosts		Attention getters	
	a	b	a	b	a	b
Number of cases Boys	19	35	16	43	38	17
Girls	7	48	18	24	27	10
cooperating on task	44.7	33.1	13.6	25.2	49.3	34.7
cooperating on routine	36.0	51.9	26.0	10.6	8.9	8.6
distracted	5.6	3.8	26.0	47.8	20.4	33.7
teacher–pupil interaction						
on task	27.0	15.1	2.5	5.3	35.0	31.8
off task	10.1	48.8	5.0	5.6	34.0	56.7
pupil–pupil interaction						
on task	4.4	7.0	1.2	8.2	5.4	3.6
off task	7.1	8.8	14.4	52.6	13.2	28.1
no interaction						
on task	13.4	11.2	9.8	11.5	10.5	2.8
off task	38.4	9.9	67.1	18.1	7.3	3.3
simultaneous interaction with teacher and other pupil(s)	0.5	0.6	0.0	1.7	5.5	26.3

It might be unfair to describe the pupils in the first cluster in Table 6.12 as task evaders. They spent significantly more time than other pupils doing routine jobs necessary to sustain their task work. They would be observed sorting out their books, collecting equipment or changing pen cartridges, for example. About 10 per cent of the sample used this style, and of these the majority (four out of five) divided their time between task (44.7 per cent COOPTK) and routine work (36 per cent COOPR) and showed significantly lower levels of distraction than other pupils. They were more frequently seen moving about the classroom, often waiting for the teacher's attention. One in five of this type showed high levels of non-task-related pupil–adult interaction (38.4 per cent). These children were likely to be either helping the teacher with a task such as giving out books, or else the teacher would be urging them to get their materials sorted out and to settle down to their work. Of these 26 'routine helpers', there were nearly three times as many boys (19) than girls (7) and the result was significant ($p < 0.05$ chi-square test). One 10-year-old boy who fitted this type, for example, managed to spend the greater part of a humanities lesson, and many other lessons, repeatedly changing his pen cartridge. Since this was not a lesson where the observer was using systematic observation she went to sit near to him and asked him about his task. The class was required to complete a worksheet about the local trades people a century previously. The boy in question was unable to read the worksheet and in the absence of adult support had decided to concentrate on fixing his perfectly functional pen. This behaviour was somewhat reminiscent of one strategy used by the easy riders of twenty years ago. They would also, on occasions, select legitimate routine activities such as sharpening a pencil as a way of avoiding work they either couldn't or didn't wish to do.

The second main task avoiding group, who constituted 9.6 per cent of the sample, were on task for less than 25 per cent of the time, at best, and two-thirds of them were off task for almost half the time, and typically chatting with other pupils. These pupils were those who started the conversations with their mates, and managed to achieve long sustained interactions without attracting the teacher's attention. The personae in this cluster were more likely to belong to boys rather than girls (43 boys to 24 girls). The other third (34 cases) appeared to divide their time between routine and distracted activities. They rarely interacted with anyone but were very frequently out of their seats, apparently waiting for the teacher while the teacher was interacting elsewhere. Together they were all essentially 'distracted ghosts', who spent considerable amounts of time off task without being noticed. Compared with the 1976–78 pupils, these distracted ghosts bore an even closer resemblance to the easy riders after transfer and the intermittent workers from the primary school. However, they were much less hard working than either of these styles. Whereas the easy riders achieved a mean task-work of 63.7 per cent, the 1996 distracted ghosts were on task on average for only 21.3 per cent of the time. This persona type was less common in the 1990s' transfer classes than in the primary classes.

The third task-avoiding style would seem to include those pupils who were observed in the 'simultaneous' pupil–pupil and pupil–teacher interaction categories and were discussed earlier in the chapter. These pupils were on task for less than half the time, and showed high levels of distraction. In contrast to their peers in the previous cluster, these may well have been the unlucky ones whom the teacher spotted. They were usually in their places, often part of the teacher's wider class audience, but were more often spoken to publicly so that the whole class could hear and take heed. The cluster included more boys than girls (55:37) but the difference was not significant (chi-square). These pupils therefore bore some resemblance to a sub-group of the *attention seekers* in the 1976 primary sample, who might have been labelled *attention getters*. In contrast to the pupils who sought the teacher's help with their work, this sub-group appeared to deliberately set out to attract the teacher's attention. We might speculate as to why these children were noticed when the distracted ghosts, who spent considerably less time on task (and kept up much longer conversations with their friends), were not. It could be that they were more noticeable, had louder voices, or were less subtle in their behaviour.

Typical examples of pupils who attracted more than their fair share of the teacher's attention might be Wayne in Mrs Whistler's class at Maid Marion, who drummed his feet on the floor during Mr Pike's PE lesson and got shouted at, or Seymour in Mrs Staunton's class, both of whom we met in Chapter 3. Another case also involved a Year 5 boy, this time at Gryll Grange, with a shock of blond hair and a tanned face, nicknamed 'Rusty' by one of the teachers. Rusty's attempts to focus on his task were continually interrupted by the rather unassuming-looking boy beside him, who asked compelling questions such as 'What would you say if your girlfriend was being neurotic?' More often than not, Rusty's reply would be noticed, perhaps as he turned his head, while, from the teacher's angle of vision, his talkative friend, who instigated the exchange appeared intent on his work. Another example might be the class 'clown', who attracted attention by making his classmates laugh. For example, a Y7 boy at Danesbury called Stephen was told to come and stand on the teacher's side of the front bench during a science lesson because he had not been paying attention to a demonstration. However, in order to watch what was happening Stephen had to face the class, and was in a prime position to make amusing facial expressions and to pretend to faint with shock as the demonstration proceeded. While the teacher laughed along with the class at first, Stephen warmed to his theme, went too far over the threshold of acceptable fooling and was duly rebuked.

To sum up, the 1996 primary and transfer personae indicate a more hard-working cohort of children than their parents' generation. Figure 6.1

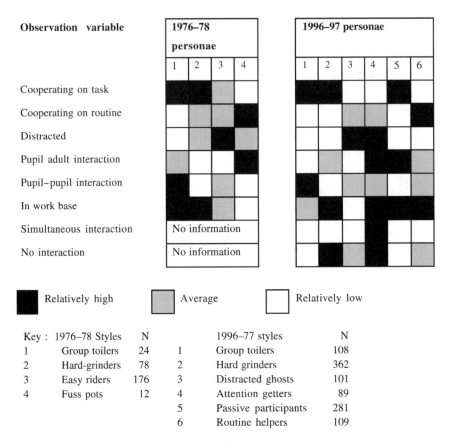

Key : 1976–78 Styles   N   1996–77 styles   N
1   Group toilers   24   1   Group toilers   108
2   Hard-grinders   78   2   Hard grinders   362
3   Easy riders   176   3   Distracted ghosts   101
4   Fuss pots   12   4   Attention getters   89
                               5   Passive participants   281
                               6   Routine helpers   109

Figure 6.1 Comparison of 1976–78 and 1996–97 pupil styles.

illustrates this by comparing the main characteristics of the 1976–78 and 1996–97 transfer personae according to whether these were high, average or low for the whole sample. The two cluster analyses were based on slightly different selections of clustering variables and the levels inserted for the 1976 styles are based on Table 3.7 and Figure 3.1 in Galton and Willcocks (1983: 54–55). The present-day transfer teachers appeared to have forced their pupils into variants of the easy riding strategy designed to cope with the fact that they were now faced by increasing amounts of whole class teaching, particularly at primary level. Nevertheless, 30 per cent of the personae used by the children were task avoiding in a variety of ways compared to the easy riders who made up 60 per cent of the 1976–78 sample. Within this minority, some children, particularly boys, spent little time on task and yet looked busy enough not to be noticed by the teacher. In the original ORACLE study, however, there were considerable variations across the core subjects and we have seen in Chapter 4 of this present volume that English teachers, in particular, adopted a different approach from either their science or mathematics colleagues. We therefore conclude this part of the analysis by looking at differences in the 1996–97 personae across the core subjects.

Pupil personae in English, mathematics and science

By grouping the various profiles together in Figure 6.1 we can contrast 'high' task and 'low' task workers. The high task-working group contains the *group toilers* together with the *hard grinders* and *passive participants*. Low task workers are made up of the *attention getters, routine helpers* and the *distracted ghosts*. Table 6.13 shows the changes in percentage of the high and low task-working personae in the three core subject curriculum areas before and after transfer. Transfer did not appear to have a significant effect on the proportion of high task-working personae in English and mathematics, although in both the original and replication ORACLE studies the trend reflected an increase in the proportions the high task-working personae after transfer. Here, in both cases the ratio of high to low workers increases from approximately 2.3 to 3.5 in English and 2.4 to 3.2 in mathematics after transfer. The results for science, however, went significantly against this trend and resulted in more 'low' task-working personae than expected after transfer. Whereas the ratio before transfer at 2.4 was in line with the corresponding figures for English and mathematics, after transfer the figure drops to 1.7. It has already been suggested in Chapter 4 that in the case of science the lessons observed in the 1977 transfer schools were very similar to those observed in the 1970s. Two decades ago science occupied a relatively small part of the primary curriculum and was not therefore a particular focus of the systematic observation. As a result, it is not possible to make direct comparisons with the earlier ORACLE study. However, as suggested in Chapter 4, today's science teaching after transfer now has much in common with the *individual monitor* style of the 1970s, which was most typical at that time of mathematics teaching. Pupils then coped by adopting either an

Table 6.13 The effects of transfer on personae in English, mathematics and science

| | English | | Mathematics | | Science | |
	Primary	Transfer	Primary	Transfer	Primary	Transfer
High task work	147 (69.3)	140 (77.8)	126 (70.4)	153 (76.5)	67 (70.5)	118 (63.8)
Low task work	65 (30.7)	40 (21.9)	53 (29.6)	47 (23.5)	28 (29.5)	69* (36.2)
Ratio	2.26	3.55	2.37	3.25	2.39	1.71
No. of personae	212	180	179	200	95	185

Notes: Raw frequencies with column percentages in brackets.
* Significantly more than expected.

179

intermittent worker or *'easy rider'* personae in order to reduce the time spent completing worksheets of 'maths examples'. Pupils might have adopted a similar strategy during the 1990s' science lessons in the post-transfer schools and this would have explained the drop in the proportions of high task-worker personae. A further hypothesis, however, is that there was a gender effect at work, so this will be considered in the next section.

The relationships between gender and levels of task work across transfer

Table 6.14 displays the effects of transfer on boys' and girls' personae and shows a decrease in the number of boys who maintained a high task-working personae, and a significant increase in the number of girls who became high task workers. For boys the ratio of high to low task workers decreased from 2.28 to 1.95 after transfer but for girls the trend was strongly in the other direction (from 2.36 to 3.61).

Table 6.14 Gender composition of high and low task-working pupil styles across transfer

Personae	Boys % personae		Girls % personae	
	Primary	Transfer	Primary	Transfer
high task workers	69.6	64.8	70.3	78.3*
low task workers	30.4	33.2	29.7	21.7
ratio	2.28	1.95	2.36	3.61
number of personae	240	286	246	281

Note: *Significantly more than expected (chi-square, based on raw frequencies, $p < 0.05$).

This finding contributes to recent concerns about boys' achievement levels in secondary schools. In the previous chapter, we saw that boys' enjoyment and motivation levels tended to decline during their first year in the transfer school. It would appear that this dip in attitude is accompanied by the adoption of various task-avoiding strategies. In contrast, girls tended to shift to high task-working types, with the increased likelihood that they will reach higher achievement levels. In the opening section of Chapter 3 it was shown that girls were mostly looking forward to English but less to science whereas for boys it was the reverse. Both boys and girls, however, were apprehensive about mathematics. It is of interest, therefore, to see how the subsequent reality of the situation matched anticipation at the time of transfer in so far that attitudes to the subject are reflected in part by the pupils' behaviour in class. We can pursue this matter further by looking at the distribution of high and low task-working personae by gender across different curriculum areas.

Table 6.15 Transfer pupil personae in the core curriculum areas. (Actual numbers of personae, with column percentages in parentheses)

Personae	English		Mathematics		Science	
	Boys	Girls	Boys	Girls	Boys	Girls
high task work	145	142	130	149*	83	102
	(72.5)	(74.0)	(69.1)	(78.0)	(60.1)	(70.8)
low task work	55	50	58	42	55	42
	(27.5)	(26.0)	(30.9)	(22.0)	(39.9)	(29.2)
total	200	192	188	191	138	144

Note: *Significantly more girls than expected in high task-working personae in mathematics (chi square $p < 0.05$).

Table 6.15 shows the proportion of boys and girls in high and low task-working contexts in the three core subjects. In English, boys' and girls' personae are equally represented in both high and low task-working types. In mathematics, however, significantly more girls were in high task-working personae, while in science the relatively high proportion of boys in the low task-working group just failed to reach statistical significance. Perhaps science afforded more opportunities, such as when getting equipment or appearing to be doing practical work, for these boys to be diverted from their tasks. Both Tables 6.13 and 6.15, however, only provide the subject totals irrespective of whether a pupil who was a high worker in mathematics after transfer was also included in the mathematics group before transfer. This would only have come about if at least a substantial number of observations on that pupil in the primary school had taken place during mathematics lessons. A more exacting measure of how pupils fared when they moved schools is to include only pupils who have a persona in a subject both before and after transfer. Although the sample is reduced, there is more control over other possible extraneous factors. In the next section, therefore, we look more closely at the personae of children who were observed in the same curriculum areas in both primary and secondary classes.

What happened to individual pupils and their personae after transfer?

In the original ORACLE project, the observers tracked the same sample of target children throughout the project. This policy had led to some difficulties in locating these pupils after transfer. In the present study, therefore, a new policy was adopted in which observers selected a new random sample of targets for each observed lesson. Subsequently, 149 pupils were identified who had been observed in both primary and secondary classes, and these constitute a small longitudinal cohort within the large overall sample. The effect of transfer on these children's classroom personae was traced and showed a general movement away from high task-worker personae to the more distracted, low task worker types. Although the effect failed to reach significance, the trend away from the high task-working type is noticeable.

In English for example, 39 pupils were observed in both phases. Of these, 6 kept the same personae, 9 pupils moved from high to low task-working styles, but 4 were 'rescued' and became 'high task' workers. In mathematics, among the 37 pupils with pre- and post-transfer maths personae, 10 did not change style, but 6 pupils moved into the 'distracted ghost' task avoiding persona. In science, only 17 children were observed with pre- and post-transfer personae. Three of these pupils kept the same high task-working styles, and 5 were 'rescued' from low task work styles to becoming 'passive participants'. Six, however, moved to the distracted, low task work personae. Although the numbers are small, it does confirm the trend seen in Table 6.13.

We have shown here that among the children who were observed before and after transfer in the same curriculum areas, some made gains after transfer. However, between one in seven, as in English, and one in three, as in science, appear to have been unable or reluctant to adapt their classroom strategies to the needs of the transfer school regimes and as a result moved to the distracted personae. While this might be expected to have cumulative and deleterious effects in time on their attitudes to school and their motivation, it is also likely to be critical for their future achievements. Before leaving this topic, therefore, we examined the relationships between personae and achievement levels for those children for whom an adequate data set was available.

The children were divided into three attainment groups, on the basis of the tests of basic skills administered in this project, according to whether their test marks placed them in the top 25 per cent, the bottom 25 per cent or the middle 50 per cent of the sample. When the attainment groups were broken down across all six main persona types, the differences between the clusters were not significant at either primary or secondary levels. When they were combined, however, into high and low task work groups some significant differences did emerge by the end of the first year in the transfer schools. Pupils were given a score of 3 if they were in the top quartile, 2 in the middle range and 1 in the bottom quartile. Hard workers averaged 2.15 (SD = 0.74; $n = 101$) compared to a figure of 1.79 (SD = 0.62; $n = 29$) for the low working cohort. This difference was significantly different ($t = -2.36$, $p < 0.02$) in favour of the high task workers.

In conclusion, this chapter has shown that on moving from the primary classroom, children have to adapt to spending more time on task, and to spending an even greater amount of the day listening to the teacher, usually as a part of a whole class audience. In addition, they have to adjust to working with a variety of different teachers, in different curriculum areas, with each teacher interpreting his or her role accordingly. At the same time many of the children are trying to make friends, but now have fewer opportunities during lessons for conversation with their new classmates either to talk about their work, or about other things. When pupils do attempt to communicate with peers, some of them are more likely to be noticed by the teacher. When these conversations are not about work, teachers will be quick to nip them in the bud. About 70 per cent of the children, and particularly girls, appear to have managed to maintain or to adopt work-styles which dovetail with their teachers' requirements. They become adept at listening or looking as though they are listening, at answering questions when asked but rarely taking the initiative by asking questions. Alternatively, or at different times, they work individually, refusing to be distracted by friends, and often unnoticed by the teacher. At times they will often watch the teacher or other pupils to see what they are doing while not interrupting the latter. The single largest group of classroom personae was of this 'classroom ghost' variety.

The children who were able to adopt these passive, subdued classroom styles achieved higher attainment levels at the end of their first year in the transfer schools. The remaining children, three in every ten, were not able to adapt so successfully. They were on task for less than half the time they were observed and in some cases almost a little as 10 per cent of the time. They adopted one of three styles, becoming teacher helpers, or doing routine chores rather than working at the same level as hard workers. By managing to work intermittently they were able to find some opportunities for chatting with friends. A third highly interactive group were frequently the subject of the teacher's attention while communicating with their peers. In terms of change over the past two decades, while a higher proportion of children are working harder, those that opted out of this arrangement showed even lower levels of time on task and moved to more extreme types of task avoidance behaviour. Inevitably, there were negative effects on their attitudes to school and their attainment levels. For those who succeeded, their experience of learning had become one of passive acceptance of teacher talk, and solitary work. Most of these distracted pupils were boys.

Transfer in today's schools are places where it is possible to observe greater extremes of pupils' behaviour than twenty years ago. More pupils are on task even if these tasks are not particularly challenging. These pupils seem to have absorbed the message from one of the 'New School Gates' activity where a girl wrote that she was coming to school 'because her mum said she needed her education'. When, however, the behaviour of the group of pupils who reject this message is linked to the findings of other studies concerning the dips in attitudes of Year 8 pupils, it is clear that some attention needs to be given to the curriculum and teaching in the early secondary years. We turn to this issue in the concluding chapter.

Note

1 The 1996 figures may differ by 1 or 2 per cent from those given by Galton *et al.* (1999b) because further analysis in which observation sheets with simultaneous interaction codings resulting in sums greater than 100 per cent were identified in the transfer data. This small proportion of cases was excluded from the analyses comparing primary and transfer pupil data. None of the discrepancies is substantive and they do not alter the conclusions in Galton *et al* (1999b).

7

TRANSFER

A future agenda

Maurice Galton and Linda Hargreaves

The findings set out in the preceding chapters, hopefully, make interesting reading for both teachers and for those charged with the management of our education system at various levels. In some respects, when compared to what took place two decades earlier, the business of moving from primary to secondary school has changed a great deal. In other respects, however, particularly when considering pupils' day-by-day experiences in the classroom, fewer changes are detectable. This is despite the introduction of the National Curriculum and the operation of a rigorous accountability system involving both regular inspection and testing. Classrooms appear to possess some of the properties of a semi-permeable membrane in the physical process of osmosis. It is difficult to upset the equilibrium between the solutions on either side of the membrane unless considerable external force is applied. In the same way classrooms seem to resist all kinds of external pressure for changes in practice, with the result that the curriculum experiences of the present day Year 7 pupils appear to be remarkably similar to that of their parents who entered secondary school in the 1970s.

As described in Chapter 2, some major changes, mainly concerned with liaison arrangements between the feeder and the transfer schools, have been instituted since the original ORACLE transfer study took place in the academic years 1977–78 and 1978–79. Twenty years ago, it was not unusual for pupils in their last year at primary school to make a brief half-day visit to their new school in the final weeks of the summer term before transfer. There, a 'volunteer' older pupil, who did not usually regard the task with any great enthusiasm, would take these 'new kids' for a 'guided tour' of the various buildings. Both the tour and the commentary were often perfunctory. It was not unusual for the crocodile to stop outside a classroom and for the new pupils to be merely told that 'This is where you do French'. The teacher might come to the door of the classroom and inside would be thirty pairs of hostile eyes daring the newcomers to cross the threshold (Delamont and Galton 1986: 29). For parents there would be an introductory meeting at the transfer school at which they could bring their children. The main item on the agenda would be school uniform. Parents were informed about what it was legitimate for their son or daughter to wear and provided with the names of approved retailers where such items might be purchased. They were given strict instructions about where to sew name tabs. Then would follow an unsupervised tour of the school where senior pupils were to be found carrying out experiments in the science laboratory, mounting displays in history or geography and baking cakes in what was then known as the domestic science area. Not surprisingly, levels of anxiety among the new pupils were fairly high.

In today's schools, however, all this has changed. Partly, because of the need to compete for pupils, schools now commence the liaison programme at the start of the pupils' final year in the primary school. Parents are welcomed to the transfer school during the autumn term and provided with a glossy information brochure. Throughout the year feeder schools are encouraged to make use of secondary school's special facilities such as the drama studio, the computer room and the science laboratory. Teachers from the transfer school regularly visit the pre-transfer pupils to talk with the pupils and sometimes to teach a lesson. Teachers, including headteachers, meet regularly to exchange information. Some pyramids have special INSET days when staffs from different schools meet to share ideas. All these liaison activities were described in Chapter 2. Over and above these various activities, and more importantly, nearly every transfer school in the country now holds at least one induction day. On these days children get an opportunity to familiarise themselves with their new surroundings before the summer holidays. In most cases pupils will be given the experience of what are said to be some typical lessons, use the gym facilities and learn how to choose and pay for school dinners. Since the survey of pupils' likes and dislikes, presented in Chapter 5, showed that school dinners, sport and PE were high on the list of things pupils were looking forward to with anticipation, the result of all this effort has been that anxiety levels have fallen considerably. Indeed, it could be argued that it would be unprofitable to do more in this respect since some degree of anxiety or, more properly, apprehension tinged with excitement, must be a consequence of the move from primary to secondary school. This is because, as explained an earlier chapter, transfer marks a 'status passage' from childhood to young adulthood. Such passages must be marked by a certain degree of discontinuity so that those involved can fully appreciate the change in circumstances. Thus schools have a difficult task of balancing the need to ensure that transfer is administratively straightforward, and not too disturbing for children, while at the same time maintaining sufficient difference so pupils are aware that they are now entering into a new phase of their 'life course cycle' (Kvalsund 2000: 402).

In the original ORACLE study the decision by some of the schools to isolate children in the first year from the rest of the pupils and to deliver the curriculum in a similar manner to that in their former school was not altogether successful. Although, initially, these pupils were concerned that work in the transfer school might be too hard and difficult, making it seem too much like that undertaken in the previous school did create a problem since some of the more advanced pupils complained that they were 'wasting time doing old work'. Most of the schools in this present study opted for the alternative strategy and from the first days provided a curriculum which was structured along traditional secondary lines. Whatever approach was taken, however, there were few fundamental changes in either the content or the delivery of the curriculum compared to that offered in the same transfer schools two decades earlier. At the same time the promotion of specialist subject teaching in primary schools and the consequent increases in the proportion of whole class teaching have made lessons in the top year of the pre-transfer school appear very similar to those that pupils experience after transfer. In Year 6 of the primary school the need to ensure good results in the National Curriculum Tests has, in many instances, led to a dominance of teaching as direct instruction with less emphasis on creativity and intellectual challenge. This was precisely the situation that existed at lower secondary level in those schools which took part in the original ORACLE study. The fact that there has been little change in the delivery of the curriculum in these transfer schools over the two decades now means that there is little that is unfamiliar to pupils when they move schools. This, as we have seen in Chapter 5, appears to be accompanied by less enjoyment of school, less enthusiasm for the teachers and their methods, and a drop in motivation. As a result, there still exists a hiatus in some pupils' progress, albeit on a smaller scale than two decades ago.

An important difference from the original ORACLE study is that this decline in attitudes and in motivation manifests itself mainly amongst the high attaining group rather than within the group of pupils who make less progress after transfer. This is particularly true of boys who do well academically. Both Chapter 5 dealing with attitudes and Chapter 6 dealing with behaviour identify important gender differences that go some way to help explain why the gap in achievement between boys and girls widens at this age.

As Jean Rudduck's work demonstrates, time in the lower secondary school is often regarded by these de-motivated pupils as 'fallow years' (Galton *et al.* 1999a). Pupils do not appear to make connections between the work they do in Years 7 and 8 and the results they are likely to obtain some years later in their GCSE. Indeed, one is sometimes struck, when interviewing pupils about transfer, by the relatively undemanding standards that they apply in order to reach a judgement that their school and its teachers are 'OK'. To the question, 'What does OK mean?' they often reply 'They [the teachers] don't shout at you' and 'the work is the same we did at primary school but more complex'. In the case of mathematics, more complex work turns out to mean that instead of doing a 'half by a quarter fractions' we do a 'half by a quarter by one eighth'. Even given that pupils of this age, particularly boys, are prone to understatement, it is intriguing, nevertheless, that so few children report that they are excited by the teaching of their favourite subjects and stimulated by the challenge. Most of the pupils interviewed adopt a pragmatic viewpoint. To the question, 'If you're not enjoying school why are you still trying to do well?' they will often reply, 'Because I need my education'.

Structural deficiencies in the present transfer system

Given what has taken place in the primary sector over the immediate past decade, particularly the development of a 'shame and blame' culture with the former Chief Inspector of Schools in the vanguard, there will be some who wish to lay the blame for the weaknesses in the transfer process on the schools and in particular on the teachers. But as a recent review by Anderson *et al.* (2000) shows, the situation described in the English schools in the previous chapters has parallels elsewhere, particularly in the United States. Like our own educational system, that in the United States is fragmented. There are transitions out of elementary school into the middle or junior high school and then from the middle or junior high school to the high school. Most students experience some hiatus in progress (Blyth *et al.* 1983; Petersen and Crockett 1985; Roderick 1993; Catterall 1998). Less positive attitudes towards subjects and an increasing dislike of teachers have also been reported (Haladyna and Thomas 1979; Hirsch and Rapkin 1987). Self-esteem also declines (Eccles and Midgley 1989; Wigfield *et al.* 1991). In the United States, for most children, these setbacks do not appear to be permanent handicaps and this is probably also true in this country, although there is no systematic evidence to support this assertion (Midgley *et al.* 1991). As in the present study, however, where about 7 per cent of the pupils experienced a serious hiatus in progress (greater than two standard deviations), there were also some pupils in the United States where the transfer from one school to another had serious consequences (Lord *et al.* 1994). These children were followed over a number of years and were highly likely to drop out of school before graduating (Roderick 1993; Scott *et al.* 1995). Students who learned to manage their time and could work independently of the teacher had the best chance of success (Ward *et al.* 1982).

Anderson *et al.* (2000: 326–327) attribute most of these problems to a number of factors. Among these are the increased size of the campus and the large number and the complex mix of students, streaming, less tolerance by the school authorities of 'high spirits' with greater emphasis on rules and a decrease in the students' personal relationships with their teachers. Before transfer, American pupils have many of the same concerns as those reported in the present study. They worry about getting to class on time, finding a space to put their books, dealing with crowds and getting lost (Weldy 1991; Mizelle 1995; Wells 1996). They are also very concerned about receiving lower or failing grades (Mizelle and Mullins 1997). But there are also some differences. After transfer American pupils report that their courses are more difficult, their teachers more strict and that they find it harder to make new friends (Scott *et al.* 1995; Wells 1996).

It would seem, therefore, that the transfer problem is not specific to English schools. This would suggest that it is not merely a case of teachers not taking the issue of curriculum continuity sufficiently seriously. It is abundantly clear that most teachers do their best to ensure that the move to the 'big school' is a reasonably enjoyable experience for new pupils. Visits to the pre-transfer schools are often undertaken in the time allocated for marking and preparation resulting in the loss of precious free periods. Considerable amounts of time are spent processing test results and writing reports to ensure that the pupils are placed in appropriate bands and sets. As we have demonstrated, this has resulted in considerable improvements in the way that transfer is organised in most English schools. In this they appear to have progressed much further than their American counterparts (Anderson *et al.* 2000). To tackle the remaining transfer problems, particularly those identified in the previous chapters, it may therefore be more important to explore whether the structural limitations inherent in our school system are preventing further progress rather than merely seeking to place all the blame on teachers for the present hiatus.

One of the key structural impediments would appear to be the National Curriculum as it is presently constituted and, in particular, the supposed links between Key Stage 2 and Key Stage 3. As discussed in the opening chapter, one of the aims of instituting a National Curriculum was to ensure increased curriculum continuity between primary and secondary school. The evidence from this present study suggests that this particular aim has not been fully realised. Part of the reason for this failure can be attributed to the manner in which the then National Curriculum Council (NCC) went about its task. Back in 1989, the then Secretary of State for Education, Kenneth Baker and the chief executive, Duncan Graham, took the decision to dispense with a special committee to plan the Key Stage 1 and Key Stage 2 curriculum in the core and foundation subjects. This followed the experience of constituting an Interim Primary Committee which, as related by one of its two University members (Galton 1995), was hurriedly disbanded within a year of being formed and its report handed over to NCC officials for redrafting. Despite the strong pleas of the dismissed committee members that the NCC should retain a working party with specific responsibility for primary education, albeit with new membership, the then Chief Executive of the National Curriculum Council, Duncan Graham, proceeded to reject this view. Instead, nominal primary representatives were invited to participate in the deliberations of the various subject panels. Secondary representatives drawn from schools, the advisory service, Higher Education and members of the Inspectorate dominated these panels. As argued in the Introduction, one of the main consequences of this decision was that, inevitably, the curriculum at Key Stage 2 increasingly took on a secondary look with the emphasis on the subject matter content. This approach was consolidated with the eventual replacement of Duncan Graham by Chris Woodhead.

Constructing a National Curriculum

When planning a curriculum, particularly where the subject has a linear development, secondary teachers tend to approach the task as an exercise in formal logic. They start at the desired end point and then work backwards so that, for example, if it were thought necessary in science that pupils of a certain age should be able to understand the concept of density, then they would first have to study pressure. To do this they would need to understand forces and for this they must be able to distinguish between mass and weight. Those building a primary curriculum, however, tend to start at the beginning by asking what it is a child already knows and then seeking to expand this knowledge. Primary teachers do not now conceive of the child's mind as an empty vessel waiting to be topped up. Rather they accept that most children have acquired, at least, a partial understanding of phenomena that they encounter in their daily lives. Thus, for example, 9-year-old children when asked what a shadow was had different ideas (Bennett 1991: 9). Some thought an object blocking out the sun caused one's shadow. Others thought that a person acted as a mirror and reflected the sunbeam onto the floor. One pupil thought it was a 'little black thing' that was attached to your leg like a balloon. The Interim Primary Committee accepted this 'constructivist' approach and argued it was therefore important to leave teachers to choose the subject matter but to establish clear frameworks within which children could gradually understand what it was to work as a scientist, historian, a writer and so on. Thus in history it would be important within this framework that children should appreciate the nature of historical evidence and in doing so learn how to retrieve and interpret documents from the past. To achieve this goal it appeared sensible to harness the children's own experience by setting the framework within the context of some local history project rather than Julius Caesar's invasions of Britain. In similar manner the importance of understanding ideas such as fair testing in science could best be approached as part of a local environmental topic so that children in rural primary schools would explore an aspect of farming such as crop rotation, and so on. It was hoped that pupils leaving primary school with these understandings, allied to a firm grasp of the 'so-called' basic skills would be in the best position to profit from a challenging secondary curriculum. In the view of secondary experts, however, particularly those representing the then Conservative government on these various subject committees, this approach was a non-starter. Each committee therefore set about the task of selecting content from the early secondary years' curriculum which was deemed suitable for primary-aged children. The criteria for inclusion appeared to be, first, that it was thought by these adults to be sufficiently interesting to stimulate the pupils' imagination and, second, it formed a logical progression so that one topic built upon another.[1] This subject matter was then incorporated into the statutory programmes of study.

This decision had two main consequences. First, it created an over-prescriptive, overcrowded primary curriculum which Ron Dearing (1993) attempted unsuccessfully to rescue. Second, it left Key Stage 3 in some confusion. Key Stage 4 was virtually untouchable since it was firmly grounded in the demands of the public examinations at 16. The universities through the various Examining Boards largely controlled GCSE content. Key Stage 3 was left with all that was not included in Key Stage 4 or which had not been transferred down to Key Stage 2. Not surprisingly, it lacked any overall clear structure or a set of principles which might have provided teachers with an explicit rationale for their lesson planning. This uncertainty then had a knock-on effect in the development of the assessment targets and the levels of attainment which were linked into the programmes of study. At no point in the development of these programmes, other than applying criteria based on face validity, was there any serious effort to assess the degree of comparability of these attainment levels between the different Key Stages. Many Key Stage 3 teachers having previously established a curriculum in science or history which had a degree of coherence therefore continued to retain this structure, and in so doing re-taught some of the work which was now part of Key Stage 2. Giving this approach they did not see the need to liaise with their primary colleagues.[2]

Making a fresh start at transfer

There are other reasons why the view that it is best to begin at the beginning, even if this means revising work previously done at Key Stage 2, is such a strong imperative among teachers in the transfer school. First, the books which primary schools pass on to the Key Stage 3 subject coordinators often contain pupils' 'best work' which in the course of time has been corrected, discussed and then redrafted. As such it does not compare with work produced in the middle of a 40-minute lesson or as a result of a hurried homework session between tea and *EastEnders*. Second, scores obtained on the National Curriculum Tests at Key Stage 2 are often the product of excessive coaching prior to the examination because of the high stakes involved. As any reader who has sat a public examination, and absorbed large amounts of information prior to the event, will know such detail is not retained in significant amounts within the long-term memory. Furthermore, the extended summer vacation also has a further limiting effect on the pupils' capacity to retain what has been learned in the final year at primary school. It is not therefore surprising if pupils in their first few weeks at the transfer school are unable to perform at their predicted levels.

191

All the above factors reinforce the strong ingrained belief held by many teachers that starting from scratch again is fairer to pupils because 'it gives everyone a chance to show what they can do'. For this reason some teachers in both the original ORACLE transfer study and its more recent replication told observers that they 'didn't look at the pupils' records till Christmas' for fear of activating so-called 'expectancy effects'. Thus an uncertain curriculum with no clear perceived rationale, which has been the subject of constant review, coupled with the belief that every pupil should be given a 'fresh start', helps to explain much of what the observers saw during their visits to the transfer school, particularly the increased amounts of testing which took place at the beginning of the school year.

The limiting effects of the secondary timetable

There are also other structural impediments that help to explain why the pupils experienced the curriculum and the teaching described in our study. The secondary school timetable, as it is currently arranged in most schools, is relatively inflexible. In the transfer schools in this present study teaching periods generally lasted between 40 minutes and an hour. At least 5 minutes of this time was taken up with pupils moving down corridors in order to leave the room where they had done French to get to the room where they were going to do music, science or PE. Since most secondary teachers prefer to teach across the widest possible age range, so that they have some of the better motivated examination classes, it often means that the person taking history in Year 7 sees the class two times in a week. By the time that the Christmas vacation arrives this teacher will be lucky if when writing the end of term reports he or she can put names to all the pupils in the class. This will be particularly the case if the pupil concerned happens to be fairly shy and reserved and has not attracted the teacher's attention, either by volunteering to answer questions more frequently than others in the class or engaging in occasional bouts of unacceptable behaviour. In these circumstances teachers will tend to balance the time it would take to get to know individuals in the class, by going through lists of pupils' test scores and the comments from the feeder schools, against the possible damage done to the pupils' attitudes by several lessons of revision. Unlike their primary colleagues these teachers do not have the luxury of extending the length of a lesson in order to allow pupils to finish off a particular task. What can't be done in one period with the class must be left at the point where it can be picked up at the next lesson. Mrs Diepers' lesson on the Battle of Hastings in Chapter 4 illustrates this dilemma perfectly. Allowing the time for pupils to engage in speculation and develop their ideas often conflicts with the need to reach a convenient point where a lesson can be terminated successfully. Time must also be allowed for stragglers to catch up before the next lesson. Hence the practice of letting the quicker children begin homework towards the end of a session

192

which allows other slower workers to complete the work done during class before the next lesson.

Linking the primary and the secondary school

A further limiting factor concerning primary–secondary liaison has to do with the roles and responsibilities of middle management within the secondary school. The Head of First Year's role is primarily a pastoral one. His or her task is to make certain that the transition takes place smoothly and with the minimum of anxiety for pupils. This study has demonstrated that First Year Coordinators have been very successful in fulfilling these roles. While they may appreciate the need for greater curriculum continuity, they will be conscious that this lies outside their remit since it is the responsibility of the Subject Coordinators. Heads of first year will be anxious lest their efforts are perceived by subject leaders as interference. While it is true that many schools have tried to solve this problem by encouraging more of these subject specialists to visit the feeder schools, and even on some occasions to teach lessons alongside the primary teacher, it remains often the case that the subject leaders do not teach Year 7 classes. They cannot therefore put these experiences directly into practice. Instead they have to rely on passing the messages on to other colleagues.

Where such initiatives have been developed within the subject areas, there has been little formal evaluation of their effect. This is partly because teachers are too busy coping with the daily demands of teaching, marking and administration and partly because there are few materials available which can be used by teachers to elicit the required information about the effectiveness of their curriculum initiatives. In these circumstances, where informal evaluations are attempted, it is all too easy to rate an initiative successful, particularly when the teacher concerned has devoted an immense amount of personal effort at the development and implementation stages.

There are also untested assumptions about the effectiveness of teaching methods in the primary schools. These often militate against a smooth transition between the primary and secondary phase. Two decades ago it was not uncommon for secondary teachers to think of primary schools as centres of 'undisciplined' learning: 'It was fun but not too serious.' Since the introduction of the National Curriculum and the increasing number of visits that secondary teachers pay to the primary schools, this view has changed. Within our study it was common to hear the First Year tutors or other visiting teachers praise what they saw in the primary school. They would often refer to the quality of the group work, the questioning techniques employed by the teachers and the value of the relationships established between the teacher and the pupils. But the data in Chapter 4 clearly show that this is, in part, a misreading of the situation in today's top junior classrooms. The demands of the National Curriculum and the National Curriculum tests, the pressure by OFSTED to increase the amounts of whole class teaching have all combined to establish a very secondary-style curriculum in Year 6. It may be, of course, that many of these visits take place in the final weeks of the summer term when the preparations for the tests have been completed and the atmosphere is more relaxed. Nevertheless, this present study clearly demonstrates that from the pupils' perspective the pedagogic diet in Year 6 and Year 7 is remarkably similar. Pupils are asked approximately the same amounts of factual questions. Teachers make approximately the same amounts of statements, again mostly to do with the acquisition of facts. There are relatively few opportunities where children are challenged. While the classroom organisation varies, although with the advent of the Literacy and Numeracy Hours, the disparities will be even less, the intellectual demands made appear to be very similar. Thus the idea held by some secondary teachers that it is acceptable to do more formal work because pupils have already had considerable experience of working in informal settings is no longer true even if it ever was. The net result, compared to two decades ago, is that it is now among high attaining pupils where motivation and enjoyment of school have seriously declined during the first year after transfer. It is these pupils who before transfer said they were looking forward to new subjects and increased challenge at secondary school. When they fail to discover this intellectual stimulation they appear to become demoralised, although continuing to work hard because they realise the importance of achieving good grades at the end of secondary school.

The dilemmas of transfer

Finally, in constructing a suitable programme for the first half of the autumn term after transfer, schools face a dilemma. Some pupils want everything to be new and exciting and very different from their previous school. These pupils appreciate the resulting discontinuities because they associate them with their change in status which marks the transition from child to young adult. Other pupils may be less enthusiastic about the move to the big school and are reassured when they find that some things, particularly the teaching and the schoolwork, resemble what took place before transfer. Between these extremes are other children who want things to be different but not too different. Schools appear to find it difficult to strike the correct balance in the attempt to meet the new pupils' needs. Thus the preferred strategy at Maid Marion to begin the normal timetable once the formalities of writing names on homework books and copying out the classroom rules had been completed, was part of an attempt to get the children settled as soon as possible into the new ways of working. Teachers and senior pupils hovered over the newcomers at lunch time making sure that there was no excessive queuing so that nobody was late for afternoon registration and classes could start on time. After two days the system was running as normal and the new pupils were indistinguishable in appearance from their older peers.

At the other extreme, schools such as Channings allowed time to pass before beginning to insist that the new pupils conformed to the established structures. In Channings, during the first few weeks of the autumn term, dinnertime was often extended and the first lesson period after lunch cut short to allow children to familiarise themselves with unfamiliar routines. Pupils were at first allowed to talk while waiting for Assembly to begin as they had done at their previous schools. Teachers only began to stop this practice and to insist on silence after several days had passed. These differences in approach may also influence the ways in which pupils who are 'at risk' as the result of transfer are identified and supported. Schools that believe in stressing the discontinuities between the pre- and post-transfer school from day one of the new term tend, from the outset, to lay stress on obeying the rules and good academic performance. Pupils at risk are therefore those who either misbehave or who do badly at their work. Schools that adopt a more relaxed approach at transfer tended to focus on the pupils' capacity to deal independently with problems that arose without recourse to the teachers. Thus at Cannings and Gryll Grange teachers rarely commented when a pupil arrived late for school, or failed to bring the right books or equipment. For example, a pupil who forgot his pen would be expected to borrow from a neighbour. Pupils at risk in this situation are those who can't easily establish supportive networks with their peers and become too dependent on adults for support.

What schools are doing about transfer

It should not be thought, however, that schools have not tried to respond to the challenges outlined in the previous paragraphs. In the last few years there have been a number of national initiatives designed to reduce the hiatus in progress and the resulting consequences. Such schemes include the summer schools for literacy and numeracy, sometimes referred to as 'catch up classes', which take place during the holidays, and the development by the QCA of so-called 'bridging units'. Many LEAs and schools have either adapted these curriculum materials or developed their own. In science, a booklet called *Bubbles*, designed by Cheshire teachers has proved very successful and has been taken up by other LEAs. Another example, entitled *Moving On Up* has been produced by Birmingham LEA. These bridging units are begun in the feeder schools once the National Curriculum testing has finished. The books are then handed over to the transfer school and the work continued when the pupils arrive at the beginning of the new school year. Some LEAs have units in all three-core subjects. This is because there is evidence to suggest that a successful experience in, say, English is rarely, if ever, communicated to colleagues in other subject departments of the secondary school.

The decision to make use of bridging units is related to the earlier discussion about the balance schools must attempt to strike between improving continuity while, at the same time, making life after transfer sufficiently different. The existence of these differences are important in that they can provide pupils with external criteria to judge whether they have successfully accomplished the 'life change' from child to young adult (Pietarinen 2000: 386). It is likely, therefore, that a school such as Maid Marion would hesitate before using units of this kind, because it delayed the new pupils' total immersion into the secondary culture, while at Channings staff might find them a more attractive proposition. In Phase Two of the DfEE project, *The Impact of Transitions and Transfers on Pupil Progress and Attainment*[3] (Galton *et al.* 1999a), pupils' reactions to bridging units have been solicited. While some have enjoyed the work others have complained that 'They don't see why they should do primary school work in the secondary school.'

There are also logistical problems in handling such units in that it is sometimes left to the pupil to ensure the work done in the last few weeks in the primary school accompanies them when they arrive in secondary school on the first day of the new academic year. Where there is a well-established pyramid it is usual for one of the teachers, either the subject coordinator in the feeder school or the first year coordinator in the transfer school, to arrange collection. However, the breakdown of the traditional pyramid because of increasing competition for school places may often mean that some pupils have not done this work prior to coming to the new school. They then have to be paired with another pupil or asked to do extra work to catch up. In some cases teachers in the feeder schools fail to mark the books before handing them on so that colleagues in the transfer school have little idea about the standards being applied across the pyramid. These problems may be exacerbated where pupils attempt all three units in science, mathematics and English. Less valuable outcomes result when the purpose of doing such work is not totally clear to all the teachers, particularly those in the transfer school. The original intention of the QCA in developing these units was to transfer work that could then be built upon in the secondary school in ways that ensured a smooth progression was achieved for each pupil. It appears from the preliminary evaluation carried out for Phase Two of the DfEE Transfer and Transition Project that many teachers do not always appreciate the QCA's purpose. They regard the unit as valuable because it provides familiar work and therefore has the potential to quell any concerns the pupils may have about the demands that may be made upon them after transfer. Thus bridging units are seen as a distinctive transitional activity rather than part of a developing curriculum. This perspective was nicely illustrated by one pupil who when asked 'What happened when the bridging unit was finished?' replied 'Mr Hayes put on his white coat and we did the Bunsen burner.'

Nevertheless, even where bridging units are not regarded as part of a developing curriculum, they can still produce positive outcomes. Setting up the activities will involve a certain amount of planning between the teachers from the pre- and post-transfer schools. This can lead to fruitful discussions on such issues as presentation and assessment and raise important questions about the demands that the work makes upon pupils. It might, for example, help to overcome some of the difficulties experienced by the science and mathematics staff at Kenilworth when attempting to relate to the primary teachers' assessments which were described in Chapter 2. It is not unusual to discover, for example, that when primary teachers and secondary teachers sit down to design a worksheet for a particular activity, it is the primary teacher who provides the more challenging intellectual demands. For example, a typical secondary science worksheet, such as the one designed by Miss Mowbray, will not only tell children what to do but also sometimes tell them the expected result. The primary teacher is more likely to begin by asking the pupils what they have seen and then require them either to offer an explanation for these observations or to come up with further clarifying questions. Discussions between teachers about the respective advantages and disadvantages of these alternative approaches have the potential to raise fundamental questions about pedagogy and can only benefit the transfer process.

The effects of increasing competition

Schools where a close-knit pyramid no longer operates because of increased parental choice, with the result that a relatively small number of pupils transfer from a large number of feeders, have special problems. The bridging unit option will be difficult to organise and implement successfully. It is also likely to mean that it is difficult to agree a date on which every pupil can attend the induction day. Maintaining adequate liaison with all the schools will be time-consuming and costly. It is hard to justify a subject teacher visiting a feeder school if only five or six children from each class are likely to take up a place after transfer. For all these reasons, some schools have begun to set up extended induction programmes during the first weeks of the new term after transfer. One objective of these programmes is to give pupils a clearer sense of identity as members of the 'lower secondary' school. For this to happen pupils must achieve a better understanding of the relationship between the work undertaken in Year 7 and Year 8 and that carried out later when they begin to study for the public examinations. The programme also provides an opportunity for the new pupils to develop appropriate study skills and can help to foster the notion of independent learning so that they become, in the words of Lahelma and Gordon (1997), 'professional pupils'. One school, for example, has dispensed with the guided tour which usually takes place on the first morning of the autumn term (as was the case in most of the transfer schools in the present study) As a means of reinforcing

197

messages about 'managing one's own learning' pupils were given a map and told that during the course of the first day they must locate the various points marked upon it. They also had to work out the shortest way of getting from their form room to other areas in the school, such as the laboratories, the gymnasium, the art and craft rooms, etc., taking care to use legitimate routes which did not conflict with the normal traffic flow. At the end of the day pupils were brought together and results compared in order to establish the best solution. As Lahelma and Gordon (1997: 134) argue, 'students do not come to secondary school from nowhere' but 'they come laden with experiences from primary schools where they have been learning to become pupils for six years'. The aim of these extended induction programmes is to build upon these experiences.

Other transfer initiatives for schools

For Phase One of the DfEE Transfer and Transition study, which reviewed existing practice, a survey was carried out by the Centre for the Study of Comprehensive Schools (CSCS) to find out what strategies schools were currently using to overcome problems of transfer and transition. As reported in that study (Galton *et al.* 1999a), approximately 100 per cent of the schools that responded to the request for information now had a liaison programme. Activities included at least one induction day in the final term before transfer, visits by teachers between schools, special attention for children with special needs and meetings and counselling sessions with parents. It is significant that schools were asked not to describe their existing practice but to list recent initiatives. It is clear, therefore, that the main thrust of work on transfer is still concerned with smooth administrative arrangements and with the lessening of pupils' sense of social isolation and anxiety during the move to the bigger school. Only 20 per cent of the schools engaged in any form of curriculum initiative designed to improve continuity and ensure progression. If the same survey were to be carried out now, then undoubtedly, because of the popularity of the bridging units, this figure would probably be nearer 80 per cent. What has not changed appreciably, however, has been the attention given to pedagogy or to aspects of pupils' learning. In the CSCS survey such initiatives, usually some form of team teaching or exchanging classes so that the primary teacher took Year 7 and vice versa, totalled less than 2 per cent of responses. The evaluation of the current Phase Two of the DfEE Transfer and Transition Project suggests that little has changed in this respect since the above data were collected.

It is clear from the findings presented in Chapter 4 that this is an area which is in need of serious attention. Whereas most schools, as part of the inspection process, produce detailed schemes of work showing progression across the various transition points within the school, few have attempted to construct similar plans with respect to pupils' learning and the links to pedagogy. In the final chapter of *Inside the Primary Classroom: 20 Years On* (Galton *et al.* 1999b), a suggested framework was provided linking aspects of learning with appropriate teaching strategies so that pupils who transferred to secondary school would be 'metacognitively wise' (Galton 2001). Part of the framework called for the increased use of collaborative learning in groups to support the development of pupils' conceptual understanding.

Given the evidence presented in Chapter 4 that collaborative group work, both in the primary and secondary phases, was used relatively infrequently when compared to whole class teaching, it could be seen as a strategy ripe for future development (Webb and Palincsar 1996). It might be argued, for example, that for work in groups at Key Stage 1 children require training in straightforward skills such as listening carefully to one another and taking turns at speaking. At Key Stage 2 the evidence suggests that pupils need to learn how to structure discussions more carefully so that they do not wander off the point (Bennett and Dunne 1992). When pupils do digress they need strategies to help them refocus the discussion. At Key Stage 3 it might be argued that the issues discussed in groups become more controversial (Cowie *et al.* 1994). This will certainly be true of citizenship topics such as fairness and justice, racial equality and the like, which are part of recent government initiatives. For the teacher to operate groups successfully in such circumstances, pupils need to learn how to handle conflict without resorting to verbal abuse or even physical violence. Discussions among teachers across all three stages might be able to develop a comprehensive training programme that built upon what pupils had been learnt and practised at the previous stage. Similar initiatives might be undertaken in other areas where classroom research has demonstrated potential weaknesses. This might include, for example, an attempt to develop the pupils' ability to respond to challenging questions and even, on occasions to interrogate the teacher!

The impact of recent government initiatives

No discussion of transfer, particularly from Key Stage 2 to Key Stage 3 can fail to take into account recent government initiatives, particularly those concerned with Literacy and Numeracy at Key Stage 2 and the recent implementation of a similar set of projects at Key Stage 3. At present the evidence about their impact on pedagogy is mixed. Mroz *et al.* (2000) have argued that the impact of the Literacy Hour has not noticeably changed the levels of questioning when compared to those reported in the ORACLE replication study (Galton *et al.* 1999b). By way of contrast, Linda Hargreaves and her colleagues in a yet unpublished study of primary interactive teaching have noticed a significant increase in the level of questioning. This research has videotaped lessons of 30 primary teachers using interactive teaching in the Literacy Hour, and 15 of these teachers teaching other curriculum areas. Comparing the Literacy Hour observations at KS2 with the 1996 ORACLE findings for English showed that questioning had almost doubled (from 16 per cent to 29 per cent). Closed challenging questions had risen from 4 per cent to 10 per cent. However, these Literacy Hour lessons were selected by the teachers for videotaping to illustrate best practice, whereas in the ORACLE replication the observations were spread over three terms and the timing of these visits was made by the researchers. The evidence from the National Curriculum Tests does suggest that these initiatives have had an impact and that primary schools will have little difficulty in meeting the government's target that the most pupils will achieve Level 4 by the end of Key Stage 2.

At Key Stage 3 the future is less certain. Among English teachers, the emphasis on skills-based approach rather than teaching the subject through literature has not been enthusiastically received. Indeed, it could be argued, given the success of the Key Stage 2 programmes, that children in Year 7 are now better equipped to approach the study of English Literature because their reading and comprehension skills have improved dramatically. While, therefore, raising levels of basic competence are undoubtedly important in helping children to cope with the move to secondary school, there is a danger in thinking that with improved literacy and numeracy standards the rest of the KS3 curriculum will adapt in ways that offer pupils greater challenges. Thinking skills have been introduced at Key Stage 3 but not specifically at Key Stage 2 where one might argue the groundwork should be laid. Measures designed to improve self-confidence and self-esteem are to be incorporated into the citizenship programme in the belief that the benefits will then permeate into the remaining areas of the curriculum. The more recent reforms of the National Curriculum have tended to blur the key questions of how to meet the pupils' entitlement to a broad and balanced curriculum while at the same time raising levels of competence in the core skills. The allocation of five mornings a week entirely to mathematics and English at Key Stage 2 makes it difficult to provide adequate coverage of the remaining subjects, particularly in the Arts where the position of music and drama is threatened.

Back in 1988 when the Interim Primary Committee first began its deliberations it recognised that only through some form of topic-related or thematic programmes of study could adequate coverage of the whole curriculum be achieved. The committee's intention was to end the rigid demarcation between the core subjects, which were taught separately, and others such as history and geography which were organised around themes. The present arrangements are forcing many primary schools to go back to this rather restrictive thematic approach when what is required is to integrate more of the core skills into these other subject areas thereby promoting challenging inter-disciplinary work. The world of the twenty-first century will be one where knowledge is not compartmentalised in the manner of the present National Curriculum. This is the kind of approach that our economic rivals among the Pacific Rim countries, such as Hong Kong and Singapore (Sharp and Gopinathan 1997) is adopting. This results from this present study suggest that the long-standing problems of transfer will only be solved if the National Curriculum is radically transformed in ways signalled in a recent review conducted by the Hong Kong Education Commission (2000). Under former British rule Hong Kong's curriculum was a mirror image of the English National Curriculum. Now as a fully autonomous region of the Republic of China, the subject-based approach is being discarded in favour of greater integration. Similar changes will be necessary in this country even if the process of implementation proves painful for those teachers and administrators who have struggled hard to make the present system work.

It also appears improbable that the problems of transfer in the lower secondary school can be solved within the rather rigid administrative structures that pertain at present. These structures have remained virtually unchanged since the Education Bill of 1918 made attendance at school compulsory up to the end of the term in which a pupil reached the age of fourteen. Throughout their thirty years existence, comprehensive schools have found the task of encouraging specialisation while maintaining entitlement to a broad and balanced curriculum extremely difficult to manage. Making it possible for every child to achieve their maximum potential in areas where they excel conflicts with the principle that no child should be denied opportunities to sample a wide range of human experience. This is even more difficult to accomplish within a system that divides children rigidly into year groups and then into bands and breaks down the curriculum into discrete 40-minute periods. Prior to the introduction of the National Curriculum some comprehensive schools were beginning to address these issues through the use of modular curriculum in which pupils were free, having completed a minimum core, to pursue various options which matched their interests and their current level of attainment. Such arrangements were only found to work if some flexibility was introduced between year groups so that, for example, Year 7 and Year 8 were organised as a single unit rather than two separate entities.

The various schemes currently being adopted by many schools, such as the 'catch up' summer programmes, mentoring by older peers, bridging units, extended induction programmes and teacher exchanges, incorporating peer observation, should all help to make transition and transfer more effective. Of themselves, however, these initiatives will not solve the long-standing problems that have existed, on present evidence, for at least two decades. For this further systemic reform of our education system is required. We owe it to the pupils who have yet to make the move to secondary school to undertake these reforms.

Notes

1 Sometimes these two principles appeared to conflict as when the English panel attempted to compile 'approved' reading lists. It was acknowledged that few children might wish to read some of the recommended authors on their own but that a teacher could read to the class in such cases. Baker (1993: 201 and Graham (1993: 48) offer different perspectives on this issue.

2 There was an interesting occasion at Channings, described in Chapter 2, where the headteacher arranged a liaison meeting between the various subject teachers to which an observer from the project was invited. The meeting was held in the school's library and tea and cakes were provided. The science staff from Channings turned up wearing their white laboratory coats and conversed among themselves for almost the entire evening until the headteacher intervened.

3 Phase Two of the project involves working closely with nine LEAs. In each local authority schools have decided on particular interventions that are designed to overcome some of the problems associated with transfer. Many of the schools involved make use of the 'bridging unit' strategy. The research team provides schools with help to evaluate these initiatives in the form of attitude surveys and simple observation checklists.

REFERENCES

Alexander, R. (1997) *Policy and Practice in Primary Education*, 2nd edn, London: Routledge.

Anderson, H. (1939) 'The measurement of domination and of socially integrative behaviour in teachers' contacts with children', *Child Development*, 10, 73–89.

Anderson, L., Jacobs, J., Schramm, S. and Splittgerber, F. (2000) 'School transitions: beginning of the end or a new beginning?', *International Journal of Educational Research*, 33, 4, 325–339.

Baker, K. (1993) *The Turbulent Years: My Life in Politics*, London: Faber & Faber.

BEDC (1975) *Continuity in Education: Junior to Secondary*, Birmingham Education Development Centre Project No. 5, Final Report, Birmingham: City of Birmingham Education Department.

Bennett, N. (1976) *Teaching Styles and Pupil Progress*, London: Open Books.

Bennett, N. (1991) *Managing Learning in the Primary School,* Chester: Trentham Books.

Bennett, N. and Dunne, E. (1992) *Managing Classroom Groups,* Hemel Hempstead: Simon and Schuster.

Bernard, M. and Joyce, M. (1984) *Rational Emotional Therapy with Children and Adolescents: Theory, Treatment, Strategies, Preventative Methods*, New York: Wiley & Sons.

Beynon, J. (1985) *Initial Encounters in the Secondary School*, Lewes: Falmer Press.

Blyth, D. A., Simmons, R. G. and Carlton-Ford, S. (1983) 'The adjustment of early adolescents to school transition', *Journal of Early Adolescence*, 3, 105–120.

Boydell, D. (1974) 'Teacher pupil contact in junior classrooms', *British Journal of Educational Psychology*, 44, 313–318.

Boydell, D. (1975) 'Pupil behaviour in junior classrooms', *British Journal of Educational Psychology*, 45, 122–129.

Brighouse, T. (1997) 'Leading and managing primary schools: the changing world of the local education authority, in C. Cullingford (ed.) *The Politics of Primary Education*, Buckingham: Open University Press.

Brophy, J. E. and Good, T. L. (1986) 'Teacher behaviour and student achievement', in M. C. Wittrock (ed.) *Handbook of Research on Teaching*, 3rd edn. New York: Macmillan.

Brown, J. and Armstrong, M. (1986) 'Transfer from primary to secondary: The child's perspective'. In M. Youngman, (ed.) *Mid-Schooling Transfer: Problems and Proposals,* Windsor: NFER-Nelson.

Bruner, J. S. (1966) *Towards a Theory of Instruction,* Cambridge, MA: Harvard University Press.

Bruner, J. S. (1996) *The Culture of Education.* Cambridge, MA: Harvard University Press.

Campbell, J. and Neill, S. (1994) *Primary Teachers at Work,* London: Routledge.

Catterall, J. (1998) 'Risk and resilience in student transitions to high school', *American Journal of Education,* 106, 2, 302–333.

Cohen, L. and Manion, L. (1980) *Research Methods in Education,* London: Croom Helm.

Cowie, H., Smith, P., Boulton, M. and Laver, R. (1994) *Cooperation in the Multiethnic Classroom,* London: David Fulton.

Croll, P. (1983) 'Transfer and pupil performance', in M. Galton and J. Willcocks (eds) *Moving from the Primary Classroom,* London: Routledge & Kegan Paul.

Croll, P. (1986) *Systematic Classroom Observation,* Lewes: Falmer Press.

Croll, P. (ed.) (1996) *Teachers, Pupils and Primary Schooling,* London: Cassell.

Cuban, L. (1984) *How Teachers Taught: Constancy and Change in American Classrooms, 1890–1980,* New York: Longman.

Dearing, R. (1993) *The National Curriculum and its Assessment,* Final Report, London: Schools' Curriculum and Assessment Authority.

Delamont, S. (1981) 'All too familiar? A decade of classroom research', *Educational Analysis,* 3, 1, 69–84.

Delamont, S. and Galton, M. (1986) *Inside the Secondary Classroom,* London: Routledge & Kegan Paul.

Demetriou, H., Goalen, P. and Rudduck, J. (2000) 'Academic performance, transfer, transition and friendship: listening to the student voice', *International Journal of Educational Research,* 33 4, 425–442.

DES (1977) *Education in Schools: A Consultative Document,* Cmnd. 6869 London: HMSO.

DfEE (1999) *Statistics for Education: Schools,* London: Her Majesty's Stationery Office (HMSO).

Dutch, R. and McCall, J. (1974) 'Transition to secondary: an experiment in a Scottish comprehensive school', *British Journal of Educational Psychology,* 44, 3, 282–289.

Eccles, J. S. and Midgley, C. (1989) 'Stage-environment fit: developmentally appropriate classrooms for young adolescents', in C. Ames and R. Ames (eds) *Research on Motivation in Education: Goals and Cognitions,* volume 3, New York: Academic Press, pp. 139–186.

Education Commission (2000) *Learning to Learn: A Report of Changes Necessary for Schools in the Twenty-First Century,* Hong Kong: Curriculum Development Institute (CDI).

Flanders, N. A. (1964) 'Some relationships among teacher influence, pupil attitudes and achievement' in B. J. Biddle and Ellena, W. J. [Eds] *Contemporary Research on Teacher Effectiveness,* New York: Holt, Rinehart & Winston.

France, N. and Fraser, I. (1975) *Richmond Tests of Basic Skills,* London: Nelson.

Gage, N. (1985) *Hard Gains in the Soft Sciences, The Case for Pedagogy,* CEDR Monograph, Bloomington Indiana: Phi Delta Kappa.

Galton, M. (1981) 'Teaching groups in the junior school: a neglected art', *Schools Organisation,* 1, 2, 175–181.

Galton, M. (1995) *Crisis in the Primary School*, London: David Fulton.

Galton, M. (2001) 'Dancing in Oklahoma: the pupil as a professional learner in the twenty-first century', in C. Richards (ed.) *Changing English Primary Curriculum: Retrospect and Prospect*, Stoke on Trent: Trentham Books.

Galton M. and Croll, P. (1980) 'Pupil progress and basic skills', in M. Galton and B. Simon (eds) (1980) *Progress and Performance in the Primary Classroom,* London: Routledge & Kegan Paul.

Galton, M. and Delamont, S. (1985) 'Speaking with forked tongues? Two styles of observation in the ORACLE project', in R. Burgess (ed.) *Field Methods in the Study of Education*, Lewes: Falmer Press.

Galton, M. and Fogelman, K. (1998) 'The use of discretionary time in the primary classroom', *Research Papers in Education*, 13, 119–139.

Galton, M., Hargreaves, L. and Comber, C. (1998) 'Classroom practice and the National Curriculum in small rural primary schools', *British Educational Research Journal*, 24, 1, 43–61.

Galton, M., Gray, J. and Rudduck, J. (1999a) *The Impact of Transitions and Transfers on Pupil Progress and Attainment*, Research Report RR131, Nottingham: DfEE Publications.

Galton, M., Hargreaves, L., Comber, C. and Wall, D. (1999b) *Inside the Primary Classroom: 20 Years On*, London: Routledge.

Galton, M., Simon, B. and Croll, P. (1980) *Inside the Primary Classroom*, London: Routledge & Kegan Paul.

Galton, M. and Willcocks, J. (eds) (1983) *Moving from the Primary Classroom*, London: Routledge & Kegan Paul.

Gardner, H. (1983) *Frames of Mind*, New York: Basic Books.

Gillborne, D. and Gipps, C. (1996) *Recent Research on the Achievements of Ethnic Minority Pupils*, London: HMSO.

Glaser, B. and Strauss, A. (1971) *Status Passage*, London: Routledge & Kegan Paul.

Good, T. and Brophy, J. (1994) *Looking in Classrooms*, New York: HarperCollins.

Gorwood, B. (1986) *School Transfer and Curriculum Continuity*, London: Croom Helm.

Gorwood, B. (1991) 'Primary-secondary transfer after the National Curriculum', *School Organisation*, 11, 3, 283–290.

Graham, D. and Tytler, D. (1993) *A Lesson for Us All: The Making of the National Curriculum*, London: Routledge.

Hargreaves, A. (1980) 'The ideology of middle schools', in A. Hargreaves and L. Tickle (eds) *Middle Schools: Origins, Ideology and Practice*, London: Harper & Row.

Hargreaves, D. H. (1982) *The Challenge for the Comprehensive School: Culture, Curriculum and Community*, London: Routledge & Kegan Paul.

Hargreaves, D. H. (1995) 'School culture, school effectiveness and school improvement', *School Effectiveness and School Improvement*, 6, 1, 23–46.

Haladyna, T. and Thomas, G. (1979) 'The attitudes of elementary school children toward school and subject matters', *Journal of Experimental Education*, 48, 18–23.

Hirsch, B. J. and Rapkin, B. D. (1987) 'The transition to junior high school: a longitudinal study of self-esteem, psychological symptomatology, school life and social support', *Child Development*, 58, 1235–1243.

Husband, C. and Bridges, D. (eds) (1996) *Consorting and Collaborating in the Education Market Place*, London: Falmer.

Joiner, R., Littleton, K., Faulkner, D. and Miell, D. (2001) *Rethinking collaborative learning*. London: Free Association Books.

Kvalsund, R. (2000) 'The transition from primary to secondary level in smaller and larger rural schools in Norway: comparing differences in context and social meaning', *International Journal of Educational Research,* 33, 4, 401–424.

Lahelma, E. and Gordon, T. (1997) 'First day in secondary school: learning to be a "professional pupil",' *Educational Research and Evaluation*, 3, 2, 119–139.

Lord, S. E., Eccles, J. S. and McCarthy, K. A. (1994) 'Surviving the junior high school transition: family processes and self-perceptions as protective and risk factors', *Journal of Early Adolescence*, 14, 162–199.

Maccoby, E. and Martin, J. (1983) 'Socialization in the context of the family: Parent–child interaction', in E. Hetherington (ed.) *Handbook of Child Psychology: Socialization, Personality and Social Development*, Vol. 4, New York: Wiley.

McCallum, B. (1996) 'The transfer and use of assessment information between primary and secondary schools', *British Journal of Curriculum and Assessment* 6, 3, 10–14.

Maines, B. and Robinson, G. (1996) *B/G-steem: A Self-esteem Scale with Locus of Control Items*, Bristol: Lucky Duck.

Marsh, C. (1980) 'The emergence of 9–13 schools in Worcestershire', in A. Hargreaves and L. Tickle (eds) *Middle Schools: Origins, Ideology and Practice*, London: Harper & Row.

Marshall, B. and Brindley, S. (1998) 'Cross-phase or just a lack of communication; models of English at Key Stages 2 and 3 and their possible effects on pupil transfer', *Changing English*, 5, 2, 123–133.

Measor, L. and Woods, P. (1984) *Changing Schools*, Milton Keynes: Open University Press.

Midgley, C., Eccles, J. and Feldlaufer, H. (1991) 'Classroom environment and the transition to junior high school', in B. Fraser and H. Walberg (eds) *Educational Environments*, Oxford: Pergamon Press.

Minnis, M., Seymour, K. and Schagen, I. (1998) *National Results of Years 3, 4 and 5 Optional Tests*, Slough: NFER.

Mizelle, N. B. (1995) 'Transition from middle school to high school: the student perspective', paper presented at the Annual Meeting of the American Educational Research Association, San Francisco.

Mizelle, N. B. and Mullins, E. (1997) 'Transition into and out of middle school', in J. L. Irvin (ed.) *What Research Says to the Middle Level Practitioner*, Columbus, OH: National Middle School Association, pp. 303–313.

Mortimore, P., Sammons, P., Stoll, L. D. and Ecob, R. (1988) *School Matters: The Junior Years,* Wells: Open Books.

Mroz, M., Smith, F. and Hardman, F. (2000) 'The discourse of the Literacy Hour', *Cambridge Journal of Education*, 30, 3, 379–390.

Murdoch, A. (1982) 'Forty-two children and the transfer to secondary education', unpublished PhD thesis, University of East Anglia.

Murdoch, W. (1966) 'The effects of transfer on the level of children's adjustment to school', MEd thesis, University of Aberdeen.

Nash, R. (1973) *Classrooms Observed*, London: Routledge & Kegan Paul.

Nisbet, J. D. and Entwistle, N. J. (1969) *The Transition to Secondary School*, London: London University Press.

OFSTED (1998) *Standards and Quality in Schools 1996/97* (Annual Report of the Chief Inspector of Schools), London: HMSO.

OFSTED (1999) *Standards and Quality in Schools 1997/98* (Annual Report of the Chief Inspector of Schools), London: HMSO.

Orsborn, T. (1977) 'Talk about our problem', *ILEA Contact*, 5, 25.

Petersen, A. C. and Crockett, L. (1985) 'Pubertal timing and grade effects on adjustment', *Journal of Youth and Adolescence*, 14, 191–206.

Pietarinen, J. (2000) 'Transfer to and study at secondary school in Finnish school culture: developing schools on the basis of pupils' experiences', *International Journal of Educational Research,* 33, 4, 383–400.

Plewis, I. (1991) 'Pupils' progress in reading and mathematics during primary school: association with ethnic group and sex', *Educational Research*, 33, 133–140.

Pollard, A., Broadfoot, P., Croll, P., Osborn, M. and Abbott, D. (1994) *Changing English Primary Schools*, London: Cassell.

Reynolds, D. (1998) *'Teacher effectiveness'*, presentation at the Teacher Training Agency Corporate Plan Launch 1998–2001, London: TTA.

Roderick, M. (1993) *The Path of Dropping Out*, Westport, CT: Auburn House.

Rosenshine, B. and Meister, C. (1994) 'Direct instruction', in T. Husen and Postlethwaite (eds) *The International Encyclopedia of Education*, 2nd edn, vol. 3, Oxford: Pergamon.

Rosenshine, B., Meister, C. and Chapman, S. (1996) 'Teaching students to generate questions: a review of intervention studies', *Review of Educational Research,* 66, 2, 181–221.

Rudduck, J., Chaplain, R. and Wallace, G. (eds) (1996) *School Improvement: What Can Pupils Tell Us?*, London: David Fulton.

Rudduck, J., Day, J. and Wallace, G. (1997) 'The significance for school improvement of pupils' experiences of within-school transitions', *Curriculum*, 17, 3, 144–153.

Sammons, P. (1995) 'Gender, ethnic and socio-economic differences in attainment and progress: a longitudinal analysis of student achievement over 9 years', *British Educational Research Journal*, 21, 4, 464–483.

Sammons, P., Hillman, J. and Mortimore, P. (1995) *Key Characteristics of Effective Schools: A Review of School Effectiveness Research*, London: Office for Standards in Education..

SCAA (1996) *Promoting Continuity between KS2 and KS3*, Middlesex: Schools Curriculum and Assessment Authority.

Scott, L. S., Rock, D. A., Pollack, J. M. and Ingels, S. J. (1995) *Two Years Later: Cognitive Gains and School Transitions of NELS: 88 Eighth Graders*, Washington, DC: National Center for Educational Statistics.

Sharp, P. (1980) 'The origins of middle schools in the West Riding of Yorkshire', in A. Hargreaves and L. Tickle (eds) *Middle Schools: Origins, Ideology and Practice*, London: Harper & Row.

Sharp, L. and Gopinathan, S. (1997) 'Effective island, effective schools: repairing and restructuring in the Singapore school system', in J. Tan, S. Gopinathan and Ho Wah Kam (eds) *Education in Singapore: A Book of Readings*, Singapore and New York: Simon & Schuster.

Spelman, B. (1979) *Pupil Adaptation to Secondary School*, Publication No. 18, Belfast: Northern Ireland Council for Educational Research.

Stables, K. (1995) 'Discontinuity in transition: pupils' experience of technology in year 6 and year 7', *International Journal of Technology and Design Education*, 5, 157–169.

Stillman, A. and Maychell, K. (1982) *Transfer Procedures at 9 and 13*, Slough: NFER.

Strand, S. (1999) 'Ethnic group, sex and economic disadvantage: associations with pupils' educational progress from baseline to the end of Key Stage 1', *British Educational Research Journal*, 25, 2, 179–202.

Suffolk LEA (1997) A *Report on an Investigation into What Happens when Pupils Transfer into Their Next School at the Ages of 9, 11 and 13*, Ipswich: Inspection and Advice Division, Suffolk Education Department.

TGAT (Task Group on Assessment and Testing) (1988) Three Supplementary Reports, London: Department of Education and Science/Welsh Office.

Tomlinson, J. (1992) 'Retrospect on Ruskin: prospect on the 1990's', in M. Williams, R. Dougherty and F. Banks (eds) *Continuing the Education Debate*, London: Cassell.

Ward, B. A., Mergendoller, J. R., Tikunoff, W. J., Rounds, T. S., Mitman, A. L. and Dadey, G. J. (1982) *Junior High School Transition Study*, Volume VII: *Executive summary*, San Francisco: Far West Laboratory for Educational Research and Development.

Webb, N. and Palincsar, A. (1996) 'Group processes in the classroom', in D. Berliner, and R. Calfee (eds) *A Handbook of Educational Psychology*, A Project of Division 15, The Division of Educational Psychology of the American Psychological Association, New York: Simon & Schuster.

Weldy, G. R. (ed) (1991) *Stronger School Transitions Improve Student Achievement*, New York: William and Mary Greve Foundation.

Wells, M. C. (1996) *Literacies Lost*: *When Students Move from a Progressive Middle School to a Traditional High School*, New York: Teachers College Press.

Wigfield, A., Eccles, J., MacIver, D., Reuman, D. and Midgley, C. (1991) 'Transitions during early adolescence', *Developmental Psychology*, 27, 4, 552–565.

Wood, D. (1998) *How Children Think and Learn*, 2nd edn, Oxford: Blackwell.

Woodhead, C. (1995) Teaching *Quality*: *The Primary Debate*, London: OFSTED.

Woods, P., Jeffery, B., Troman, G. and Boyle, M. (1997) *Restructuring Schools, Reconstructing Teachers*, Buckingham: Open University Press.

Worcester LEA (1997) *Key Stage 3 Survey*: *Headteachers' Responses*, Worcester: Quality Division, Inspection, Advice and Training Service.

Youngman, L. and Lunzer, E. (1977) *Adjustment to Secondary Schooling*, Nottingham: School of Education, University of Nottingham.

Youngman, M. (1978) 'Six reactions to school transfer', *British Journal of Educational Psychology*, 48, 4, 280–289.

INDEX

179; teacher's audience 120, 177; teacher-centred classroom teaching 118; teacher exchanges 201; whole class instruction 104, 118

test: beginning school year 192; core subjects 78; formal 76; mental arithmetic and English 80; routine class-based 88; for 'sorting out the sets' 78; time spent processing results 189; use of 88–92; *see also* assessment

timetable 60, 62, 64; completion 61; copying 63; filling in 65–6; fixed system 77; limiting effects of secondary 192–3; reproduction 60; timetable proper, introduction of 76

transfer: age 155; clean slate approach 91; dilemma 194; 'expectancy effects' 192; fresh start 191–2; initiation myths 17; from Key Stage 2 to Key Stage 3 199; LEA initiatives 24; 'level playing field' 88; other factors 17–18; recurring themes 24–6; remaining problems 189; *rite of passage* 3; start from scratch 88, 192; as 'status passage' 17, 56, 186; structural deficiencies in system 188–90

transfer day: *see* induction day
transition 26; year-by-year 12

Webb, N. and Palinscar, A. 199
Worcester LEA 89; survey 25

Year 8: 'fallow year' 11
Youngman and Lunzer 5, 6